EA #108
Love In Christ!
Pamella Simmons
EA #92

EH #105
Love du Ghiaz'
Donnetta Simmons
EH #92

Rise Up, Recount Love

BECKY SPELL

iUniverse, Inc.
Bloomington

Rise Up, Recount Love

Copyright © 2011 by Becky Spell.

All rights reserved. No part of this book may be used or reproduced by any means, graphic, electronic, or mechanical, including photocopying, recording, taping or by any information storage retrieval system without the written permission of the publisher except in the case of brief quotations embodied in critical articles and reviews.

iUniverse books may be ordered through booksellers or by contacting:

iUniverse
1663 Liberty Drive
Bloomington, IN 47403
www.iuniverse.com
1-800-Authors (1-800-288-4677)

Because of the dynamic nature of the Internet, any web addresses or links contained in this book may have changed since publication and may no longer be valid. The views expressed in this work are solely those of the author and do not necessarily reflect the views of the publisher, and the publisher hereby disclaims any responsibility for them.

Any people depicted in stock imagery provided by Thinkstock are models, and such images are being used for illustrative purposes only.
Certain stock imagery © Thinkstock.

ISBN: 978-1-4620-7144-9 (sc)
ISBN: 978-1-4620-7148-7 (hc)
ISBN: 978-1-4620-7146-3 (ebk)

Printed in the United States of America

iUniverse rev. date: 12/15/2011

Acknowledgments

$\mathcal{M}$Y HEART IS FILLED WITH much love and appreciation as I write the most important page in this book and edge closer to a dream come true, my first published book. This book has been a lifelong work in progress, taking shape in my young heart when I would write love stories long before I understood the power of God's greatest commandment. Time has toughened and tendered this heart of mine, giving me courage to Rise up and Recount love through seasons of sunshine and sorrow. Rising up boldly and commemorating love is pleasing to the Lord and loved ones. My strength to move forward in faith comes from my Father who gave me life, liberty, and love. I am grateful to Jesus, my Lord and Savior. Your amazing grace and endless love makes all well with my soul. Thank you for guiding me and giving gifts that enrich my life here and prepare me for heaven.

My family and loved ones deserve endless bear hugs and pats on the back. You inspired the stories that started at home with our big, happy family and have kept me lifted and loved through each chapter of my life. With heartfelt thanks, I am grateful for your loving devotion to God and my family. Cameron and Clint, you are the greatest gifts God gave your Dad and me. I will love you, believe in you, and enjoy writing our love stories forever. It really is better when we are together.

Among my greatest treasures are the friends who share life's adventures with me and season my stories deliciously. Many friends are mentioned by name in this book. Some people I don't know personally, but all those referred to in Rise Up, Recount Love are special and their shining examples and experiences are uplifting to me, to us all. I am thankful to all the people who have touched my life and inspired a story or two along the way.

Those who work alongside me at Tim's Gift Inc. and The Learning Station have made the journey of writing and publishing this book much easier. Thank you for supporting me and carrying the load when deadlines loomed and tears threatened to replace my smile. I am grateful for a loyal, loving staff. Cameron Spell and Loren Hawley, who support Tim's Gift and me with endless energy and expertise, I will love you forever.

The stories in this book were inspired by many people and experiences throughout my lifetime. I don't remember the exact source of every story or example shared. I am grateful for each person and season that has enriched my life and added details to my stories. My heartfelt desire is to pass along stories that will be a blessing and glorify God.

Two main sources used in writing this book are my favorites.

<u>The Holy Bible</u>—King James Version, Thomas-Nelson Inc. Nashville, TN 1976

<u>Tuesdays with Morrie</u> by Mitch Albom, Bantum Doubleday Dell Publishing Group Inc. New York, N.Y. 1997

I am thankful for the opportunity to share this book, for everyone who touched my life and added love and details to each story, and for the inspiration and story line from my heavenly Father. With much love and many prayers, I thank you and God for guidance and blessings through all seasons and for stories waiting to be written. I am humbled and honored to rise up and recount love forever and ever.

Forward

*A*S A YOUNG CHILD GROWING up I knew deep inside my inner being that I had been given to a wonderful, loving family, at least at times I thought I knew that. I have great memories of my family from my childhood, memories of lots of work with few vacations. I can remember going into the woods with my mom and dad as the leaves turned beautiful colors and the air began to have a cool nip as the season changed in an effort to find wood to burn in our fireplace. I can remember "camping out" in sleeping bags as a family in front of that wood burning fireplace on cold winter nights. It sure seemed like a lot of fun, what I didn't realize is, at that time, it was our only means of staying warm at night when heating oil was far out of reach for my family. I remember vividly the Saturday routine which consisted of getting up to a biscuit as I watched the morning cartoons. Then a couple of hours were filled helping my mom fill orders for Avon. We would unpack and sort the beauty items that filled the huge pile of boxes left by the delivery man that day before. Then it was off to the yard to help my dad clean and load up the trailer with trash that would lead to a father-son trip to the local dumpsite. This was a highlight because I knew the first stop would be the Scotchman, just down the road, for a Mountain Dew and a giant Tootsie Roll. I can remember helping mom make evening visits to other homes and laying out jewelry that she would sell. There was even a span where we sold and delivered Encyclopedias. At the time I did not know that it was Mom's second and third jobs she had taken on to help pay our bills, all I knew is that is what we did, and Mom made it fun. We would take day trips to the beach and every year or two we made it all the way to Myrtle Beach for two or three days. I never knew that we didn't have a lot of money to do things that a lot of other families did; I just knew we worked hard as a family and my parents made it fun family time with me and my younger brother. However, as I began to get older I began to realize that other families did do, and have, more than we did. I guess the first time I noticed this was when I was about ten years old and went to McDonald's with a childhood friend and his mom. When his mom approached the counter to place our order she turned to me and asked me what I wanted to eat. I was completely and utterly confused as I answered "a hamburger". When my friend told his mom that he would like Chicken McNuggets, I was completely floored. When I finally got home, I ran in the house as fast as I could because I was certain my Mom had not heard the news. As I slung open the back door I yelled. "Mom they have chicken at McDonalds!"

To my surprise my mother was already aware of my stunning revelation. What I didn't realize is that I just never had that choice, a hamburger was all I really ever needed, and all we could ever really afford. By the time I hit my early teens my family's financial situations were certainly changing as my father's business began to grow along with my mom's second business. He had started an insurance career and she was a school teacher and had opened an afterschool care program. We were able to live a little more comfortable, but my parents never forgot their humble beginnings.

Now, I am now all grown up with a family of my own and am finding myself reverting to many of the things that were instilled in me as a child. I strayed out on my own course, like most of us do, throughout my late teens and early adulthood. But now that I have a wife and two beautiful children I see the importance of what my parents taught me as a child. I can now see the value of how I was raised. Certainly, we still have times that we laugh about how I found out that McDonalds had chicken nuggets and how most of our clothes came second hand. At family gatherings we still tease my mom that we always ate leftovers but could never remember the "original" meal they should have come from. Although we laugh about these things now, I realize that we were never "poor". Surely, we did not have all the materialistic things that many have today, but I understand what we did have, and it is something that money can never buy. Looking back, and looking forward into my own family, I realize that my parents taught me hard work; they taught me how to always do and be your best, but most of all they taught me how to be thankful for what you have and to love others. I guess I had to be at least twenty-five years old before I ever saw, or heard, my parents arguing. Now, I am sure they had many times, but growing up I never saw it. I saw how they both strived to make the little everyday things special memories. This is something that seems to be lost in most families today.

As an adult, I most certainly realize how very fortunate that I am. God blessed me simply by giving me the family that I have. My father, though he has now passed, was a man of integrity and virtue. My mother is one of the most phenomenal women that I have ever met. Together, they shared a love that many couples never experience. Looking into my mother's life, I see the true gifts within her and there is no denial that God has placed his true love deep inside of her. Her passion and fuel has been, and still is, to help others and share His love with them. She is a woman that never gives up on a challenge, always finds the way to make things work, and is continually giving of herself. She continues to be one of the few that still believes in the goodness of people. She has a desire to reach out to those in need, and continues to work hard instilling the same values in children today that she did in me and my brother.

As you read into the following pages of Mom's stories, you will laugh and you will cry. You will see into the life of this amazing woman and you will find encouragement and strength. And just maybe, by the time you finish this book, you will, as I do now, begin to see that though I consider her amazing, this is how God has made each and every one of us to live our lives.

Introduction

*T*AKING THE FIRST STEP IN writing and self publishing this book took more courage than the lion ever thought of asking for in The Wizard of Oz. Since childhood, the desire to write a book has stirred within my heart. My life stories started at home, a rural crossroads where our house sat across the road from the country store, where we grew up learning to appreciate a good life and giving quality customer service. My family loved deeply and lived devotedly to the Lord and one another. We worked hard and shared triumphs and trials through seasons that wove us tightly together and gave us wings to fly away and build our own nests in God's perfect timing. I am thankful to my mother, Mary Dean; father, Harold Brunt; siblings, Glenda, Billy, and Gaye for living and loving passionately and sowing seeds that sprouted into stories stored in my heart and shared in this book.

My once upon a time began on March 30, 1975 when I married my high school sweetheart on Easter Sunday. We stood before our Father, family, and friends in Union Grove Church, where I grew up loving the Lord and looking forward to the day when I would walk down the aisle and marry the love of my life. Timothy and I kept our promise to love and cherish one another until death parted us. My best friend became my husband the day we entered into a covenant of love with the Lord and one another. Saying 'I do' was the beginning of a beautiful love story that has blessed my life and birthed this book. Tim and I were crazy in love until our love story here ended on April 22, 2007. He lost his battle with cancer here but received God's best healing, heaven.

Tim and I shared a fairytale love filled with adventures that kept us young and in love through all seasons of our lifetime together. January 10, 1979, our first son was born. Cameron Odell Spell was a blessing we prayed for and thanked God for every day. Together, we witnessed the miracle of his birth and the joy of loving him and training him up in the way he should go. Cameron has given his Dad and me sacrificial love and endless stories for his proud mom to write about. Cameron lives in Clinton and is director of Tim's Gift Inc. The ministry is God's gift to us. Our mission is to give help and hope to people in need and open their hearts to love and cherish the Lord and loved ones deeply and devotedly. Cameron is my sunshine every morning when he enters the door at Tim's Gift Inc. The happiness and love we share and our joy of serving God grows stronger each day.

December 2, 1983, our second son was born. Clinton Harold Spell was another blessing we prayed for and thanked God for every day. We shared the miracle of his birth and rejoiced when his little cries filled our hearts with happiness. Clint's gifts of laughter, love, and honor for God, Tim, me, and his brother have kept us grounded through storms and sunshine. He quit his job to come home and care for his dad and me as we battled cancer. He lives in Charlotte and enjoys working as a district sales representative with US Foods. Clint keeps the family lifted and in good spirits with his quick wit and connected closely with his desire for us to always remain a 'big happy family'. Clint brightens up the cloudiest days with loads of love and laughter. I will love him forever.

Tim's family has loved, supported and been the source of some amazing stories in this book. His two brothers and their families have weathered storms and shared sunshine with our family. Tim's mother, Agnes, has been a good mother to me. Politically correct titles would be mother-in-law and daughter-in law for the two of us. For many seasons, we were not close and missed lots of blessings while trying to understand one another. I felt more like an outlaw, as Tim did with my family, in our first years of marriage. One of my sweetest stories shares how time and prayer worked things out and connected us closely to the Lord and one another. The story of Ruth and Naomi parallels with our lives. Today, I am proud to call her mom and love her with a heart full of thankfulness and appreciation. The best part of the story is, she loves me like a daughter and tells me so. Showing and sharing love for those God has placed in our lives is proof we understand his greatest commandment.

Family is the core of our lives, the source of love stories, and the sparks that keep our fires going through seasons of sunshine and sorrow. Cherishing family is necessary and needed in our world more than ever. I am thankful for supportive family members who color my world with love and laughter.

One of the greatest gifts God gives is fabulous friends. Every day I bow my head with thanksgiving for the good friends who add spice and spirit to my stories. Having friends to share life's journey with makes every adventure a memory to be cherished, a story to be written. My life stories are peppered with wonderful friends who have stuck with me like glue through tough times and happy hours. I am grateful for all the friends who have contributed to my love story.

Rise Up, Recount Love is a collection of love stories that has given heart and happiness to my life here and hope for my forever and ever in heaven. My prayer is for these stories to encourage and inspire you to live life crazy in love with the Lord and your loved ones, to rise up and write your own love story. We aren't promised tomorrow and should embrace each day with gusto and guts to rise up and recount love . . . to remember, commemorate, and give praise to God for the good life he has given. This book is just one more step of faith. I promise there are many more to come. God has given 'wings' and is working out all things according to His purpose for all who love Him, and I do!

Rise Up, Recount Love

*T*HE TITLE OF THIS BOOK recounts my life in a nutshell. Since childhood, I have embraced the challenge of rising up and sharing stories of love. Growing up in Rebel City, a country crossroads community nestled in the plains of eastern North Carolina, girded my love for faith and family. Threads of tender love stories—laced with thrills and tears, sunshine and sorrow, headaches and happiness, gumption and growth, reassurance and romance—grew deeply and gave wings to the woman I am today.

The true stories in this book reveal the blessings of living out loud in love with the Lord and my loved ones for more than half a century. Making mention of every character that has enriched my life and inspired my stories would be an endless list of precious people I cherish and count among my biggest blessings. I salute each person who has seasoned and colored my life with love and laughter. Your name may not appear here, but it is written in my heart and in God's storybook in heaven.

The tender family love stories are my favorites. Childhood stories rewind the times shared with parents who taught me to work hard and love two sisters and a brother who stuck up for me and still stick by me, my older sister watching from heaven, a bunch of kinfolk who remain closely connected as we journey different paths, and a whole host of faithful friends who have become family by choice. Strangers have woven their way into many of my stories, showing the strength of faith when we reach out and reel in the blessings of being a part of the family of God.

The tight-knit stories showcasing the journey of life with my husband, Timothy Cameron, and my two sons, Cameron Odell and Clinton Harold, share the strength of our Father's love and family's love through all seasons. Tim and I began our life together on Easter

Sunday, March 30, 1975. We loved with a love that never grew cold—even when cancer came and our time together on earth ended on April 22, 2007. The legacy Tim left refuels our family's tanks every time the enemy tries to tarnish or tamper with God's plans for our lives. Our family circle has grown to include Angel and Jamie, the two women our sons chose to share their lives with, and two grandchildren, Corie and Connor. We truly are one big happy family—a one-liner Tim made our motto when we welcomed each gift from God and watched the wonders of love at work in our lives. Our circle has been broken, but link by link we will reconnect again in heaven as we are called home to live together forever and ever.

The time to rise up and recount love is now. Share your love stories and witness the sweet spirit of the Lord saturating your heart and home. Watch as loved ones read and remember, wondering how so much time slipped away while tending to things of this world. Stand up and share stories of how God has brought you through seasons of change and kept His promises. Show the world He is Lord of your life by the way you live and the love you share.

The true stories in this book have been written in obedience to God's nudging my heart to give my best to my Lord and loved ones. He heard my cries in the middle of our battles with cancer. Tim received God's best healing—heaven. Four months after he entered heaven, God healed me here. Why? I believe He has called me to help others cherish relationships with loved ones and the Lord and to share my love story.

God reveals things to us in His time and place. Perhaps our answers will come only when we get to heaven. When will that be for me—for you? Why take the risk of dying unsaved? Accept Jesus and make him the main character in all your love stories. Rise up and recount love before it is too late to share your stories with those who color your world. Write your stories, sing your songs, dream your dreams, teach your lessons, reach out in faith, and be bold and brave as you commit to Christ's calling. Rise up and recount love.

Giving in Love

*D*O YOU GIVE GIFTS GRACIOUSLY? Often, we give and receive in a spirit not pleasing to our Father or to our family and friends. Many people feel guilty for having good things and enjoying them. Others are apathetic or flamboyant, never understanding or appreciating the blessings of the good gifts they have received or those they possess and can pass on. God desires that we enjoy what He gives. In Ecclesiastes 3:12-13, we are reminded to rejoice and do good, enjoying the gifts of God. The idea that Christians should not enjoy life does not come from the Bible. Scripture often speaks of the blessings God gives His people. That doesn't mean enjoyment is our primary goal in life. We shouldn't mainly seek out wealth and become obsessed with things of this world. God describes these things as fleeting; putting our trust in them will only lead to sorrow, but that does not mean we should not rejoice when God gives us worldly goods. When we thank God for His blessings and use them properly—to help others and support our families in a responsible Christian lifestyle—those temporary things become blessings He can use through us. That's exactly what God intends to happen when He gives gifts.

There are gifts we can give that cost very little but are treasured for a lifetime. These gifts keep on giving and bless us even more than those who receive them. Enjoy giving in the spirit of love and good things will come back to you in ways you have never imagined.

The first good thing we can give is our time. Many give excuses for not having enough time to do things for others, to give to charitable events or visit rest homes, even to get all done they desire for themselves and their families. Our time is precious, can never be called back, is the same for everyone, and should be used wisely. We must be good stewards with it. Invest in others. Give time to do things together as a family. Give God the first fruits of your time. Start your day with prayer and praise. You will be amazed by how your steps will be ordered and you'll get much more done with your time. Stay closely connected to God. Don't make excuses; make time—invest in the good things that bring heavenly rewards.

Another gift we can give is our talent. God blessed us with abilities—gifts that we can use to improve our own lives and to help others. Many possess artistic talents. Giving someone you love a personalized sketch or decorated flowerpot would be awesome. Some have talents to de-clutter or decorate. My daughter-in-law was blessed with these gifts. It's amazing to watch her transform a cluttered room into a charming, cozy creation. Everyone has talents to use or lose. Share them and see blessings bloom in your life. Giving gifts that carry a price tag of priceless do not have to cost a penny. Many people near and dear to your life would love the gift of spending an afternoon with you or receiving a handmade card that expresses your love and appreciation for their impact on your life.

God is pleased when we use our talents and time to honor Him and bless His children. You are one of His children. If you have been stingy with sharing the gifts He has given to you, it is not too late to change the way you live and give. Start with God. He is a loving Father who longs for more of our time. When we start our day, our week, our year, our vacations, our meetings, our family reunions, our everything, giving God the first fruit of our time, our steps will be ordered as we proceed with our schedules and situations at hand. Watching us use wisely the talents and gifts He blessed us with makes God proud of our faithfulness to be doers instead of doubters.

Singing is a gift that God gave me. Since childhood, singing has been one of my favorite things to do. One of my first jobs at our country store was pumping gas for customers. When neighbors would pull their cars up to the gas pumps, I would rush out the front door and greet them with a grin. While the gas flowed, I would stand on a little cement platform between the tanks and sing them a song.

My Uncle Mack still remembers a song I would sing to him and his date about being a little girl with curls on my shoulder but stand back fellas till I get a little older. I don't remember singing that song, but Uncle Mack and Aunt Betty Jo sure do. That makes us aware that what we say and do, sing and share does impact others—even when we forget about what we did. Wallace Beals tells how I would stand on that little platform as he pumped his own gas and sing to him, "Here I stand on this stump, please come and catch me before I jump!"

When I go home and share time at the country store, I am reminded of how time changes things, but some things stay the same. My brother and his wife and son own and operate the store and carry on the family tradition of serving others. Uncle Mack and Aunt Betty Jo are retired and live right down the road, as do Wallace and June Beals. We still share stories of yesterday with smiles and cherish the closeness of people who still care for one another. That's a good gift. The price of gas on my daddy's old pumps does not read thirty five cents per gallon anymore. No one rushes out to pump anyone's gas. The fast pace of living keeps everyone moving quickly and missing simple pleasures, such as stopping to listen to a little song and slowing down to talk to people in our paths.

Singing has given me joy and opened doors for opportunities I never expected. As a teenager, I sang at weddings, funerals, and church services. Mrs. Amalie, my choir director, and her son, Dennis, and I sang together at many events. We had fun singing and sharing the love of our Lord. Singing love songs in a talent competition at my high school beauty pageant was an unforgettable memory. I will forever treasure the gift God gave me that night. I stood onstage and belted out words about what our world needs now is love, sweet love, asking people to take a look around, if they were looking down, to put a little love in their hearts. I wore the crown home that night, but God had greater plans in store. I would sing His songs and share that powerful message throughout my lifetime in ways I never imagined. The greatest crown we can attain will be the one when we go home to heaven. Then, we will take our crown and place it at Jesus's feet. Receiving a crown is the ultimate gift from our Father. Living our lives out loud for the Lord, using our gifts to give help and hope to others, obeying and honoring our Father, staying connected to the vine while rising up and reaching out in love will bring crowns when we get to glory.

After our preacher pronounced that Timothy and I were man and wife, I sang the prayer that God had joined us together in covenant with Him and one another. We held hands with the look of love in our eyes. That moment grows sweeter as time passes, for God honored our prayer. He did seal us with His Holy Spirit. And when death parted us, the love we shared did not die. True love conquers all things—even death. God's love is greater than anything. He loves unconditionally. When we honor His sacred love, we will live forever and sing our songs for eternity.

Singing in the choir at my home church is a blessing. Yet, when our sons were small and our schedules were packed to the brim, I decided that choir took too much time. Telling Jean, my choir director, wasn't easy, but she understood. What I did not realize was how easy it would be to stay away from choir—even when our sons were older. For years, I enjoyed sitting with my family and enjoying the services together. Then, God got hold of me one day and showed me I was not using my gift to glorify Him. At Mrs. Parker Thornton's funeral, He spoke to my heart. The choir stood to sing that day after the preacher explained how Mrs. Parker shared the gifts God blessed her with all her life. My heart pounded like a jackhammer, sweat poured from my brow, and my knees knocked when I stood to leave. My choir director played at that funeral. Family and friends gathered for lunch after the service. I rushed to Jean and told her how God had spoken to my heart to use my gift of singing or I would lose it. The next Wednesday night, I sat in the same seat I had left many years earlier. Many things had changed in my life since those days when our sons were small and our dreams were big. Our sons are grown, my husband has gone home to heaven, and our dreams were fulfilled as we were sealed in His Holy Spirit. I'm still singing His songs and loving it.

We can also give our treasures. It isn't the magnitude of what we give, but the attitude toward what we give that matters most. It is the spirit in which we give that makes it a good gift. Jesus was at the temple where a rich man gave a big gift, while the poor widow put her two pennies in the offering. He taught a powerful lesson on giving graciously.

Are we giving our best? God sees what we give to others and the spirit in which we give. He also sees what we give to Him. Our tithes are His. It's not that He needs just the 10 percent because all that we have is His. Giving beyond our tithe pleases God. Give him the first of your time, talents, and treasures. Give in faith and the fruit will flourish. Blessings will flow and you'll know that these gifts are from God.

Giving is not always easy. Many people hoard the blessings and hold onto the money we possess. Often, we justify selfish spending with the money that settles in our billfolds and bank accounts. Many times we sit in the pew as the plate is passed without being prepared to give. Often, we hold back what is rightfully God's gift. Pleas are often ignored when people God has raised up to do His work are placed in our path. Giving is the greatest gift we can give to ourselves. When we help others, give generously of our time, talent, and monetary treasures, we will be blessed bigger than we could ever imagine. God promises—and He is a promise keeper.

I am frugal by nature. I still clip coupons, watch my spending, and look for specials. Shopping is my passion, especially when my best friend, Rhonda, and I hit the road and stop by every shop on our way. I head for the clearance racks, always looking for the best bargains, being cautious and careful of how much I spend. If the cost of what I want is too high, I leave it and justify why I didn't need it anyway.

Often, we opt for something cheaper—or something to replace what we know is the best—and we are disappointed in what we get. That's the way it is with God and the good things He gives. We look for a cheaper way, not believing we should give back 10 percent. We give a little here and there, but we fail to commit and carry through with giving what we know is God's portion of our possessions. We can't skimp and expect God's best. I am learning the joy of giving without worrying. I have failed my Lord many times when I gave a little when He blessed me with a lot. Not anymore! My life changed when cancer came and death stared me in the face. In the twinkling of an eye, I realized that we can be gone, all we have can be gone, and my frugal ways went by the wayside. God healed me through gifted doctors and His healing touch. I will never be the same, nor will I go back to business as usual, failing to give my best back to Him and to those I share life with here on earth. I promised to give and share generously my gifts from God.

Don't let life be less enjoyable because you are overwhelmed and burdened about the gifts you're giving or receiving. Mark that off your list forever! Embrace and enjoy the gifts from God. Strive to develop gifts of time, talent, and treasures. Appreciate God's gifts and enjoy giving. Invest your gifts—your time, talents, and treasures—wisely. Give graciously to others and build up your treasures in heaven. Your burdens will be lifted and blessings will bring happiness forever and ever.

Love Will Always Win

*D*O YOU BELIEVE THAT LOVE makes the world go round? It may not, but love sure makes the ride worthwhile. Enjoying the journey, staying closely connected with loved ones and the Lord, and keeping covenants make life grand—and love great! The Bible teaches the importance of faith and hope, but touts love as the greatest gift of all.

Try reading 1 Corinthians 13: 4-7 and insert your name wherever the word love appears. "____ is patient and kind; ____ is not jealous, or conceited, or proud; ____ is not ill mannered, or selfish, or irritable; ____ does not keep a record of wrongs; ____ is not happy with evil, but is happy with the truth. ____ never gives up."

Go ahead; go through those three verses one more time. Read slowly and reflect on your life as you say your own name in the place where love is found in this powerful scripture. Happiness comes when we are willing to look inward, confess our wrongdoings, and live our lives with God first—and never give up on love, on us, or on His plans for us.

These words assure us that love will win if we do our part. When we walk in love, we are lifted to heights of happiness. We make choices to love and spread sunshine. Bathing ourselves in pity smothers love. Basking in His light and spreading love's rays warms hearts and heals homes. Are you smothering or spreading love? Why do we say we're all about love, but our actions reflect the things Corinthians said love is not? Think about your actions and reactions to those you love. Do you show anger, bitterness, or selfishness toward family members—neglecting to honor and cherish, respect and protect. Often, loved ones are overlooked, offended, and offered leftovers.

Love is happy with the truth. Busyness and burdens of overextending and outdoing others become addictive. The Bible teaches us to honor covenants in order to live in peace and prosperity, happiness and honor. When we fail those we love and follow the ways of the world instead of the Word, love is slowly smothered—and quietly killed. We must fight for love, defend and stand strong in our love for God and those He gave us to love.

Nine months after my husband went to heaven, I boarded a plane for Belize. Joy filled my heart for being a team member on the mission trip, but sadness settled while watching the world celebrate Valentine's Day. Looking out my window while flying over Miami, compassion flowed as did tears. I felt insignificant and in awe of God's grandeur and greatness. I began talking to Him as if He were seated by me on the crowded plane. Peace settled in my heart. When we landed, Michele—a close Christian friend—rushed to me with a message that God had spoken to her heart: "Tell her I see her broken heart and I love her."

My sadness melted supernaturally. For the rest of the trip, I wasn't lost in yesterdays; I didn't worry or wonder relentlessly about my tomorrows. Today is the gift to cherish. Walking in love, stepping in faith, getting out of the boat as Peter did, keeping our eyes on Jesus and showing a willingness to share His love out loud will ensure love and joy all the days of your life. Even when there's rain mixed in with the sunshine, you'll get a rainbow when you let go and let God!

Love does make the world go round. Yesterday I sang that song, uncertain of my future—but believing in love. Today, I sing with joy and peace, for He is protecting my tomorrows—just as He did when I was young and unsure of what waited beyond the safety of my home and family. I am His; wherever He leads, I'll go to share His love with a hurting world. This lasting love is our ticket to happiness and heaven when our time here is done. Keep your covenants; stay closely connected and in love with the Lord and your loved ones! Follow His voice within your heart. Then, love will always win and you will be happy from within!

Cherishing Close Relationships

*D*O YOU ENJOY AN INTIMATE relationship with God? Many people question the possibility of a personal relationship with Christ. It is not farfetched; it is fabulous and free for the asking. Jesus made this possible when He came to earth and shared the Good News of a loving God and life eternal. He paid the price and is the only way to the Father.

Sharing a personal relationship with Jesus doesn't happen haphazardly; it comes from trusting and obeying. Giving God time each morning starts the day off right. Spending time with the Lord and with loved ones is wise. Many marriages suffer when time spent together is taken for granted. Couples become complacent as their love grows cold. They wonder why distance, discord, or depression plagues their hearts and homes. When we steer clear of intimacy and fail to cherish time together, relationships are ruined quickly.

God is always there for us and desires first place in our lives. He gives graciously—while we grumble and grow accustomed to His goodness. We can empathize with our Savior, understanding the pain when loved ones distance themselves from us. Why do we hurt those who love us most? Father God so loved us that He gave His Son to die for our sins. Surely, we would never hurt Him, but we do. Devoted, loving parents should never be disrespected or distanced by their children. The same is true for our Father God. How much time do you spend daily with God, reading His Word, praising Him, thanking Him, praying, and pleasing Him? What is your answer to Him—and to your loved ones who long to spend more time with you? Your relationship with the Lord and loved ones is personal and precious. Never should the sun set on anger and wrong relationships. Waiting too long ruins your treasure and happiness here and in heaven.

Commitment and closeness to Christ and one another kept my husband and me crazy in love until God called him home. We were sealed by his Holy Spirit, living closely connected through triumphs and trials. We made mistakes. We had seasons when we were weary and worn out, especially when raising our children and wondering how we could do it all. Tim helped me realize that doing it all isn't the answer to happiness and can drive us and our children crazy. Our generation is guilty of overextending our children, inflating their self-esteem, and getting them involved in more things than they can handle effectively. Our sons taught these lessons to parents who were trying hard to do it right. Quality and quantity time for the Lord and loved ones are essential and endangered. Many parents and children miss the warning signs that shout the dangers of packed schedules. Being an educator, my children endured lessons at school and at home. My oldest son felt I put him on a pedestal and helped me see how a parent's expectations can endanger a healthy relationship. We only wanted to give our best in order that they might have more in life than we had—what all parents want, right? Most of us fall victim to the demands of society and forget that our time with God and loved ones is where He wants us to be first and foremost. Safeguarding and cherishing that time together fosters family bonding.

Children are all different. They do not always do things as we think they should or use wisely the gifts and blessings bestowed upon them. Often, we live our children's lives through our dreams and desires without their choice. God gives graciously and could do the same thing with us, for we are all His children. However, He does not choose our path. He knows His plans for us and desires for us to follow them, but He never forces His way on us. He never forgets us when we wander. When we wake up, weary from our wrong choices and sinful ways, His arms are open and so are His blessings. He is a loving God who never gives up on us or forces us. We must be careful not to wait too long if we are lost and wandering in the desert. He is the Good Shepherd who is concerned for all His children—even one lost sheep. He loves and allows us to choose to love and follow Him. He made us different and enjoys how we serve Him differently with the gifts we are given. God doesn't dwell on boredom; He wants us to enjoy life and share the Good News with smiles and sunshine lighting our paths.

Cameron, our oldest son, breezed through Bible Drill and enjoyed choir. Clint followed in his brother's footsteps in many areas but not to Bible Drill and choir. I baited him with rewards if he would just go. It was a battle every Wednesday when Pastor Mark came by the Learning Station to pick up Clint for choir. On one Wednesday, I walked over to Tim's office to vent my frustrations. His smile told me that we weren't alone. He patted his leg, my cue to take a seat on his lap. He tenderly told me what I needed (but didn't desire) to hear. I was more concerned about Clint being in choir than Clint was. He didn't enjoy singing and my forcing him to do it was wrong. He motioned for me to look under his desk. Our Clint sat curled up, safe and secure from all alarm, in his daddy's domain.

Clint popped up and said, "Daddy said that I could stay with him and everything would be okay."

I learned a lot that afternoon: a great appreciation for a husband who understood the principle of God's love and made sure his family was close and connected, a whack on my hardheaded belief that our children had to do it all, and a praise to my Father for connecting me with the man He chose to be my husband and the children He entrusted us to raise up as mighty men of God—not mighty men doing everything that came their way. Every mother and father reading this understands the blessings of being closely connected to those you love—and the burden and beauty of balancing. Whatever we do in life, we must strive for balance while being the best we can be.

Luck isn't a factor in happy, healthy relationships. You've got to make the right choices, respect one another and the One who gave you life, stay closely connected, and live out loud in love—through thick and thin. Renew your relationships with a spirit of love.

Singing Love Songs

*D*O YOU HAVE A SPECIAL song that colors your world? Music is important in our lives; special songs preserve cherished memories and messages in our hearts forever. Why do some stick to our souls and bring sunshine every time the lyrics start to play? Why do words surface from out of nowhere on any given day? We associate certain songs with significant people and places in our lives. Songs of Christmas fill our hearts and homes in December. Favorite carols and traditional tunes keep us in the spirit. Special songs make all the seasons of our lives sizzle with memories from yesterdays and promises of tomorrow.

Childhood songs made their mark before we realized the tunes would always stay in our hearts—just as the memories of growing up would. My love for singing creative songs came from my daddy. He would sing instead of argue. Silly as that seemed, when he would break out in a comical little song, it replaced growling with giggles. Mama would be all stirred up over this or that only to hear my daddy singing and smiling; soon, she was happy too. Time has taught me what a smart man my daddy really was. Singing and smiling instead of fussing and fuming is music to God's ears.

Visiting my grandparent's church instilled a deep meaning for the message of a song; Granddaddy Baggett directed singing at Hornett Primitive Baptist Church. Since they had no musical instruments, his singing set the tone. Imagine my joy when I found his old songbook in a box of treasures that had almost slipped into a yard sale pile. The words to the old hymns preach sermons on every page.

Good music made for great dates. Tim and I thought we were in rock and roll heaven when we'd slide in an eight track and sit back to enjoy the tunes. Special songs gave meaning to our young lives—and to our divine love. "Still Waters Forever" by The Four Tops became our signature song. We loved it, learned it, and lived by it. Every time I hear our song, my heart smiles. The words are eternal:

> P is for the privilege of loving and being loved.
> E is the ease it gives the soul and mind.
> A is the absence in the search to find yourself.
> C is the calm you feel if you like what you find.
> E is everlasting. Let this love never cease.

Those words bring peace to all who inwardly embrace them and openly live them. Peace comes from our Father God who is *love*. When we know Him, peace will rest in our hearts, enabling us to love and enjoy our journey through life. Finding your true love—the one who touches your heart so profoundly that your love never ceases—brings peace and songs that will stay with you forever.

I wasn't embarrassed or afraid when I stood to sing a special song to my husband at his fiftieth birthday party. Even though I mixed up the words as the band played on, I felt led to stand and sing to the world how we loved and believed. In our minds, love really didn't come any stronger than his and mine. I believed in him, he believed in me, and that made us one of a kind. Material things didn't make our love right, but if I could have given him the world on a string, that would have been all right. Those words have been sung to lovers all over the East Coast by the Coastline Band. At my husband's last birthday party, I stood and sang them to him. Three years later, we would be parted by death, but our love shines further and brighter with each passing day. Love is stronger when we believe in our Lord and one another.

As our time together grew short, Tim and I listened to our special songs—especially as we drove to Chapel Hill for treatments. Tim turned up one of his favorites about a train whistle blowing your name, ready to take you to heaven's hall of fame. I told him I'd be gone before him. How do you talk about death with loved ones? We avoid it as if that whistle won't really blow our name—or a loved one's name. But it does. That's why we should make every day a beautiful memory; never go to bed ill or mad at one another or leave a loved one when you're angry. We should take time to be together and share special days, special songs, and grow love that will last forever.

Communicate openly and honestly in a spirit of love. Remember the things you did when you first fell in love—and do those things for one another. Remaining in love with your first love is powerful and precious—just as it is when you stay crazy in love with God.

Tim lost his voice a few weeks before he went to heaven. One day, a special song started playing as I was driving us home from a cancer treatment. He reached for my hand. No words were needed; we knew our moments were numbered, but our love would never cease. His strength and dignity held back my tears. I was privileged to have shared an everlasting love.

Celebrate life with special songs. Love deeply and devotedly.

A loving, close relationship with your Heavenly Father and your loved ones will color your world and give you peace. Cherish such love and it will never cease.

Be Grateful Not Greedy

*H*AVE YOU MARVELED AT THE obedience of ordinary people following God's instructions? Biblical stories share such times of trials and triumph for those who loved the Lord and listened. Can you imagine being given a command to dip in the pool seven times for healing or walk around a city seven times for victory when the walls would fall down? What about telling your ninety-year-old wife that God said she would have a baby or being told to get out of the boat and walk on water! Then there was Debra who obeyed a command in battle that brought defeat to the favored enemy. Imagine being in the camp of Israelites seeking the Promised Land for forty years. Not following God's instructions kept them wandering. Manna fell to feed them daily. They thought, as we do, gathering a little extra to save for a rainy day made good sense. Greediness isn't smiled upon by our Father. Sometimes what we work so hard to save is lost to things beyond our control. We are wise to watch out for our tomorrows—but not to become obsessed piling up riches here on earth. He tells us our wisdom is in storing up treasures in heaven.

How foolish Noah felt building that ark per God's instructions. He was jeered and mocked by friends and family, but he stayed true to his conviction that rain would come. Imagine the Noah jokes that were told in social circles for years as the boat took shape and ridicule soared. Noah had his moments when he wondered why—why him, why an ark with no rain in sight, why such scorn to be endured—yet he took it in stride. God gave him specific instructions for two-by-two and family members to get on board. When the rains came and those who laughed lost their lives in the flood, Noah enjoyed the ride.

During Moses's time, God's people were instructed to put blood over the doorposts to protect their firstborn. This might have seemed foolish until cries of death filled the air. Things that might seem silly to some can save your life or secure protection and promise for your family. We should never feel foolish when following what God puts on our hearts, yet we must strive to serve Him in ways that will be pleasing to God. We must also remember that even people in the Bible didn't always listen and do things as instructed.

One young woman heard instructions from God and pondered them in her heart. She faced ridicule—even the threat of being stoned—but she remained faithful to what was planted in her heart by her Lord. She kept quiet, persevered, was protected by Joseph and God, gave birth to our Savior, and proved to the world that God keeps His promises when we listen and obey. Mary's bravery and faith in God while facing adversity made it possible for us to share an intimate relationship with Jesus Christ today. She wasn't overbearing or bragging about being chosen to do this great work for God. She heard His voice, believed, and followed what God downloaded in her heart. There was no fanfare, no baby shower, no friends and family preparing an adorable nursery for her son—only God giving her strength and showing Joseph the way to the lowly stable where angels, shepherds, and Wise Men would proclaim the birth of God's Son. How happy we are that she listened to her heart.

Have you felt God's gentle nudging and instructions to do something for Him that others might find fault with? He still speaks to His people. When we covenant with God, He expects our best efforts and unconditional love as we follow His lead and listen with our hearts. Often, we fear people might think it silly—even stupid—to believe God would want us to do something so not normal or out of the box. How normal is it for a young girl to give birth as Mary did, for one to build an ark and a flood to finally come, or for a son with a coat of many colors to obey and move from pit to Pharaoh? Nothing is impossible when we follow God's calling—believing and being all we can be for Him.

Safe through Life's Storms

*H*OW DO YOU HANDLE STORMS? Summer is synonymous with storms. Some storms are predicted—giving us time to prepare, but others are unexpected—catching us off guard. We are safe from all storms when we keep our eyes on Jesus.

My parents taught lessons and gave good counsel that has helped me weather storms of all kinds in my lifetime. Having a godly fear of storms was modeled by my mother. She wanted all her children gathered safely inside with reverence for the storms raging outside. Being quiet and respectful during storms was instilled at an early age by my dad; it's still with me in my sunset years.

Memories of storms surface when least expected. These past experiences, in the tempest, provide tales to intrigue listeners and lessons that can change lives and bring people closer to Christ. Daddy told stories and shared pictures of Hurricane Hazel that frightened me. However, no pictures or recollections could ever prepare one for the wrath when such powerful storms rage in your presence. Recalling the decade of the nineties, I am reminded of destruction and deliverance from storms destined for our nation's eastern shores. We were hit hard by one storm after another. Clean up was barely completed when news of another brewing storm brought dismay and prayers that it wouldn't come our way. No one wants to be in the path of a storm. We grew tired of intense preparation, unseen danger, routines uprooted, waiting and wondering, force and fury of storms tearing down what we spent lifetimes building up, prayers for protection, reverence for our almighty Father God, and peace when the storms passed. My photo albums show pictures and flashbacks of storms that struck my family; some we were prepared for, but others hit without warning, catching us off guard and unaware of what awaited us after the storm.

One picture's caption, "Snowstorm—Sumter, South Carolina, 1979," reminds me of a blizzard that swept across the state where we had been residents for only two weeks. Our four-week-old, Cameron, slept peacefully between us on a small bed in a stranger's home. Our power was out for a whole week. These kind people—whose son worked with Tim—took us into their warm home so our little son would be safe and secure from the storm. Thirty-two years later, I pause to pray again for that family who showed their Christian spirit in our time of need.

Another picture reminded me of a fearful Friday night when a freak storm flooded Fayetteville. Tim was playing chess with his good friend, Ike, so I loaded our small sons for a shopping trip. Clint was attached to me with one of those Velcro leashes that kept him close. People panicked as we walked toward the exit doors in the mall. Friends warned us of an approaching storm. We tried to make it to our car, but rushing waters sent us inside for dry socks and a plan to get home.

With no cell phone, we ventured into the storm with faith and hope. I stayed calm when waters on I-95 swept inside the door of our little black Saab. Since the bridge was out on Highway 24, I slowly pressed forward to the new bridge. Cameron screamed for me to see shopping carts being swept across the parking lot by the rising, swift waters. I was afraid, but I stayed calm to reassure my sons that we would be safe. I kept my hands on the wheel, my eyes on the road, and my prayers filling our car through songs and sayings the boys understood. We talked to Jesus all the long way home. I stop today to thank Him once again for keeping us safe through that storm.

Pages of pictures bring back memories of hurricanes that hit home—hard! Almost two weeks with no electricity took a toll on our town. The pictures showed weary, tired faces of thankful families and friends joining together to clean up after the storm. Those storms brought the reality of destruction that we watch on television and read about in other places to our back door. Our fate was in our Father's hands. We kept our eye on the weather station until power was lost; the silence was deafening. We waited in the darkness. The only peace and promise was in keeping our eyes on Jesus. He brought us through that storm—and through all the storms that hit us throughout our lifetime together. He is still the One who keeps me safe now that the captain of my ship is with Him.

Drawing closer to Jesus in stormy times, sunshiny days, and circumstances that can drown our hopes and dreams pleases God and puts us in safe harbors of peace and protection. Never be caught off guard; storms come at us from every direction. Keeping our eyes on Jesus will take us through the best and worst of times with a rainbow waiting to remind us of His promise. He will never leave or forsake us; He is with us through every storm when we keep our eyes on Him.

Reading about Peter and the fishermen's ordeal in a fierce storm shows what can happen when we try to deliver ourselves by our own methods instead of reaching out to Jesus. In Matthew 13:22-33, brave friends are fishing while Jesus goes away to pray. When night came, so did a storm. Their boat was tossed by the waves, the wind was contrary, and they thought Jesus was a ghost as He walked toward their boat.

Jesus watched as Peter came down out of that boat and walked toward Him. He was walking on water until the winds roared louder and he was afraid. Then, he did what we do when fear grips and the enemy taunts: he took his eyes off Jesus. Jesus was still there to reach out and save Peter—just as He does for you and me when we get off track and begin to sink.

Jesus taught a great lesson of His love and protection for those fishermen who declared He was truly the Son of God. Jesus saved them from the wrath of the storm while reminding them they were of little faith and should never doubt.

This Bible story shows a picture of Christ walking on the water and the one disciple who was brave enough to get out of the boat and walk with Him. Yet, there is a greater message for all of us than having the faith to walk on water. The command to come was not exclusive to Peter; Jesus was addressing the whole boatload of disciples to look to Jesus in sunshine and storms. I can see this picture in my mind so vividly, can't you? Jesus is holding out His hand while Peter takes baby steps on that roaring sea. This would be a great snapshot for all our picture albums—one to store in our hearts for when we face stormy circumstances in our own lives.

The disciples were afraid of losing their lives. I've been there. Have you? Jesus understood that fear had overcome their faith. Do you face storms in fear or faith? Our pictures show storms that have hit our homes and hearts with memories so painful that we choose to keep the picture albums closed. Jesus opens our hearts and helps us when we cry out for Him. Things may appear to worsen as we reach out to Him—just as it did for Peter. We step out in faith, believing the Word of God, but conflicting emotions, which war against our faith, will rise up against what God promises. We must stand firm and stay true to the One who can deliver us from anything that tries to drown us in sin and keep us from the good life and blessings He freely gives. Storms will come and go, but we will be safe and secure when we keep our eyes on Jesus.

Believe Boldly

*D*O YOU HAVE A SPECIAL saying or story that colors your life? Everyone has a story. The choices we make determine the setting, characters, details, climax, and conclusion of our stories. Is your love story one that features your main characters in a wonderful way and gives honor to your Creator? We write the story, the songs, and choose the words we live by. When our storyline changes, we decide to keep writing and bring beauty where bad things happened or to end our story before it is finished. Enjoying the journey as we write and making sure the end is where "we've only just begun" to live happily ever after with our Father in heaven is most important of all.

This story is about my favorite word: *believe*. This word holds my world together every time the enemy rears his ugly head. We can't elaborate on bitterness, bad reports, or good-byes, but we can choose to believe and put our script in His hands.

It's easy to believe when life is good, but our light must shine even brighter when life isn't good. Believing was a special word to old Abram as he pleaded for a child in Genesis. He was a very wealthy old man with no child to inherit all his riches. The Lord told Abram to look up in the night sky and count the stars to see the magnitude of his offspring.

God's words are easy for us to believe in the story of Abraham and Sarah because we know the ending. They didn't know, but they believed they would have a child and many descendants. Do we believe God even when circumstances seem linked to a story many would call fiction? We can't pick and choose; we must believe in God the Father, Son, and Holy Ghost—the whole story from beginning to end.

Not all people believe. In John 12, we are told that despite all the miraculous signs Jesus had done, most of the people didn't believe in him.

It's hard to believe people don't believe—until we look at our own stories. How many chapters have been written in silence instead of standing up and shouting that we believe and trust Him to guide and give all that He promises? God is bigger than any mountain we face. When we believe, He sees and sends His blessings while we write our stories.

Believe can be all around us, but if it's not inside us, we can't understand the power and peace of the Holy Spirit. The most important place *believe* can be found is in our hearts! One day soon, He is coming to take all believers home to heaven where we will sing our song forever and ever. *I believe!*

Locked Out

*H*AVE YOU EVER BEEN LOCKED out? Writing about losing things and finding them brought a message to my heart about being locked out and how we handle it. Of course, how we handle anything in life is what matters, but being locked out is never lovely—or is it?

The times you've had troubles being locked out—or in—stick with you forever. My family has difficulty keeping up with our keys, which contributes to the numerous locked-out adventures we have endured.

Are you thinking of adventures, shared with special people, that seemed desperate but left lovely memories?

On an icy day in December 1985, Tim left home early for an out-of-town conference. The boys and I pulled on heavy coats, hats, and gloves, and rushed out the door to tell him good-bye. He drove away, leaving us to enjoy leftovers from a recent snowfall. We romped through the snow for hours. Frozen and exhausted, we headed inside to warm by the fire. The back door was locked; the keys teased us, hanging right beside the locked glass door that kept us prisoners in the cold.

Fear gripped my frozen body. What would we do for seven hours? God gave me a peace and plan; our locked-out adventure became a precious memory. We searched my van and found enough change to buy lunch. Cameron and Clint huddled on their sled; I pulled them down the icy street. We stopped to visit friends at their used furniture store. They made room beside the potbelly stove for us to warm our frozen feet. We stayed for hours, browsing and talking, until Clint and Cameron had an icicle fight and I knew it was time to leave. McDonald's was our next stop for a long, long lunch with burgers, fries, and water. The boys colored and played at our table until their restless little bodies begged to be rescued. We crossed the street to K-Mart for an extended shopping spree with no money to spend. The afternoon sun slipped lower in the sky as we headed home. We made another stop to warm up at the furniture store—and then we were off to skate on our neighbor's little frozen pond. The thin ice broke and Clint came up soaked and screaming. We heard a horn honk and what to our startling eyes should appear? Tim drove up in his shiny red car with his smiling face. What could have been an awful day became an awesome adventure with my sons.

Does every locked-out adventure have a fairy tale ending? More end miserably than lovely. My keys were locked inside the house again one summer morning in 1992. Tim was at a sales meeting in the western part of the state. I rushed the boys so I could open the Learning Station for parents to drop off their children. My house and car keys hung inside; we were locked out again. I panicked. We could walk but would never be there before parents arrived. Cameron glared at me as I told him he was about to become my hero. I handed him the key to open the door to The Learning Station and gave him directions that sounded like a James Bond adventure about to unfold. I told him to be careful at every turn, stop at every road, and look three or four times before crossing the streets on his bicycle. I showed him how the key had to be held just right to open the door and told him to tell parents I would be there very soon.

I sent my son off with a prayer that God would take care of him and help us through this locked out dilemma. Cameron rode his bike out of sight. Clint and I walked as fast as his little legs would let him and made it to The Learning Station out of breath and before a single parent arrived. Cameron was waiting at the front door, waving and wearing his proud hero grin. I wasn't very happy with myself, but the locked-out adventure turned out to be lovely when Cameron stepped up and saved the day. My sons and I will never forget that scary morning. That adventure encouraged me to be more careful with my keys—and my kids. They are both precious!

The delightful days of December remind me of Christmas adventures when losing things can drive us crazy—especially gifts bought early, hid carefully, and unable to find!

One Christmas, Tim and his friend, Willie, played friendly jokes on one another throughout the holly jolly season. On Christmas Eve,

Willie hid our Santa stash from Tim. My poor husband was terrified, thinking someone had stolen every single Christmas gift and Santa surprise from his car. Our children were little—as was our extra money to buy more gifts.

Imagine our joy when the gifts appeared and the stories we have shared from that fun but frightful adventure. What Christmas adventures are told around the table when your family and friends gather to give thanks and share love and laughter? Let us rise up and recount the greatest love story of all. It's about God loving us enough to send His Son to die on the cross and save us from our sins.

Cherish each day with those you love. Enjoy adventures of life and secure the love of Jesus in your heart. The one thing that we don't want to lose is the precious gift He so freely gave. Cling to Jesus; stay closely connected to the Lord and loved ones each and every day.

Imagine how Mary and Joseph must have felt as the days grew close for her to give birth. Surely, they felt locked out as government, guidelines, friends, even family forced them to look elsewhere for help and hope. They traveled far away where God was with them in every adventure they encountered while delivering His Son—His gift to the world. They found a way to keep Jesus safe and sound. God showed up and secured every detail in the story that would change the world.

God works things out even when we feel we have no place to turn. As we grow closer to Him, we handle things differently. In May 2008, I handled a locked-out adventure with much more maturity. My knees were red and rashed from a morning battle scrubbing my white-tiled kitchen floor with Clorox. My hair was in hot curlers and I was clad in shorts and a pajama shirt. I looked like a red-kneed alien about to attack planet Mars—and then I realized I was locked out.

I love to make every minute count, so I reasoned I would take out the trash while my hair curled. When the door slammed behind me and automatically locked, my heart sank. I had twenty minutes before the kids would hop off the bus for afterschool care at The Learning Station. My door was locked, no neighbors were home, my cell phone was inside, and I was a wreck. My backyard was beautiful, with two white tents standing and flowers blooming beautifully. I was hosting a wedding rehearsal for my niece that night and a twenty-fifth wedding reception for our neighbors the next day.

My Friday morning had been wonderful as I worked like Martha to get everything ready. When I locked myself out, I didn't fall apart or lose my mind. I prayed, planned, and verbally declared the enemy could just go take a hike. It never fails that when things seem to be going so well, the devil shows up and tries to steal our joy.

I started repeating James 4, "Resist the devil and he will flee from you. Draw near to God and He will draw near to you." I walked around my house and talked out loud as if the door would fling open anytime. It didn't, but I did look up and see the windows opened in our sunroom. My smile widened as I stood the long, silver ladder against the house and started my climb to freedom. Standing on the top rung, I realized the screens were secured and would not slide open from the outside. I started my descent to find a knife to cut the screen, but remembered they were special order screens and replacing one just to get inside the house went against my frugal upbringing.

With only minutes to spare, I had to think fast. I heard laughter near our backyard fence and recognized a dear friend's voice. Running toward the foursome preparing to take off in their golf carts, I yelled for help. They heard my cries and came to my rescue. One of them climbed the ladder and tried to release the locked screen, another tried the door. Finally, one gave me his cell phone to call for help. With all the drama, I had forgotten how ridiculous I looked—until Jackie inquired about my bleeding knees. I explained and the five of us enjoyed a good laugh before they took off to finish their game of golf and my spare key arrived just in a nick of time. My curly hair and red knees were a hot topic that night, but the enemy didn't spoil the party. I was thankful for the people God put in my path to share my adventure.

God is always with us, watching over us and helping us through life's adventures. We should make sure we have taken care of every little detail to ensure we don't get locked out of heaven's gates. Accept Jesus as Lord and Savior, trust and obey, and stand firm in faith until our journey here ends. Then we will have no worries about being locked out of paradise.

Instead, we will celebrate the beginning of a never-ending adventure in heaven with Jesus and all the saints who've gone on before us. We will be locked in with no more keys to be found, no worries or sickness, no sadness or bad news, no terrorism or torture, no hate or crime, no politics or prejudice, no judging or juggling, no testing or expectations to do more, more, more. There will only be God and goodness and glory forever and ever. Eternity with our Father is a great gift—and it's free for the asking.

Christmas rush and worry lock many out of the true meaning of the season. Don't let busyness and commercialism spoil the joy of holiday weeks when we should be locked into happiness with our Lord and loved ones.

Lock out craziness that kills the spirit of the season. Lock in love that ushers His sweet spirit into our hearts and homes. Relish quiet mornings reading His Word while the tree twinkles in the darkness. Communicate with family and friends; do not try to do everything or lock yourself into spend—spend—spend!

Choose to give gifts to charities and cheer up those who have no one to brighten their holiday. Designate a night for family to sing and share memories of past Christmas adventures. Attend church and look for those who might be alone to sit with at Christmas Eve services. Go caroling, visit rest homes, and take time to wear a smile. Don't worry so much about presents stacked to the ceiling.

Treasure gifts He has freely given that we easily take for granted. Lock His love inside your hearts and homes, keep your families focused on the miracle of Jesus—and the gift of Christmas will keep on giving forever and ever.

Behave Yourself

How many times have you been told to behave yourself? I can hear my mother's words echoing from heaven as I write. She never failed to remind her children to be careful and behave when we left home. We were taught to behave at home and away from home, and if we didn't, Mama and Daddy knew it before we got home. My parents were quick to correct any misbehaving from their four children—and were even quicker to give us another chance to prove we knew how to behave. Lots of love and forgiveness followed the needed discipline we received.

What is correct behavior anymore? Do we honestly teach our children to behave? Do we behave or do we blend in with the ways of the world? The Bible gives clear instructions for how to behave like a Christian.

Don't just pretend that you love others—really love them. Hate what is wrong. Stand on the side of the good. Love each other with brotherly affection and take delight in honoring each other. Never be lazy in your work; serve the Lord enthusiastically. Be patient in trouble and be prayerful always. When God's children are in need, be the one to help them out. If someone mistreats you because you are a Christian, don't curse him; pray that God will bless him. When others are happy, be happy with them. If they are sad, share their sorrow. Work happily together. Get into the good graces of important people but enjoy the company of ordinary folks. And don't think you know it all. Never pay back evil for evil. Do things in such a way that everyone can see you are honest. Don't quarrel with anyone. Be at peace with everyone. Never avenge yourself. Leave vengeance to God; He has said that He will repay those who deserve it.

Imagine the difference we would see in our lives—and our world—if everyone embraced and lived by these instructions from our Father.

Imagine families coming together each night to read God's Word and pray. You say, "But my family does read the Bible and pray." What takes priority in your home every night—television, Internet, video games, or reading the Bible and praying together?

How can our children know how to live right when they have not been taught biblical instruction? How can we hope to change our world when we fail to embrace the greatest commandment of all—loving one another as Jesus loves us? More importantly, how can we stand on solid ground when we are not living connected to the vine? We see morals and values, prayer and witnessing, honoring and upholding Christian principles being cast by the wayside. When we fail to believe, behave, and live connected to Christ, internal happiness and eternity in heaven become endangered.

God instructs and expects us to live right and behave; He is always there to forgive when we ask for forgiveness and to wrap His arms of protection and power around us, keeping us safe and secure. He never fails to love us—even when we have misbehaved and have come back to our Father for forgiveness and correction. He welcomes us with open arms.

Each of us can learn lessons on behaving by spending more time studying God's Word and being our best. When we put God first and behave ourselves, He takes care of the rest.

Promise Keepers

$\mathcal{A}$RE YOU PASSIONATE ABOUT THE promises you make to loved ones and to the Lord? Are you one who promises to do this or that with little intention of following through, or are you one held in high esteem for being a real promise keeper? If you've ever been a victim of broken promises, you understand the importance of keeping them. We break promises; God never does.

Relaxing alone in the hot tub at the Center for Health and Wellness, I closed my eyes and had a little talk with Jesus. While praying, a peaceful spirit settled in my heart, urging me to pray there again. I promised God I would pray every time I relaxed in those tranquil waters.

Being bold in our witness is important, but equally important is not chasing people away when we witness. We expect to pray in church, at the dinner table, or before bedtime, but what about times when people need prayer in places where we feel prayer wouldn't be acceptable? Do we shy away, fearful of what someone might think? Does being politically correct or prim and proper stop us from praying with people?

We must remember how Jesus taught us to pray, especially when we feel led to pray with others. He frowned on those who prayed publically as the Pharisees did. He taught us to pray to our Father, asking His will to be done on earth as it is in heaven, to forgive us and our sins as we forgive others and what they have done that's not pleasing to God, and for what they've done to hurt us. That's tough when the hurt is so deep and time has built walls of isolation. We must pray for strength to say no to temptations and for deliverance from evil, for His Kingdom is ours forever and ever. Jesus hears and honors prayers spoken from hearts in tune with Him. They may be short—even silent—but when spoken in the right spirit, they get the job done.

For months, I worked out, headed to the tub, and prayed with people God put in my path. There's power in praying with people. That's what Jesus taught us to do, even as He met the woman at the well and started a conversation when most people would have snubbed her and kept silent before walking away. Jesus's example shows that we are to reach out to all people—not a select few. Those we feel most uncomfortable with often bring the greatest blessings.

One cold morning, I shivered and stepped quickly along my path beside the pool. With the hot tub in sight, I stopped suddenly. Standing there in my stretched and most unflattering bathing suit, I was keenly aware of my sagging, pale skin in places that used to be tight, toned, and tanned; I flushed with fear and wanted to flee. How foolish I must have appeared standing there with my towel covering my face, of all places! Hiding my face did nothing to help remedy how ridiculous I felt. Knowing I must do something quickly, I spoke a silent prayer and waited.

Ever so slowly, I stepped in faith and sat down in my little corner of the tub without a word leaving my lips. I closed my eyes and thought the fears would go away, but they didn't. I prayed again and remembered my promise to God. Having a silent conversation with Him, I reasoned that these two handsome young men would be just fine without me saying a word. I remembered how Jesus talked to people about things that interested them. One of the young men spoke about studying to pass the test for the SEALS. God opened the door. I introduced myself and began talking about school. They told me how they had graduated and were pursuing careers as Navy SEALS. Their bodies showed dedication to training; their kindness revealed Christian upbringing; their willingness to stand in swirling waters and pray reminded me that God rewards us when we keep our promises to Him.

I thanked God for the time we shared on that cold morning when our hearts were warmed by His grace and goodness. Our amen was followed by a firm handshake and smiles that melted my heart. I stood without fear; I felt as if I could have walked across that pool just as Peter walked on water. My heart was happy; the enemy had been defeated that morning in the hot tub. I sucked it up and trusted my

Lord to lead me through what I couldn't do without Him—and He did!

Prayer is precious and powerful. We must rise up and allow our prayers to pepper our days. Be not afraid to pray with the people God places in your path. When your prayers are spoken in love, purely pouring from a heart that honors and hears from God, He gives just the right words and puts all things in perspective. Then, the blessings flow. He does it for me and will do the same for you. He never puts more on us than we can handle. He never asks more than we can do. He never breaks His promises to me and to you.

Be Prepared

*A*RE YOU A PERSON WHO strives to be prepared? In Genesis, we read of Noah preparing for the flood from God's directions and Joseph receiving wisdom to prepare for the seven-year famine. Gideon was shown how to prepare his army in advance of the battle in Judges. John the Baptist told the people in Isaiah to prepare the way of the Lord.

Studying Matthew 24:44, we learn to be prepared for the second coming. The riches of the future are for those who make preparation today. We are wise to draw on His wisdom, for He knows the plans for each of us. When we watch and prepare as did the three hundred men Gideon chose, God will save and deliver us. We can't procrastinate or play around when we should be preparing for our tomorrows.

Preparing our minds, hearts, and bodies for tomorrow takes daily discipline and determination. It doesn't just happen. God comes to us in various ways with direction and guidance just as He did to people in the Bible. Noah's encounter was completely different from Joseph's or Mary's or Abraham's; the list goes on of how God shared His wisdom to help people prepare for the future. Moses heard from Him with a burning bush while an angel visited Joseph in a dream. How do you hear from God? If we aren't hearing from Him, we might need to adjust our channel and stay tuned in to Him. If we don't nurture our relationship with Him by spending time in prayer, reading His Word, worshipping and praising Him, and staying closely connected, we will find static on the line and fail to hear His calling.

Our future is shaped by today's decisions. Jesus did not teach us to ignore the future but to prepare for it. His warning was against anxiety concerning tomorrow—not against preparation. And He doesn't compromise. Noah could have built that ark the way he thought it should be done, but he listened to God, making an ark of gopher wood. If He taught Noah how to build a boat able to withstand the flood, He can teach you and me what to do today that will affect our tomorrows. Listen as He speaks!

Last winter, I opened my eyes early one morning, focusing on the dormant treadmill beside my bed. We had placed it there five years earlier with good intentions of exercising every day. My excitement dwindled; there was always something else to do—actually something else we'd *rather* do. Therefore, the treadmill that could keep us in shape only took up space. That cold winter morning, I couldn't shake the feeling that overwhelmed me to prepare myself for what was ahead. The treadmill was the focus of what God was downloading. His prompting to get myself in shape grew stronger. My lukewarm exercise regime wasn't working. I gave leftover time to exercising my body, and it showed.

Finally, I followed my heart to the Center for Health and Wellness. I decided to give my best and enjoy the journey to a stronger, healthier body. My hesitation about joining the center included finding time to work out, getting my money's worth, and embarrassing myself in front of all those people in tip-top shape. Those things sound so silly in comparison to what concerned Noah, Abraham, Mary, or Joseph. They feared time restraints, friends making fun of them, and not being able to do as He instructed—but they didn't run from what He encouraged them to do. They listened to His warnings, instructions, and messages even though they didn't see clearly the plans He had for their lives. We make the choices that determine our tomorrows. I don't love to pull myself from my warm bed on cold mornings, but I love the feeling when I've worked out while talking to Jesus and good friends who inspire and encourage rather than laugh at me, spend a little time in the hot tub, shower, dress for work, and leave feeling refreshed and ready for the day. When we are engaged and passionate about what we do, it brings blessings. We must listen, look, and lunge forward in faith or we'll stay stuck in the bottom of our pits.

Do you hear His voice guiding, gently nudging you to give your heart to Him, to give Him first place, to get in shape physically and spiritually? What He speaks, He will do! He is preparing His children for what His Word reveals in end times. He is building up an army of believers . . . brave and bold. He is getting us in shape so that we might stand firm for the Lord. What preparations should we be making in our lives now? Let us not put off until tomorrow what He tells us to do today. Listen, look, and be prepared for what God has called you to do.

Sweet Holy Spirit

*A*RE YOU RESPONSIVE TO PROMPTINGS of the Holy Spirit? God sends stirrings and strength from the Helper, the Holy Spirit. He may not speak with a blast of a trumpet or a mighty wind, but when you are connected to the vine, you will hear and understand in whatever way He comes to you—a touch on the shoulder, a stirring in your heart, a picture popping in your mind, a comment from a person, or words from a song.

Are you obedient to the gentle moving of His Spirit? He works in wondrous ways in order to develop our sensitivity. He knows our frailties. This sensitive moving of His Spirit in our lives makes us strong. In His quiet way, He strengthens our faith. We must learn to live in the presence of God. At any moment, He chooses to manifest and do things in our lives that can't be explained. We may not understand; others may mock and make light of being led by the Spirit, but we should always honor and seek God. He will stir up our spirit, lead us where we should go, give us the comfort we seek, and shower us with blessings and favor for following, trusting, and obeying. When we are filled with His Spirit, we are in tune with the Holy Spirit. When we aren't connected, racing ahead, or lagging behind, His voice falls on deaf ears.

By reading Acts 20:22, we realize the importance of being bound in the Spirit wherever we go. When God wants you to go somewhere or do something, you will feel a connection to it. He aligns us in our spirit. When we pray hard, we will either be bound or released. Think of something you've done that brought confusion or chaos—it wasn't bound in the spirit. When things you do create a calm, peaceful feeling, you're receiving confidence and confirmation from Christ. Being surrendered shows Christ you are broken and bold in your witness. Surrender to Jesus; stand firm and faithful in your relationship with Him. We must believe in the Holy Spirit even though our eyes don't behold His presence. He lives within our hearts. We feel God and know His spirit is the real thing. We are led by the Spirit. By the same token, we know when it's not real by the way we feel inside. It's counterfeit when we don't get peace and promise in our hearts. Just a closer walk with Thee opens the door for the Spirit to dwell in you and me.

Get in Shape

*A*RE YOU SPIRITUALLY IN SHAPE? Recently, I sat in bed looking at my treadmill with thoughts of getting in shape. My Bible fell from my lap, opening to the Book of Jude. I felt compelled to read the short epistle before turning in for the night—and I was intrigued by the powerful message. I kneeled beside my bed, reflected, rested in His peace, and rededicated my life, promising to pursue the challenge to contend for the faith and get in shape spiritually!

Three hours later, I was awakened with a stirring to get this story going. Downloading from my Father came like a refreshing rain that replenishes and restores parched areas of our lives that have longed for relief. My prayer is that after reading this story, you will read the Book of Jude to fully embrace the urgency to obey God and leave the consequences to Him, to anticipate the Lord's return while living productively, and to realize we stand tallest and strongest on our knees.

Jude begins his short letter extending love, peace, and mercy to believers. His focus changes quickly as he challenges them to fight for the faith, beware of false teachers, and live for God. Jude's message, written between AD 65-80, is even more relevant and real for present times.

Today, we must follow that same challenge to stand up, fight, and do battle when the truth of God is attacked. Danger is all around. We see corrupt cities in our world drenched in sin, as Sodom and Gomorrah were. God calls us to move away from such sin and not look back. The force field of evil pleasures and pursuits pulls powerfully while the enemy entraps and destroys. Our glorious God gives sinners plenty of time to repent. We have golden opportunities to live for our Lord and be doers of His Word; churches are on every corner and believers work to spread the Good News. Bibles are plentiful, but are they placed on shelves until a crisis or read and studied for directions for a closer walk with Thee? If we refuse His calling, even in His grace, there will be suffering and judgment.

In these dangerous times, we must beware of false leaders and not be caught off guard. Keeping ourselves in the love of God and helping to rescue fellow believers from the deception and devastation of sin is crucial. This challenge may seem big, but even bigger is the God who is able to keep us from stumbling. Jude 24 reminds us to beware, to live for God, and to depend on the grace of God in order to keep us standing and not stumbling.

God longs for His children to honor and adore Him, to worship and praise Him, to talk with Him, and enjoy His goodness and grace. He hears our prayers and sees our faithfulness. He enjoys the times we share with Him intimately—as we do with a best friend or a loved one. Taking time to get to know him, obey him, and honor him as Lord of our lives pays huge dividends. He is always there to protect, bless, and enlarge our territories. He is loyal and loving, but He expects our loyalty and love in return.

As He loves and craves a personal relationship with us, so does He abhor sin and so does He judge. In Jude 15, we are told the Lord will come with ten thousands of His saints to judge and convict those who've been ungodly. How can we risk what awaits those who live in an ungodly way in this world? He stresses ungodliness because He hates it. It will keep us locked out of eternity with our Lord and nothing is worth missing heaven.

Today we see the same things Jude warned against thousands of years ago. We are told to remember the words spoken by the apostles of our Lord Jesus Christ: mockers of the Word and unbelievers would be rampant in end times (Jude 16-19).

The beautiful part of this message is the ending—for those who believe and be all they can be for Jesus Christ. When we keep ourselves in the love of God, we can look for the mercy of our Lord Jesus Christ unto eternal life. In all things, we should give glory to God as Jude does in ending his letter.

Times may be tough today; sin lurks at every turn. We wonder what it will take to get our attention and turn us back to God. The enemy is working harder than ever to bring division among God's people and saturate our world with wickedness. That's why this challenge to contend for the faith is crucial. We must be prepared, ready to stand firm and do battle, when the truth of God is attacked. The time is now to fight for the faith, but only those who are spiritually in shape can answer the call.

Passionate on Purpose

*P*AUL UNDERSTOOD THE JOY OF living passionately for Christ. What Paul desired for those he loved as Christian brothers and sisters, so I desire for you. Please accept these words as a challenge to come closer to the Lord and to those you love in this life.

Paul writes in the fourth chapter of Philippians that peace and joy come when we are rooted in following God's ways. Paul writes with conviction. He lives what he writes—even for those who didn't know him personally—his deep love for the Lord was evident. Paul gives encouragement, instruction, and appreciation for the help and support he received. He poured out his heart passionately for the people to be unified in a humble attitude toward one another and God. He stressed praising God and rejoicing over complaining and finding fault. Living in peace, with promise, was his choice over a life of anxiety and apathy with little regard for the One who gave the gift of life so lovingly to His precious children. Do we take this gift for granted? Are we any different than those Paul pleaded with to resist the enemy and reconnect with the Father? Do we live our days with a spirit of anxiety instead of appreciation? Paul's words reach into each of our homes and hearts; are we listening or looking elsewhere for peace and promise?

Anxiety is a Goliath in today's world. Daily routines cause worry and anxiety. Health, bills, lost jobs, healthcare, too much to do and too little time, maintaining the house and yard, gas and grocery prices, running late, and work-related demands can deafen our ears to God's calling. Dealing with issues where the enemy gets his foot in the door can be devastating. The enemy creates confusion, frustration, and separation from those we love—and from the Lord who loves us and longs for us to live in peace and prosperity. Our poor choices can paralyze the progress God has planned. If anxiety rules in your life, Paul's words offer help to keep from getting distracted by anxiety. Honoring God and thinking right and lovely thoughts enables us to grow in joy and peace.

Paul reminds us to rejoice in the Lord always, to allow others to see gentleness in our lives, and to give thanks to God as we ask Him to hear our prayers. Paul ends with my favorite verse: Philippians 4:8. His words remind us to keep our thoughts on what is lovely, pure, and right in God's sight. Think about such things and we will stay closely connected to the vine. When we are connected, we bear delicious, bountiful fruit.

Paul wants us to put our disagreements into the proper perspective and think about lovely things instead of being troublemakers and concentrating on chaos and confusion. Paul showed how the Church should operate as a partnership, being honest about joys, sorrows, burdens, and issues to be worked through together. Release anxieties, relish togetherness, and rejoice in the peace that only God provides. We can work together, worship together, and walk together in unity with joy in our hearts and homes

As prayers increase, so does the peace that God gives. Through prayer, our anxieties leave us and go to God. We release worries. We disagree in love without division. Strength unites by abiding in prayer and love for one another.

One of the last gifts my mother gave me was a sheet of stickers with special verses that she loved. I stuck those stickers in a drawer and forgot all about them—even though I appreciated the gift, agreed with their messages, and dearly loved my mother who gave me life and loved me unconditionally. This is how God must feel when we forget all about Him—even though we love and appreciate Him, agree with His message, and know He gave us life and loves us unconditionally. Keeping passion alive in our relationship with the Lord and loved ones is wise and wonderful.

Recently, I found those stickers, held them close to my heart, and spoke words of love to my mother and my Maker. Then, I stuck them inside my kitchen cabinet where I get my coffee mug each morning, by my bedside where I kneel to pray, on my mirror, in my car, even inside my billfold. Daily, I am reminded of the love of my Lord and the woman He chose to be my mother. One day, when we are reunited in heaven, I will tell her that I should have shown greater appreciation and acknowledgment for the gifts she gave me throughout my lifetime. If your parents are still living on earth, take time to thank them every day for all they have given—and for giving you life, the greatest gift of all.

Think of all the gifts God gives. How have we used them? He will recount every detail when we rise up to meet Him in glory. What will He say when we reach heaven's gates. I long to hear the words that He is pleased and He considers me a good and faithful servant. Each of us can hear those welcoming words—if we have accepted Jesus as our Lord and Savior and are doers of His Word.

May you find peace and promise from this message of love. Give God first place in your life! Stop dwelling on disagreements, disrespect, and despair. Start living out loud for the Lord, being crazy in love with Him and your loved ones, and thinking of things that are lovely. Then, you will wake up in the morning loving life and the Lord. And when He calls you home, you will be ready to meet the Master and enjoy paradise forever and ever.

Protect Your Tomorrows Today

DO YOU ENJOY CREATING MEMORIES? I live for Kodak moments, for times when my family and I do things together, for moments at work when I touch children's lives (more importantly, when they touch mine), for days when I clean my house and work in my yard and feel so close to my Father, for times with friends who color my world, for each morning when I open my eyes to His gift—another day of adventure and blessings. It's what we do with the twenty-four hours He gives daily that determines if our album of memories will be packed to the brim or have lots of empty spots. I want mine to be overflowing. How about you?

My mind has been frozen in time thinking about what I just wrote. The floodgates opened and out poured more than fifty years of memories that had been stored safely inside my heart. The picture show is in living color, starring my husband, sons, family, friends, and me. The executive director is my Lord and Savior, Jesus Christ. He made every moment possible, knowing the script, scenes, climax, and ending before our love story ever began. Scenes of our "memory making" flashed back to 1985 when we were remodeling my husband's insurance office. I could see the four of us taking a break from painting in the back room, exhausted from a long day at work, school, and renovating. Our three-year-old, Clint, grabbed his toolbox and headed to the main room where our paint buckets waited. My husband and older son, Cameron, were enjoying a snack and rest break in the back room. Clint burst through the open door, wearing a sailor hat and blue jeans covered in wet paint, and said, "Daddy, a fox turned over the paint can and ran out the front door."

Tim's new brown carpet was covered with beige paint. I can still see Tim and Cameron desperately trying to clean up the mess with

Clint still talking about that mean old fox. Clint finally repented when he realized his daddy's carpet wasn't ruined.

There's a whole series of renovation movies we created in our lifetime together, but the fox story was the one playing in my mind as I wrote this. Clint's tall tale took up precious moments we needed to be working, but all work and no play steals time to create memories that will touch tomorrow. The four of us shared long hard nights, the deadline to open, the thrill of turning a headache into a haven where we would build a business and create many memories. I thought of how God had plans for that building even thirty years ago when we were stepping in faith to grow Tim's business. God was putting it all in place even then; our children were small, but our dreams were big.

In God's time, He opened the door for a ministry to glorify His name in that building where we worked and made memories for decades. It was a decision that came after months of prayer and divine signs. The enemy worked hard to discourage us while we overcame obstacles. I spilled the paint this time—an entire gallon inside Tim's El Camino. So close to tears, I started singing, cleaned up my mess, and made the car shine. That's what Jesus does for us when we praise Him instead of pouting and putting other things before Him. He cleans us up and makes us shine from the inside.

"Tim's Gift—The Love Ministry" began as a step of faith, in obedience to glorify God. My husband's spirit of love and integrity seeded the ministry where he spent long hours serving others. God knew then of His plans for Tim's office to be a ministry today. The small building is like a lighthouse giving hope and help to people and sharing God's gifts: love, life, and light. The ministry is growing as a new season propels us to the plans our Father has for the rest of our lives. Tim's insurance slogan, "Protecting Your Tomorrows Today" seems to have been in God's plan too, for He protects our tomorrows when we choose to accept Him today.

Cherish the Good Book

*D*O YOU ENJOY READING THE Bible? This story stirred while singing a song I learned long ago about the Bible being the book for me, how I will stand alone on the Word of God, the Bible. Children still sing this little tune, but do the words ring true in hearts of all God's children. Is the Bible the main book in our lives? Are we standing alone on the Word of God?

Do you read the Bible for information or transformation? Many people feel guilty when daily Bible reading and understanding the Word is not happening. The Bible is meant to give Good News, guidance, growth, and guts to follow our Lord throughout our lifetime. If we study and read His Word every day, there will be endless lessons waiting to be uncovered and understood.

Reading the Bible for information without transformation will not secure our spot in the promised place He is preparing. We can go to every Bible Study being offered, read the Bible morning, noon, and night, memorize scripture and say them for all to hear, but still be unsaved. We can set our schedules to read designated chapters each night in order to read the entire Bible in a year, yet neglect accepting Jesus and being doers of His Word. Reading the Bible for information is important and will help us understand how legalism in the Old Testament was a part of the Good News that came in the New Testament. When we allow the words to settle in our hearts, the seed will grow—as will our faith. When we stop reading out of duty or requirements and read with a passion to learn more and love deeper, the transformation becomes apparent. Scriptures we read without understanding, before our change of heart and closeness to our Savior, suddenly become clearer and more meaningful. Relying on Biblical scholars or schools isn't necessary to understand the Bible. When we study the Bible and maintain our relationship with God, the greatest Helper will live inside us and bring insight, opening our eyes and hearts to see and understand the Word and the ways of our Father. With our transformation comes the helper Jesus promised to send: the Holy Spirit.

His Spirit will dwell in our hearts to help fight life's battles and enjoy God's blessings. He helps us read with understanding and react with active faith. We can bravely stand firm and be all that God wants us to be, knowing that we have been transformed into a treasure that our Father cherishes. Transform and enjoy being a child in the family of God.

Forgiveness Is Free

*D*O YOU HAVE A HARD time forgiving yourself? Forgiving oneself is not easy, especially when we allow sin and situations that can distance us from God to build up in our hearts. It's like plaque on our teeth; when we don't remove it daily, eventually we proceed to the dentist with problems, pain, and a price to pay. If we fail to clean our hearts of sin and forgive others and ourselves, our lives face the same fate: problems, pain, and expensive lessons about keeping our lives in order and connected to our Father. Children at The Learning Station understand the concept of cleaning out hearts daily. Each afternoon, before we begin homework, we stop to talk about the day, share prayer requests, clean out our hearts, and pray. Our younger children love to act out their daily cleansing of their hearts. We pretend we are holding a big brush that empties our hearts of anything that needs to go. They speak of heartaches or happenings of the day that have caused them pain or problems. While we brush our hearts clean, we ask for forgiveness for those we hurt and those who hurt us. We praise the Lord with loudness before getting on with our afternoon work and play with pure hearts and a much sweeter spirit. Jesus reminds us to go to Him as little children. Could we learn lessons on forgiving others and ourselves by watching innocent children carve the little sins away from their tender hearts? A cleansing a day keeps the enemy away. Practice makes pure hearts. Try it—you'll love the feeling it gives when you keep your heart spiritually in shape.

God's Word gives guidance and instructions to help us understand the importance of forgiving ourselves and others. In 1 John 1:9, we are told if we confess our sins to God, He will continuously cleanse us.

The Bible makes it clear that there is only one requirement on our part: we must freely admit that we have sinned and confess our sins.

It is dangerous to let sin sit and stew inside a heart that can quickly corrode, keeping us from God's blessings and the beauty of peace and prosperity. When our hearts aren't right with God and with one another, we repress the hurt and pain until it erupts or we keep it buried until it eats away at our happiness and relationships. Be quick to repent. Don't try to hide anything from your loved ones—and especially from God. He will never reject you because He loves you unconditionally. Why do we think we can hide a thing from Him anyway? He knows everything, but repentance releases the power of His blood on your behalf and makes it effective in your life. When we confess our sins and clean out our hearts, the blood of Jesus will cleanse us regularly. We won't worry; we'll be happy.

When we clean our hearts each afternoon, there's always at least one child who hesitates or isn't very enthusiastic about going through the motions of cleansing. Yet, that does not mean they aren't listening to the lessons of the love of God and His forgiveness when we confess and clean out the stuff inside. A mother recently shared a testimony of how her son was listening and learning about the love of the Lord. He had been bickering with his brother all afternoon. Finally, the young son hit his older brother. She scolded him and put him in time out. When she came to check on him, she heard him talking to himself as he sat in his time out chair. Standing beside his bedroom door, she heard him telling Jesus that he was so sorry for what he had done. She peeped inside to see him cleaning out his heart and asking for forgiveness. The mother's tears told a story of the unconditional love of the Lord that we can all enjoy. She held her son close and thanked him for taking his little sin to Jesus.

On the following Monday afternoon, she rushed inside to tell her story and thank us for teaching her children about Jesus and His cleansing power. That story may seem small and insignificant in comparison to big sins that saturate our world today—from murder to terrorism and evil acts that send shivers down our spines. Still, we should model the behavior of the young boy who talked to Jesus and cleaned his heart. Time out and talking it out with God is good for us. The best news is that God forgives all sins—no matter how large or small—when we seek forgiveness, confess genuinely, and cleanse our hearts. He doesn't weigh the scales to measure the magnitude of the sin we commit. We all sin—and it's impossible to remedy that sin by ourselves. None of us are above sin.

"If we claim to be without sin, we deceive ourselves and the truth is not in us. If we claim we have not sinned, we make him out a liar, and His Word has no place in our lives" (1 John 1:8-10).

The real question is not whether we sin, but what we will do when we sin. We can't get rid of our sin by ourselves. Since God knew how hard it would be to forgive ourselves, He sent His helper. His spirit lives in our hearts, walks with us, talks with us, and comforts us. God is faithful; He forgives our sins upon confession and wipes them away forever. We need to do the same. We forgive and try to forget, but the enemy keeps bringing up the pain from people who hurt us. Forgiving is easier with God's help. The only thing we can do is take it to the cross. He washes us and we are whiter than snow. Forgive yourself, forgive others, and enjoy the feeling of freedom that comes from trusting and believing in Jesus Christ.

Singing His Songs

*D*O YOU AGREE THAT TOUGH times in life are gifts from God? We wonder, wait, and welcome goodness that can come from the depths of sorrow, sadness, and situations that stew us in self-pity.

King David's life shows how sadness and sorrow helped mold him into a dynamic leader. He could have given up when his son died, when he hid in caves from King Saul who wanted him dead, when his home was burned and his family taken hostage, or when he endured years of hardships and heartaches before becoming king. He sinned, repented, and lived through the consequences of his sin, but he was always a man after God's own heart. He loved the Lord even when he was making the mistakes that led to miserable living conditions. Yet, his repentant heart and genuine desire to love and serve the Lord brought blessings throughout his lifetime. He reigned as a king who had everything. His psalms send a message that having God's guidance and love through the depths of despair and heights of happiness is what matters most. God will do the same for you and me. Our hearts are molded and hopes heralded through hurt and hardships.

David's writings share the story of God's love in our lives. He asked God for a pure heart, a steadfast spirit, and begged to stay in the presence of his Holy Spirit. David wrote and sang to the Lord—even in his deepest depression and toughest times. When he felt the world closing in on him, he learned that singing praises delivered him from despair. If we praise the Lord instead of moaning and groaning in times of despair, we will be lifted with peace and joy saturating our souls.

Writing is a wonderful way to share your love and communicate with the Lord and loved ones. Recently, I found a three-page poem I wrote for Tim on his birthday when sickness threatened to turn our world upside down. The words I wrote bring tears and confirmation that our God is an awesome God. He knew the plan for our lives even before we were formed in our mother's womb, before we were joined together in marriage and covenant with one another and Him. Sharing portions of this love song show how God will sooth our aching hearts and bring goodness from the sorrows we bear.

> To share our thoughts aloud is good for the soul. I thank God for giving countless stories to unfold.
> Keeping our family close to God is important, you see; the enemy works hard to disrupt our harmony.
> Flying home from visiting our son gives a majestic view of God's beauty from the big, blue sky.
> Thank you God for grace, for goodness, by faith we continue to live our lives.
> I am blessed with two wonderful sons and a husband; my great gift is being his wife.
> Please protect us and give Timothy strength, peace, and help him keep our ship afloat.
> We are getting older; there are things that threaten to sink our boat.
> Please grant us time to get things all worked out, then to Topsail, after retirement, we can go.
> Keep us mindful that you are our captain and all things you do know.
> Our love is strong, our dreams are big, our faith in You is true.
> My prayer is filled with thanks and praise; please keep us both in tune.
> Our journey's been a great one; the seas we've sailed our best.
> Now, we prepare ourselves for life's greatest test.
> Still waters run deep—as we age, more care our vessels demand.
> Help Timothy and me get in shape and get things done, please help us understand that we can meet the challenges and our remaining dreams can come true.

> Those dreams will become reality with our steadfast love and faith in You.

Today, I sing my song louder than ever with a thankful heart. I am humbled to share these stories with people I know and those I will not meet until glory! I am honored to serve God and use the gifts He has given to share help and hope with people in need. I am committed to preaching and teaching the Good News and singing songs of love to praise my Lord. I am filled with a passion to help people see the need to rise up and recount love, to stay closely connected to the Lord and loved ones, and to enjoy living each day crazy in love with Him and them.

I am reminded of King David when he mourned his son's death, then tore off his ash clothes and praised God. Only God can take away the pain and restore a broken heart. Our dreams of retirement and being together through our sunset years didn't work out as we planned. We don't understand why things work out as they do, but God does. He has the perfect plan for our lives. He works all things out for good for those who love Him and are called according to his purpose. I step in faith as His plans for my sunset years unfold. I am doing my best to stay in His will and share from my heart the great love stories of our Lord.

Time is short here on earth; it is like a fleeting moment, a mere mist, a season, and we're gone. Let us love God and one another with passion and purpose in our plans.

Blessings on the Beach

*E*NJOYING A WALK ON ANY beach brings blessings and rekindles memories. My favorite beach is Topsail Island, off the coast of North Carolina. Recently, I strolled down the beach, passing people of all ages, some wearing frowns, others sharing smiles. Everyone was focused on their family, their fishing, and their fun in the sun. Their togetherness turned my own thoughts to times past when my family played together on the beach.

The first beach trip after marriage ended with Tim and me searching the sandy paradise for our car keys. Our last dollars paid a locksmith to open the door to our little red car. Years later, our sons scooted across the silvery sand on boogie boards. Building sand castles and moats filled with toy boats was a favorite; burying our bodies in the sand necessitated cool, cleansing dips in the ocean. Flying kites, feeding seagulls, and finding seashells for keepsakes kept us going strong. Then, we'd flop on our towels and bake in the sunshine. It seems like yesterday when we'd drag our tired sons from the sandy shores and head home. As quickly as I strolled down memory lane, I pulled myself back to reality and continued my walk down the beach.

Seagulls soared overhead as children teased them with bits of bread. Parents closely watched their young children's daring attempts to outrun the ripples. One man posed his wife and two children for a perfect picture. I stopped my stroll and offered to snap a real family photo. Looking through the camera lens, I saw one of God's best blessings: a smiling family sharing a day on the beach. I held back tears as I handed back their camera, thinking of the family picture I worked hard to have taken the Christmas before Tim went to heaven. Having everyone in the picture was important to me. We planned times for the perfect family picture, but that pose with each member present will never happen. We waited too long. Gather your family for a holiday picture even when it's hard to get them all together. A big happy family picture will be a blessing and preserve a family memory before your circle is broken.

Many people walked alone on the beach; others lounged on chairs with no one by their side. Some stood and stared at the sea. Wondering what they were thinking, I walked faster, assuring myself the people I met were just like me. They dreamed and dared to be their best while dealing with what life dished out to them daily. They cared deeply and came here to spend time with their loved ones—or remember their loved ones. They had endured pain, shared happiness, hectic schedules, held strong to the ropes of hope, and anchored their dreams. No one spoke a word to me, yet their dreams and hopes for tomorrow could be seen in their expressions and the protection for those they loved.

The orange sun slipped behind the dunes; it was time for me to leave this place where I so easily commune with my Father. Walking the beach brings me closer to my Maker and gives me time to think about cleansing my heart and honoring my Lord. Above, clouds hovered like puffs of white smoke. I kneeled and talked to God with prayers of thanksgiving thundering above the sound of crashing waves. The beauty of such moments can never be erased. I looked to heaven, accepting my lot and thanking God for all I've got. I could picture Jesus breaking through the clouds and holding out his hands. One day our strolls will be on heaven's sands—the golden streets where we will mingle with the saints of old and meet loved ones again. We will have no worries or woes, only joy and life eternal.

Living each day in anticipation of Jesus's return gives assurance that He will welcome us home. I brushed the sand from my feet and headed for home, singing words from an old hymn about how the clouds will roll back as a scroll and all is well with my soul. What a wonderful feeling when we have peace in our hearts and a personal relationship with Jesus. It is so simple. Talk to Him today. Tell Him your troubles. Confess your sins. Ask Him to cleanse your heart and come in to stay, come in today, come into your heart, and show you the way.

A walk down the beach brings blessings, memories, and a closeness to God. Answer the question before it's too late: Is all well with your soul?

Keeping Christ in the Center of Your Life

*D*O YOU KEEP GOD IN the center of your life? That question has been saved in my computer for nine months waiting for a story to be written. Time and time again throughout several seasons, I would click on the saved question but no story spewed forth. In winter season, only a few days before Christmas, I sit in my favorite writing spot at Topsail—my heart filled with joy and a story stirring to answer the question and start a New Year with Christ in the center and commitments renewed.

Time reminds me of changes through seasons in our lives, predicaments or plans that cause procrastination in finishing what we start. Why spend time wandering and wondering, when in faith we could be doing? Giving up when the going is tough isn't what pleases God. Mary and Joseph stayed strong, even when their minds wondered while waiting for Baby Jesus. God was in the center of their lives as they walked in faith, committed to God.

Wouldn't it be wonderful if all God's children would commit to Christ wholeheartedly and rely on His guidance? Why? When we try to do things on our own, we make big blunders of intended blessings. It may take seasons to see clearly that keeping our focus and commitment on Christ is the answer to peace and promise in all things.

Are you committed to God through new seasons of your life? Long ago in Bethlehem, Mary and Joseph faced tough times and heavy burdens. Life wasn't easy for them but they kept God first, staying committed from cradle to cross. We can also commit our load to God by rolling it over to Him. It is helpful to realize that we can roll something that is too heavy to carry or to cast. God promises the yoke is easy with a comfortable, calm spirit in our hearts and homes if what we do and who we are is centered on Christ. If there is craziness, confusion, turmoil, and tenseness in our lives, the yoke will be heavy. This means Christ isn't in the center of our lives-we aren't truly committed! But what are we to commit to God?

First, we commit ourselves. Psalm 22:8 reminds us those who trust in the Lord and let Him rescue will be delivered and God is delighted. Let us delight God in the four seasons of 2012 by committing ourselves to Him in all things.

Trusting God to carry our burdens is revealed in Psalm 55:22. When we cast our cares on the Lord, he will sustain and never let the righteous fall. Burdens can imprison and keep us from seeing the beauty of living life out loud—with the Lord leading. While we will never be burden free, it's how we handle the load that makes life happy and heavenly or hectic and horrible. Watching people with loads much heavier than mine, smiling and trusting Jesus, is a sure sign that He is carrying their loads.

Committing ourselves and delighting God may seem difficult, but the more we trust and obey and be happy in Jesus—the lighter the load, easier the yoke, and happier we are.

Three years ago, I traveled to a revival in Charlotte with my sister, Gaye, and niece, Katy. The huge coliseum was packed with people who waited hours to get inside. We were in one of those long lines, but an usher saw Katy's handicap and kindly led us inside—all the way to the front. The service was amazing. Driving home, a stirring in my heart wouldn't go away—'have a revival at home and the people will come'! The seed was planted; my faithful, fertile heart prayed, questioned, planned, even postponed dates reserved for the Civic Center, and finally took the step of faith to what I believe God wants to happen worldwide . . . a great revival.

Making a commitment to God is serious business. Tossing and turning at night, planning in my mind as I'd drive down the road, listening to the Lord's leading and confirming the very things He had already revealed, asking God to put people in place to help make this happen, and keeping God in the center of this has been an amazing three year journey.

Making this commitment to follow through with what God put on my heart hasn't been easy, but running from what God wants us to do isn't easy either, especially when you have committed yourself to Him. Taking that first step and writing a check to reserve the date for the Civic Center took courage, but things started falling into place miraculously. We keep stepping in faith and believing God to make it happen. We can't do it; He can! I ask for your prayers and support for **Rise Up, Recount Love.** It can be lonesome and scary when you step out of the boat and seek guidance in carrying out His plans. I thought of how poor Noah felt building a boat with no rain in sight and lots of people wondering if he had lost his mind. God was in the center of what Noah was committed to doing, and the rain came!

Giving this event a name presented another decision to cloud my mind, but God took care of that too. We live in times of turmoil everywhere we turn. Many Christians have been silenced or watered down. God is ready for His children to rise up, renew commitments, recount love, and be revived. 'Rise Up is a great name, but where did Recount Love come from'? I asked over and over in my prayers, and couldn't even explain it to my son, who frowned every time I said the word. The dictionary tells how recount means to give details.

Karry Godwin, who God lined up to be the Worship Leader for the entire event, met with me at Mr. Weldon and Mrs. Joyce Faircloth's cabin to talk and pray about the event. He was thrilled with the name of Rise Up, Recount Love. He referred me to 1 Chronicles, where the Levites used the term recount in worship meaning to commemorate, remember, praise, share details and appreciation.

My Tar Heel grin brought blue skies to my clouds of concern; recount was just what God wanted in the name for my book and the Christian Celebration in my hometown. I was on cloud nine as we prayed and left the peaceful place where we communed with God. I drove down the path from the cabin with a happy heart, recounting all the things God has so generously blessed us with and thanking Him in detail. Sunshine filled my heart while remembering and commemorating my love for a God who loves unconditionally and delights when we commit ourselves to Him.

Is Christ in the center of your life? If not, take time today to invite Jesus into your heart and honor a commitment with the Creator. Rise up to tell the stories of how your life has been blessed. Recount your love for the Lord and loved ones. Relish each day with praise and promise.

Lookout Loneliness

How do you handle loneliness? A good night's sleep cures fatigue. A delicious meal wipes away hunger. A close connection to the Lord lifts loneliness looming over our lives like dense fog. With Christ as our companion, we can handle loneliness, sorrow, or any other situation that shows up at our door.

Most people suffer through seasons of loneliness. It may be you, a friend, or family member searching for answers to cure loneliness. Reading how people in the Bible handled loneliness gives help and hope to lonely hearts.

Mary comes to mind first. Imagine her loneliness when family and friends doubted her story; stoning her to death seemed the likely solution to the sin she was accused of. Mary suffered seasons of loneliness with faith and integrity. Her pregnancy wasn't a joyous journey, but she kept pressing forward and pondering in her heart. Her lonely times strengthened and saved her from the pits of depression and doubt.

Ruth was no stranger to loneliness. The death of her husband and two sons could have held her captive in grief for the rest of her life. Not Ruth! Her choice to stay with her mother-in-law opened doors to blessings that she had never dreamed possible after suffering such loss. Her tender words are shared in songs and sermons that tell of a love story where loneliness was conquered and commitments were honored, keeping people close to the Lord and loved ones.

Jesus also felt the pains of loneliness, but there were times when He chose to be alone, deliberately making himself unavailable so He could commune with His Father. He experienced loneliness and alienation. When the crowds grew bigger as did the demand for His teaching and healing, He carved out "me time" from His busy schedule. He didn't wait until He was completely drained and desperate; He took time to nourish his soul and spend precious time alone with His Father. It was a powerful lesson by the greatest teacher of all time—a lesson we would do well to master. Jesus didn't use his relationship with God as a substitute for human companionship. His friends were important. Spending time with his three closest disciples—Peter, James, and John—and in the home of Mary, Martha, and Lazarus gave him joy. Jesus endured lonely times. Perhaps His pinnacle of loneliness was in the garden of Gethsemane, when He needed his closest friends to stay awake. He asked if they would leave Him also.

Are you thinking of a time when you uttered those words to a family member or a close friend? Being alone in a time of trial or crisis escalates the pain. Jesus desired his faithful few to pray with him, to stand by him, to watch with him—but they didn't. They fell asleep or denied him more than once in his time of need. Are we faithfully watching and praying with family members and friends who wonder if we will stay? Stand firm by those you love, fall to your knees, pray with them, speak words of life over them, and never leave them in their time of need—or anytime.

When times seem too tough to bear and we wonder why nobody's there, God will be there to help us handle whatever we face. Some mountains may tower too high to climb, some tragedies may seem too terrible to overcome, some heartbreaks may seem too severe to mend, but all things are possible with Jesus. He turns the bad, meant to hurt and harm, into good that brings blessings and happiness. He makes it possible; we make the choice. Refusing to budge from lonely times and painful experiences keeps us captive and unproductive.

King David had every reason to stew in sorrow or shout unfairness in his quest for the crown, but he loved the Lord too much to give in to pains of loneliness, despair, and downright unfair treatment. He made mistakes, but he never lost close contact with God. He continually asked for forgiveness and guidance. His long journey to reign as king was difficult, but he didn't stop when the going got tough. He just got tougher and more determined to seek God's will and way in his life. Surely, he was lonely in the caves that hid him from King Saul or bitter when his home was plundered and family attacked, but he never gave up. He showed his men and God the power of repenting and remaining close to God.

Loneliness will come to us—even in the best marriages, the closest friendships, and greatest child-parent relationship. God created us as unique individuals and knows the best way to fill the empty places that become open doors where loneliness, depression, or sorrow can grow out of control and kill our happiness. We don't have to settle for living lonely lives. Jesus is our forever friend who is always by our side.

Death Has Been Defeated

*D*O YOU FEAR DEATH? It's natural to have some fear of death and normal to talk about going to heaven. While we plan for heaven, it's amazing how people very near that journey are so at peace. Have you witnessed such a sacred time when one of your loved ones was bidding farewell to earth and being prepared for heaven? We tend to talk little about people passing from this world into eternity, but it's something we should stress, making sure our reservations are secure and our destination is definitely heaven.

One day we will leave this life. Dwelling on death isn't good for anyone, but being ready for it any given day is wise. Many people, especially the ill and aging, see the end of life approaching. We get things in order—insurance policies, wills, savoring moments with loved ones—and make sure we have our hearts right with the Lord and those we love.

The Bible gives comforting words about death. "For this God is our God forever and ever; He will be our guide even unto death" (Psalm 48:14).

Isaiah 25:8 tells of His promise to wipe away our tears. "He will swallow up death in victory; and the Lord God will wipe away tears from off all faces."

Dealing with death can be extremely difficult. Tears flow. People come and go. Services are planned. Tomorrow without your loved one must be faced.

When I was a teenager, I was asked to sing at a funeral for a beautiful little girl. The four-year-old looked like an angel in her tiny casket. The pain and sorrow in the eyes of her parents penetrated my heart, but I could only cry and try to sing words about joy in heaven. We followed the family to their little girl's gravesite. After the prayer, her father asked for the casket to be opened. It was hard to watch the family weeping and begging their little girl to come back while refusing to leave her grave. I went home that day with dreadful thoughts of death.

It wasn't long before I sat in the same pews and listened to songs of happiness in heaven. My family gathered close to my Uncle V.B.'s gravesite. The sting of death became personal. I have learned much about grieving since those funerals in the 1960s. We can read books, listen to friends who've walked the path, seek help from pastors, and try to pass through the seven stages per directions, but dealing with death is very personal with different paths to healing. There is no right way or wrong way. It is only with God's help that we can overcome the grief and find true joy in the morning.

"My flesh and my heart failed: but God is the strength of my heart, and my portion forever" (Psalm 73:26).

Believers have no reason to fear death. God promises eternal life when we accept Him as our Savior. Where fears and frustrations of facing death tried to root in my heart, Jesus pulled the worries and weeds away. Today, I still don't understand it all, but I believe it all—especially living for eternity in heaven. I no longer fear death. Do you?

May the love of the Lord live in our hearts, take away fears, and dry our tears. When we know Jesus, we have a destination and a reservation for when our time here is done. Believers rejoice; death is defeated and victory is won!

The Joy of Knowing Jesus

Have you failed God? We fail Him every day—even if it's a wrong thought or neglecting to spend time with Him—but we can always make it right. David and Peter failed Him many times, but always repented and rallied for their Lord. Peter denied Jesus three times and felt miserable—even as the words left his mouth. However, he didn't stop at being a loser and failing His Lord. He regained his courage and composure and became the cornerstone for spreading the Good News. His faithfulness made up for his failure to stand up for Jesus when he sat around the campfire and felt threatened by the angry mob. And though he failed Jesus, he didn't resolve to sit it out the rest of his life and lament his mistakes. He got his heart right and his mission in motion. Peter's passion for spreading the gospel penetrated hearts and networked throughout Judea and to the far corners of the world. Jesus knew Peter would be a rock when He chose him to be one of His disciples. Peter brought excitement and energy wherever he went. Who else dared stepping out of the boat and walking on water? Peter trusted His friend Jesus enough to try it—even though it seemed impossible. And he did walk on water—until he took his eyes off Jesus. He may have failed in many people's eyes, but he tried; it took faith to get out of that boat and to attempt such a feat.

What are we attempting to do for Jesus today? Do we choose to play it safe or are we willing to get out of the boat and be as daring as Peter? Many never fail because they refuse to engage in anything beyond the safety net of comfort and convenience. Peter's failures were turned around by faith, passionate performances, and a willingness to give up all he had to follow Christ. He earned his coveted title: the Rock!

What about David? His failures included murder, rebellion, even adultery. He was also tenderhearted and wanted to please God. He was as bold as he was big hearted. Trouble followed him wherever he went, but he was honorable and honest, even in his failures and his earnest requests for forgiveness from his Father. David played the game of life with gusto and guts. He was the kind of guy you'd love to have on your side. He was genuine when he admitted his wrongdoings and made them right with God. His failures didn't stop him from being a mighty man for God. He didn't dwell on the wrong things he'd done. He didn't spend his days complaining about having to wait to wear the crown or being forced to hide out in caves with a renegade army. He persevered and plowed through the tough times until his time to shine came. His close connection to God came from his willingness to praise God openly and seek God's will in his life. He didn't waste his time complaining and making excuses. David sought God and spent time praising Him instead of worrying God with pitiful pleas and woe-is-me attitudes. He loved to sing and dance and praise God. His family thought he had gone overboard with all the praise and glory. David didn't worry what people thought; he continued praising and pleasing God. And God had favor on David for his faithfulness. What a life David led! Can't you imagine him dancing down the streets of gold and telling stories of the days of old?

Are you thinking of times you have failed the Lord or failed the people God gave you to love here on earth? I am typing this story the last week of the year by a warm fire and dwelling on my own failures throughout the year. It's easy to become depressed over things we wish we had done differently. Endings and new beginnings must be faced in faith—as they were by Peter and David. May you find peace and joy as you move forward in faith.

Preparing for Christmas

*D*O YOU HAVE TRUE JOY in your heart and believe Jesus is the reason for the Christmas season? When we are in right relationship with our Lord and our loved ones, joy will live in our hearts and homes; it will be Christmas every day of the year. I write this story on Easter Monday while waiting for the sun to rise over the ocean at Topsail. My family sleeps as I sip coffee and share this beautiful dawning with my Father. Birds chirp, the ocean roars, big boats slip across the sound, my computer rests in my lap, my heart is filled with prayers and praises, my body is relaxed in my favorite chair where a panoramic view of paradise emerges from the fog, and my Father puts a message about Christmas in my heart. While I don't understand His timing, I will write the words He sends.

Yesterday, my grandson and I colored hardboiled eggs with crosses and creative questions about why Jesus died and who dressed up like the Easter bunny? Connor drew the big cross on his little egg and never stopped talking about the things he pondered in his heart. His wise words captivated me.

"Nana, Jesus doesn't dress up; he is real," Connor declared as he drew pictures on his eggs.

My coloring ceased; Connor's conviction and confirmation comforted my heart. Wise words from our five year old shared a sermon greater than anyone could have preached from any pulpit on this most Holy Day.

I proclaimed, "Yes, Connor, Jesus is real."

Shifting my thinking to cold days in December, tangled lights, blinking stars, packages stacked in corners, parties being planned, stores swamped with shoppers, money being tight, children filled with delight, decorations lighting up dark nights, sadness settling in suffering hearts, and rehearsals for cantatas. Many people pretend to be happy, but few possess and practice true joy. The real meaning of the season settled in my heart. What have we done to Christmas? Where is Jesus in our celebration? Connor's words at Easter took me from the cross to the cradle. Jesus gave His Son—what greater gift could He give? His sacrificial, unselfish gift personifies the love and joy He gives to all who accept and believe in Him as Lord and Savior.

Commercialism has captured Christmas celebrations; "getting" has grown into greedy giants that grumble and growl, corrupting the sweetest season of the year. Joy comes from giving.

During the Great Depression, two families shared a house—one family upstairs and the other on the bottom floor. The families looked at life so differently. The family downstairs always invited people in to share what they had. No matter how much they gave, they always seemed to have enough. The family on the upper floor, however, scoffed at how the family downstairs lived. They chose to store up any extras in a locker in their pantry and gave nothing away. It wasn't until they found that rats had gotten into their pantry that they were sorrowful for what they had done.

Are we focusing on getting rather than giving, hoarding instead of helping? Think about these things and you will understand: pantries packed with outdated food, freezers filled with food that spoils from power outages, stock market crashes that dwindle investments, nest eggs that disappear through tough times, things taken by thieves either hungry or hunting for money to feed bad habits, savings for retirement years snatched away. Being robbed of joy by the enemy promotes selfishness and sucks the life from anyone who falls prey to his schemes.

The good news is that we don't have to live our lives in sadness and sorrow for sins of our past—things lost from selfishness or the grip of Satan. We can be freed when we repent, renewing our relationship with God. The night seems dark and dismal when we distance ourselves from our Savior. When we put God first, everything else will fall into place, and we will have a friend forever. Talking to Jesus and feeling his presence are the best gifts anyone can receive.

Take what I have, Lord, and use it for your glory. I have nothing except what you have given me. Help me share my abundance—and to give all that I can to those who are in need. Thank you for the joy and peace you sent that Christmas long ago and the promise and hope we have in knowing You and living in your will. May our hearts swell with praise as songs of joy and unselfishness He brings, the tower bells on Christmas Day ring, and the family of God worldwide sings. Happy birthday, Jesus. You're the real thing!

Forgive and Be Forgiven

*D*O YOU GLADLY OBEY THE law of love and follow through when relationships demand commitment and forgiveness? Being forgiven and forgiving others are big in God's book. He frowns when we refuse to budge and forgive our fellow man, when we stew in stubbornness and separate ourselves from people we hold grudges against, when apathy starves our desire to serve our Savior, when contrary and callous hearts hinder His plans for our lives and weaken our Christian witness, and when we distance ourselves from our Father. We wonder why we have little peace and joy in our hearts and homes; why can't we find satisfaction?

Do you have a satisfied mind? Do you head to bed only to toss and turn worrying about what tomorrow holds? When we have that precious peace of protection and promise from our Father, our sleep is peaceful and satisfaction is divinely delicious. Seeking satisfaction from the wrong sources shatters happiness and hope—no matter how hard we try to find it on our own. When we give our hearts to Jesus and stay connected to the vine, the fruit is sweet and satisfying. Jesus is the only answer to a satisfied mind. The debt of sin is paid by the love of our Lord. He paid it all on the cross; we are forgiven. His Word teaches the power of forgiveness.

"And when ye stand praying, forgive, if ye have ought against any; that your Father also which is in heaven may forgive you your trespasses. But if ye do not forgive, neither will your Father which is in heaven forgive your trespasses" (Mark 11: 25-26).

In other words, if we can't forgive them; He won't forgive us. Forgiving some things seems impossible. When it hurts the most, it blesses the best. Romans 12:20 shows how forgiving our enemies fosters our faith. "Therefore if mine enemy hunger, feed him; if he thirst, give him drink."

We claim to forgive—and, in time, most of us really do—but to go to the next level leaves us shaking our heads and saying, "Lord, what more must I do"?

Luke 6 shares what God expects: "But love ye your enemies, and do good, and lend, hoping for nothing again; and your reward shall be great and ye shall be the children of the Highest: for He is kind unto the unthankful and to the evil."

If Jesus could ask his Father to forgive the people who persecuted, mocked, and cruelly crucified Him, can we not forgive those who are hateful, hurtful, and hamper our hopes? Forgiving paves the way for satisfaction to sweep our hearts and please our Father.

Have you been faced with the tough task of forgiving someone who has deeply hurt you? Don't think it will go away, my friends; it will only devour your inner being and destroy your joy. Forgive, obey the law of love, and find sweet satisfaction with a clean, happy heart.

When Your World is Turned Upside Down

*H*AS YOUR WORLD EVER BEEN turned upside down, leaving you wondering which way to go? Mary and Joseph's world was turned upside down, yet they persevered in faith and protected the Christ child. Their child brought peace defined by the presence of God. God is not absent when storms hit. He is always present, bringing peace and promise—even to a nation "digging out" from a destructive earthquake. Many people blame God with questions and concerns that plague their minds. We should never question or blame God for the storms we face in life.

Some things we will never comprehend until we get to heaven. God doesn't enjoy seeing His children suffer and die. Knowing how much we love our own children and would give our lives in order that they might live, we appreciate our Father's willingness to give His Son so that we might have life everlasting. We should never say we understand how one feels when we haven't walked in his or her shoes. This settled in my heart this morning as I worked on card ministry at Tim's Gift. While searching for envelopes, I found a card in the corner of my drawer and felt compelled to open and read the message. It was a sympathy card from my cousin, Monte Smith. His words of truth touched my heart,

> *So sorry to hear of Tim's passing. Even though I'm sure you expected the possibility of this, I wouldn't know if it is easier for one to bear. Really, I find myself searching for the words to say to make you feel better, but I simply don't have them. I care deeply and pray to God that you will get through this adversity a stronger woman.*

Peace settled in my soul as I read the message inspired from God. Monte penned those timely words four months before he went to be with Jesus. He searches no longer; all understanding and joy is his for eternity.

Those who choose to reject Jesus wither and die by removing themselves from the vine. Though they live, they have no life. Those who choose to trust Jesus and forge forward in faith move beyond the grave. Our only hope, precious peace, true happiness, and glorious grace come from staying connected to our Father—even when we're buried deep in depression and life seems dark and dreary.

A recent interview with an earthquake victim showed a woman portraying a faith in God much bigger than the earthquake that had turned her world upside down. Her three children clung to her as she answered questions that preached a sermon all mankind should embrace. The reporter asked if she felt forsaken.

Anyone watching knew her relationship with God was strong. She looked in the camera and told the world she had not been forsaken. She'd watched her home crumble on her three children. She shared how God had helped her dig them from the rubble. Her five-year-old son's leg was torn open from his foot to his knee. She had to stay on top of him while the doctor sewed up her baby's leg. There was no anesthesia—no comfort for her little boy. His operation was possible because his mother loved him enough to hold him down—even as he screamed in pain. She assured the reporter that she had not been forsaken; God had given her the strength to pull her children to safety and He would not forsake them. What amazing faith in the face of death!

Why did some survive while some met Jesus? Only God knows. Yet, we can't bury ourselves in grief. We must follow the example of Christ and forge forward in faith.

Ending this story has been a challenge. My five-year-old grandson is in front of my desk eating his chicken nugget meal as I seek the right words to conclude. When his questions begin, my concentration ends.

"Nana, why won't you eat one of my French fries? Why are you fasting? Doesn't Jesus like French fries? What are you writing? What does this button do? Can I type a word? Are you finished? What is an earthquake? Why did Jesus shake the earth?"

His questions and childlike faith end my story. We bombard God with never-ending questions (some silly) and wait impatiently for answers. There are things we will never understand until we get to heaven, but we can be assured that God is always with us; we are not forsaken!

God can bring good from the bad things that torment and threaten to bury us alive. Important questions to ponder can make the difference in where we spend eternity. Do you know Jesus? Are you ready to meet your Savior in the twinkling of an eye?

Tomorrow could be the day your world is turned upside down. Don't let the sun set without asking Jesus into your heart and home. He will never forsake you.

Looking Beyond Losses

DO YOU EVER WONDER WHY bad things happen to good people? It seems that some people really get zapped with tough times. Recently, we were studying the Book of Job. Explaining how Job lost everything seemed effortless. How can we comprehend such loss, especially little children who view life with such innocence? We talked of Job losing it all while remaining faithful and firm in his love for the Lord as if being strong like Job was without worry or weariness.

I thought of the heartaches and headaches Job weathered when the devil took all that he had, laughing at Job's predicament while loathing his devotion to God. God knew Job would stay true to Him—even when everything was gone in his life. God waited while the devil tormented and took Job's loved ones, his flocks, his land, and all his possessions, but he couldn't take away his love and dedication to his Lord. Surely, you have studied the Book of Job and marveled at the magnitude of his faith while wondering what you would have done in that same situation.

How much would we have to lose before we would cry out to God and give up—or turn against Him as Job's wife suggested. When Job's wife didn't stand strong with her husband in the tough times, he walked a path many people do each day in marriages. She felt her family had been treated unfairly, unjustly, and unprotected by God. She begged her husband to curse God. Would we do as Job did or as his wife did, if we lost all that we love, all we have worked for all our lives, and all that we claim to be ours? How much would we have to lose—a little or a lot—before becoming bitter and badmouthing our Father? To make matters worse, what if our friends pointed fingers and accused us of doing wrong?

Job stood his ground and stayed true to God. How did he prevail through such persecution? Surely, he wrestled in prayer through long treacherous nights, wondered how he would ever smile again, felt depressed and desperate, like a lone ranger, yet he believed he would win the war against the devil. And he did! God was with Job through every loss and hateful assault from the enemy. He watched and waited to celebrate victory with Job, bringing blessings and a good life for the man who had lost it all, but had gained honor in the sight of the Lord. Job was a hero who had a crown loaded with jewels waiting for him the day he entered heaven's gates.

What have you lost? How have you handled your losses? Have you lost everything you love and own in this world? Studying the Book of Job minimizes what we have lost, yet the pain of losing someone you love or possessions you've worked hard for threatens to take away our desire to live life with the faithful spirit that opens doors for blessings. Job survived his hard times. Will we?

Recent happenings cause us to wonder what must be lost before we give God first place in our lives. He is shaking the earth to get our attention. While walking the beautiful beach at Topsail recently, I pondered these questions while looking over the vast ocean. I thought of how God had made an awesome earth for our home. How sad He must be to see our foolish ways; waste, pride and prejudice, apathy, and busy schedules keep us stressed and distanced from Him. We fail to honor mothers and fathers and love neighbors as ourselves. As believers, we should be shouting from the mountaintops about how great our God is! I stopped to gaze into the beautiful, clear waters with whitecaps glistening in the sun. His mighty power is seen and heard in the sea. God gave all we have and can take it all away—with one shaking of His earth, one storm that sweeps our shore, one war or economic crisis where we lose our land, or one crisis that turns our world upside down.

Could we lose it all? Surely, Job asked that same question before everything in his world withered and died before his eyes. Do we throw in the towel and declare defeat when losses come closer and Satan seems to have control? More pleasing to our Father would be throwing out the ways of the world, claiming victory over the enemy, and restoring God to first place in our everything!

Bad things may happen to good people and losses may come our way, but we must choose to trust God and stand firm in our faith. God blessed Job abundantly for his faithfulness. He will do the same for you and me. We can never lose when we stay true to Jesus to the end. He is our Lord and very best friend!

God Is Always With Us

*H*AVE YOU EVER LOST GOD? This story downloaded in one of those all night dreams, you know the kind you wake up and wonder if it's a dream or did it really happen? Dreams can be so ridiculous, even scary, especially if you're dreaming someone or something (like a snake) is chasing you. Other dreams leave you wondering how the message might affect your life or what the meaning of your dream reveals. While we may never understand, God can use dreams to deliver meaningful messages.

The Bible proves the power of dreams. My favorite is when the angel came to Joseph in a dream that made all the difference in the love story of Christmas, the birth of Jesus, the life of a young girl who willingly accepted what seemed impossible, when God spoke it to her own heart. Joseph needed a little more proof that his sweetheart was the innocent Mary he loved and longed to marry. God saw Joseph's inward struggle and sent a sign through a dream. Aren't we glad Joseph listened? Mary was. Joseph's love and loyalty for the woman chosen to bear God's Son became solid as a rock.

When we read the beautiful story of Christmas, one might think Joseph should have been more faith filled from the beginning. Put yourself in Joseph's place. How often have you or I been where pure faith is required to stick with a loved one or step into the unknown believing and being committed to God's calling? Joseph needed extra assurance; an angel in a dream was just what the Master ordered. And it worked! The Christmas Story gives goose bumps and great expectation every time I read it, tell it, even think about how His love tenders our hearts.

Preparing messages and writing stories to uplift and encourage people to stay closely connected to the Lord and loved ones are my favorite things to do. Teaching how God colors our world with peace and purpose is a calling I cherish.

Recently, I prepared my stack of essentials for the next day and placed them near the door. This routine ensures a smooth morning without searching high and low for what's needed to make it through the day. I checked the stack twice making sure my GOD cards were secured, they would be the visual for a children's sermon the following day.

Climbing in bed, I should have buckled up and braced myself for the dream that would keep me tossing and turning all night long. People I hadn't seen in years were in the dream, along with those I see every day. Materials for the sermon to be shared were gone. The G O D cards were nowhere to be found. People laughed as I searched frantically, going all over the community with a plea to please give back GOD. Everyone was busy; no one offered to help in my time of need. The world went on without worrying about my dilemma. I had lost God and no one seemed to care. Exhausted from my search, my dream found me driving to the place where I was scheduled to share God's Word . . . without GOD. Arriving at my destination, I reached for my Bible on the passenger's seat; GOD was right there underneath a stack of 'stuff' that blocked Him from my vision. Then, I woke up!

When my feet hit the floor, I rushed downstairs making sure my stack of stuff included GOD! There were the three cards proudly showing the letters that spell "GOD" . . . Lord and Savior, Messiah, King of Kings and Lord of Lords, The Door, Living Water, Shepherd, Teacher, Holy One, True Vine, Carpenter, Healer, Helper, Redeemer, Bright Morning Star, The Way, Truth, and the Life . . . Jesus Christ.

Breathing a sigh of relief, I headed for a quick shower to wash away the weariness of the draining dream and start my day off right. Talking to Jesus as the cool water refreshed my body, His sweet spirit soothed my soul. The message He really wanted me to share was birthed in that dream. We never lose God, but it feels like it when we stray. He can be seen in everything when we keep Him on top of our lists, not buried underneath stacks of stuff that can distance us from our Father and separate us from the Vine.

Have you lost GOD? Many times we search frantically when stepping in faith is so simple. God never leaves us. We don't lose God; we bury Him under stacks of 'stuff' that overpower our good intentions and take His place in our lives. God longs to be first, included in whatever we're doing, honored and praised, and put on the pedestal where we place 'things of this world' we think we can't live without. Everything will one day pass away, not GOD. God is always with us. It's our choice to enjoy a personal relationship and honor Him as Lord of our lives. He is forever and ever.

Crazy in Love with Life

*A*RE YOU CRAZY IN LOVE? I am. Enjoying life and those God blessed us with to love is a great gift I cherish. Recently, Clint called with an invitation to accompany him to a wedding in Murrell's Inlet, S.C., where he would provide the music for the wedding and reception. I hesitated at first. Our North Carolina Tarheels were playing Michigan State for a spot in the NCAA final game. I love the Tarheels but love sharing time with loved ones more. What a great gift from God, spending the day with my son and hearing him D.J., plus enjoying an outdoor ceremony of love. Guests were greeted at the southern plantation with towering oak trees and azaleas painted pink and white. The silhouette of the wedding party looked heavenly as sunlight glimmered across their faces and a cool wind sent ripples across the waters of the Waccamaw River.

Wedding watchers waited to hear the couple say, 'I do"! The preacher struggled to be heard over wedding crashers . . . sounds of boats and a helicopter that hovered overhead. The enemy tries to spoil the best of times in our lives, but this preacher understood James 4:7 well; the deafening noises went away, fleeing like the devil does when we resist him. He told how distractions tried to steal the joy of their wedding ceremony just as distractions will always be present in their lives. It is how we handle distractions that determine our happiness or heartaches. The preacher waited, whispered words to the couple that made them giggle and went on with the service. Everyone could hear clearly the words binding the covenant of love between this man, woman, and God. He shared a message that reached deep down in my heart telling how God commands us to love Him first, to leave our father and mother to become one. He shared three sets of words to help their marriage stay strong until death would part them . . . 'I'll be there, I am sorry, and I love you.' He charged the couple to share these words endlessly and live them passionately forever and ever.

The beautiful surroundings and serenity of the ceremony saluted the newlywed's first walk together down a green carpet created by their Father. Family and friends followed the grassy land to the reception hall. I walked to the banks of the river to enjoy some 'me and God' time . . . thanking Him, listening, lingering in the sunshine and letting my Lord know that I am crazy in love with Him and with my life.

Clint greeted guests with a smile and soothing music. I headed to his truck to retrieve my computer and write this love story. For hours, I sat in the corner of the reception hall and had a blast talking, typing, and thanking the Lord for my two sons who love good music and the good Lord . . . like their dad did.

When Clint played the train song, I left my writing to join the train of happy people who weaved all around the beautifully decorated banquet hall. I felt like family even though I knew few of the people present for this happy occasion. That's how it is with God's love. We will want to go and pass it on, enjoying ourselves instead of being grumpy and growling over things that can steal our joy, or sitting in the corner and missing a blessing. God is pleased when we step out in faith, love with all our hearts, and recognize Him as God the Father and Son. John 22:5 came to my mind. ' . . . love the Lord your God, walk in his ways, obey his commands, hold fast to him and serve him with all your heart and all your soul.'

The best blessing came at midnight when the last piece of equipment was loaded and the bride's parents stood beside Clint and me with checkbook in hand. Clint took his pay and put it in his pocket; I listened to their words of praise for my son and tucked them in my heart. The bride's dad said, 'Clint is a gentleman, always sharing a sweet spirit and thinking of others.'

The three hour drive home gave my son and me time to talk and enjoy time together without interruptions and to thank God for the memories we made. We stopped for coffee halfway home; I offered to drive since Clint was so tired. Parents are happy to help their children, just like God is thrilled to help His children. Driving the long winding roads gave me time to think as Clint dozed. I watched him sleep and remembered times our family traveled with two, tired boys in the back seat.. Clint would always fall asleep on the way home, most of the time in my arms. His dad would lift him and tuck him safely in bed. Those times are cherished memories stored in my heart.

We pulled in our driveway in the early hours of a new day, tired and thanking God for bringing us home and for our loved ones who are safe at home in the arms of Jesus. I finally stretched out in my warm bed, closed my eyes, and thanked God again for the time I shared with my son. I whispered softly to my Lord, *'I am crazy in love with life and with You.'*

Make the most of opportunities to spend quality time with your loved ones and the Lord. Remember to always be there for Him and them, say 'I'm sorry', and love deeply and devotedly. Then, you will truly understand the beauty of being crazy in love with life and the Lord.

Friends of Gold

*A*RE YOU A GOLDEN FRIEND? Remembering a character education activity I do with my students helps visualize circles of friends. Try it. Draw a small circle, a larger one around it, and one huge circle around both smaller ones. Write the names of casual friends in the larger circle, the names of friends you see often in the middle circle, and the names of those friends you seldom see, but are always there for you . . . . fair or foul weather, in the small circle. That is where you will find your golden friends. The golden chain of friendship is a blessed tie, binding hearts together as storms and struggles go by. Do you have friends in the small circle? Would your name be written in the small circles of those who know you? Being a golden friend brings blessings one could never purchase.

While writing, I listen to water cascade from the lovely fountain in our garden. Friends from our beloved Sunday School Class—*Love, Laugh, Lift*—placed this treasure in the center of our garden in memory of Tim. The tranquil waters fall from the three tiers, bringing peace and promise to my heart and memories of golden friends who were faithful to our class and to Tim and me. Every Sunday morning Tim walked around the room giving a firm handshake to our golden nuggets, while I taught lessons from the Good Book and told how Jesus is our best friend.

Those good friends are still golden today, though some of them are walking the streets of gold in heaven. Butch left us first. He fought cancer bravely and talked openly in class about the importance of doing kind deeds for suffering friends. He recounted how some people would avoid talking with him, while others would give a pat on the back and offer prayers. He taught us never to walk away from a friend in need. Instead, give a handshake or kind note with prayerful

Rise Up, Recount Love

sentiments that bolster faith when fighting for one's life. Butch never met a stranger and touched lives wherever he went.

Tim was next to go home to heaven. His battle with cancer was long and hard too, but he never complained. Once he told us how he would change nothing in his life except the cancer. Golden friends, some my sons and I never knew, stopped by Tim's insurance office after he passed to share stories of how Tim helped them in their times of need through the years. Tim did good deeds without seeking recognition. Friends told Cameron and Clint how their Dad paid insurance premiums when their families were going through hard times, gave gas money for family members to drive to Duke or Chapel Hill for cancer treatments, or just listened and helped friends in need. Those are golden memories of a loved one that will never die.

Travis left us in a hurry, not like Butch and Tim who suffered for many seasons but had time to say good bye. Travis was the golden, singing friend. His voice was a gift that gave joy to multitudes of people through the years. When Interstate 40 came through our eastern North Carolina community, state officials planned a huge grand opening at the Warsaw exit. Travis was asked to sing, *God Bless the U.S.A.* After the ceremony, Travis' sound man was approached by a well known media person who requested an interview with Al Green. Travis was honored but his humor had everyone in stitches saying, *'me, Al Green . . . you gotta be kidding.'*

Travis shared love and laughter wherever he went. His small circle of golden friends was huge. Only weeks before he went to heaven, he shared bits of wisdom with *Love, Laugh, Lift* friends at our good friend's daughter's wedding. He told how a neighbor at Topsail Beach had been very sick for a long time. Travis said, *'when the good Lord is ready to take me home, I hope I go fast.'* Travis touched many lives, leaving a legacy of happiness, love, laughter, and songs that continue to be music to our ears.

Having faithful, understanding friends is worth much more than gold. As I grow older, I appreciate friends much more and judge folks a lot less. We should remind our friends how much they are appreciated, never assuming they know how we feel about them.

Writing notes and sending cards to friends, even folks I don't know in need of a good word, gives me much joy. A golden friend, Brenda Nordin, assists me in a card ministry we began at Tim's Gift in

2008. Weekly notes of encouragement and support are sent to people throughout our communities. This ministry, sharing words of life, is powerful and proof that writing love notes and sending cards makes a profound, positive difference in peoples' lives. It has in mine. Brenda began sending cards to Tim and me when we battled cancer. Her cards shared special handwritten messages to brighten our days. Those cards are still coming—days when I know God whispered in her ear, *'Becky needs words of encouragement Brenda, send her a card with a special 'I love you' from Me.'* A file with hundreds of cards from Brenda is among my most prized possessions. Do you share words of love with your golden friends? Do you receive love notes from friends? When you share words in a spirit of love and concern, the blessings come back to you ten fold.

Golden friends often become family by choice. Bobby and Rhonda are golden friends who became family soon after we moved beside them. Recently, Rhonda heard me talk of how I craved a piece of hot pound cake. I told her how my mother made Crisco pound cakes and let me sneak a piece of hot cake while it cooled on the counter. Later than night, while writing a story, Rhonda called and asked me to walk over to her house. The urge to make excuses not to go danced in my head, but my heart said, *'get up and go even though it's almost midnight; she called to borrow a cup of flour earlier. Surely, she's baked you a cake.'*

My heart was right. Entering their house, the aroma of pound cake filled the air. The two of us sat down to Pepsi and warm pound cake as the clock struck twelve. She told me to remember my mama while eating her treat made just for me. Her pound cakes and friendship are golden. Rhonda's husband, Bobby, is the best golden friend one could ever hope to have. He has stood by my family and me through seasons of sunshine and sorrow. He is a modern day Good Samaritan. Wherever he and Rhonda go, I always feel comfortable tagging along. That's a blessing when you don't feel comfortable going places by yourself. Cameron, my son, works with Bobby as a sales representative for their business, Group Benefits. Recently, they were driving to do an enrollment in the western part of North Carolina. Bobby and Cameron were talking as they traveled. Cameron looks to Bobby as a father figure now that his Dad has passed. Bobby stayed by Tim's bedside, sat up long nights, stood by us through his death and still looks out for us. Bobby shared with Cameron words he told Tim before he died, *'don't you worry about Becky or the boys Tim. I will take care of them.'* And he does! Bobby is an honorable, humble, helpful, big-hearted, golden friend that has a special spot waiting for him one day in heaven.

I thank God every day for golden friends and try my best to be one for others. DO you appreciate your friends and be the best friend you can be? Start today by sharing words of love and support with friends who will be thrilled to have a card or call from a good old friend like you. Good friends are gifts that can't be bought or sold and are worth far more than gold.

Wait on the Lord

Have you ever grown tired of waiting for something and made a mess of things in your life? This story stomps my toes before the words hit the page. Waiting is not one of my strengths—the post office, traffic lights, the grocery store, doctor appointments—and the list goes on, as do the stories of waiting.

Watch the expressions of most people waiting in line; the inner turmoil roars silently. Waiting a long time for something you really want can seem like an eternity. Sometimes, in the waiting process, we lose our perspective and make the wrong choices.

The best choice is waiting on the Lord and working things out together with those we love. When we follow His stirring in our hearts, the wait is worth it. Somehow we don't wait well. Our generation is no different than the Israelites who roamed the desert for forty years. We try to do it our way, spending more time fixing the messes we made and waiting even longer to receive the blessings.

Oh, the tales I could tell of times I've waited. Plenty of my waiting experiences could have ended in disaster due to my stubbornness and immaturity. When it seemed Tim and I would wait forever for things to work out for marriage, we almost eloped. Believing in His Word etched in our hearts, we waited with courage; God strengthened our hearts and made all things right and good with us and our loved ones.

Making the right choice to wait worked a miracle in our lives. Our life together began and ended with us crazy in love—honoring our covenant with God and one another. We waited for paychecks, weekends, vacations, jobs, and children. We waited to get out of diapers, daycare, college, for retirement—and some things we waited for never came. Yet, God's plan blessed us with a beautiful life and everlasting love.

His plans continue to unfold in my life—just as they do for each of you who have faced troubles, trials, and tragedies. When God is in our plan, we can overcome anything and move forward in faith. He has great plans for us, yet we must be careful not to get ahead of Him, nor lag behind what He calls us to do.

I am eager to do His will for the rest of my life—while waiting and knowing that Christ's timing makes all things work out for those who love Him. Do you wait on Him or take things into your own hands? I have repented a gazillion times for being unable to hold my horses.

In 1985, we worked together building a big barn in our backyard. It took forever because we had to wait for the time to work on it and the money to finish it. We loved our barn, but I wanted to put another door on the side facing our house. Tim told me we were fine with one door. Yet, I could just see that extra door being what we needed. I waited and waited for him to change his mind. The thoughts of that door wouldn't leave me. I should have remembered the Word where we are reminded not to let thoughts become imaginations.

Years later, our neighbors were doing some renovations. I walked over and asked the carpenter to take a look at our barn and give me advice about adding a side door. He assured me the door would work well and add value to our building.

The enemy worked quickly in my mind, telling me I had waited so long and could surprise Tim by doing it and not worrying him with it. I gave the carpenter the go ahead. He came early the next morning, cut a huge whole in our barn, and by late afternoon the door was in place with molding waiting to be painted.

Tim came home after a long day at work and saw what I had done. He wasn't happy. I had hurt him deeply, but because he loved me so much, he forgave me. Yet, we paid the price for my actions. When it rained, water ran under the door in our barn, creating all kinds of problems. What I thought would be a good thing made a big mess. That door was a constant reminder of my wrongdoing, an Ishmael. I knew I was forgiven, but my heart ached to see how I had disappointed Tim and the unforeseen headaches that side door brought.

Have you done things that made a mess for you and for others? When we allow Ishmaels in our lives, we must deal with the consequences.

In Genesis, we read about Abram and Sarah's happy life together—and how they became tired of waiting for a child. Sarah decided to see if Hagar, her handmaid, would conceive a child by Abram. She had all good intentions, thinking this was the only way for Abram to have a son to carry on the family name. She took things in her own hands. Hagar gave birth to Ishmael, not the child of the promise. Abraham and Sarah waited fourteen more years before Isaac was born. What Sarah thought would be the right thing turned into a big mess. Things worked out for them, but with unnecessary heartaches and tough consequences.

We would like to carry out our plans and have God bless them. God has great things in store for us. He loves to see His children waiting on Him, having courage, trusting Him to bring about the good things promised. He isn't happy when we take things in our own hands and do them according to our plans. What we do without Him is all in vain. Yet, when we mess up and confess our sins, He forgives and has favor—as He did with Abraham and Sarah. God's got great things waiting for us—and He will bring them in His perfect timing. Just wait and see!

Passing the EOL

*D*O YOU BELIEVE THAT GOD provides tests as measures of progress? Are you thinking of tests you've endured in the past, tests that face you today, and knowledge that tests will never stop in this lifetime? Some we pass; others we fail. The rewards are awesome when we stand firm in faith and pass the tests.

Testing is tough! Some people breeze through tests in school, work, family matters, and faith. They enjoy blessings beyond belief. Others fail miserably, wondering what went wrong. Testing is handled differently by all of God's children.

This child dreads tests. My global nature makes me a prime candidate for not fitting the mold of good test-taker, while my desire to do my best propels me to work hard in order to pass my tests. Testing isn't easy for me. I second-guess myself when answering multiple choice questions, wondering who in the world makes these tests anyway. You should try taking one of the end-of-grade tests that tosses out tons of tremendous pressure for those little folks who know they must pass in order to progress.

Recently, I helped a perplexed third grader search for a correct response for his reading passage in preparation for the end-of-grade test. The story told of an animal family enjoying a picnic with friends. Every answer had been highlighted in the passage except the one that asked the color of the tablecloth. We read, reread, and were ready to give up when I spotted a clue that sparked that higher level thinking we desperately try to teach our children. The story told how the family sat on the grass in the bright sunshine and ate their food. The answer popped out like a jack-in-the-box, hiding and waiting for someone to look closely, connect, and cast the right response. I explained; he circled green! He would pass that little test, but what about all those who don't have someone guiding them until they reach the season when they are independent learners?

Do we ever get to that point in life? Testing will be with us until the day we die. We must be prepared. When we stand the test and do our best, God is pleased and will propel us to new heights, adventures, blessings, and triumph in passing continuous tests.

Abraham passed one of the greatest tests a parent could face. In Genesis 22, we read how he climbed that mountain with thoughts that tormented every step he took. Yet, his obedience to His Father took precedence. When God saw Abraham ascend Mount Moriah to sacrifice his beloved son, He knew the father of Isaac would be willing to do anything asked of him. God was pleased that Abraham passed the test.

Be obedient and following God's guidance, remain faithful in a world where the enemy tempts and torments, and prepare daily for the EOL—End of Life Test. That's one test no one wants to fail. Passing is simple. We must accept Jesus as our personal Savior, repent, and live our lives in obedience to His calling. Does Jesus live in your heart? Do you know His voice, plans, and peace for you? When we give the time to prepare and keep God first, we always make the right choice and pass the test.

Singing His Song

*H*AVE YOU EVER FACED A test you thought was just too tough to tackle? One tremendous test for my Learning Station teachers and myself came at our End of the Summer Program in 2010. We had prepared, practiced, put in action the theme of our program—Paying It Forward—and placed it in God's hands. Clint came home to work the sound system. We had practiced all summer using my small CD player; Clint's larger, more powerful system would be the perfect solution for everyone to hear clearly in the huge auditorium.

The day of the program finally came. Everyone reading this story will understand the pressure of passing the test when producing a church play, a community event, a dance recital, or anything involving people and aimed at pleasing an audience. We prayed all summer for our program to be a blessing, to bring people closer to Christ, to appreciate our community, and to take the good things we do for others and for our Lord to the next level. We even prayed over the seats where family members and friends would watch our children perform. Paying It Forward brought blessings to our Learning Station family the entire summer season. Now, we were ready to shine for our Lord and all those who were waiting in the foyer of Sunset School's auditorium.

Parents and guests enjoyed watching our summer video while waiting for the doors to open. Backstage our children pottied, played as children will do under pressure, and positioned themselves on the bleachers for the start of our program. Different children prayed and we were ready to get the show on the road. Problem number one was that the CD with all our music wouldn't work on Clint's system. No sound meant no show. I panicked as thoughts of disaster plagued my mind. Ms. Emily Sutton, the choreographer for our show, fought back tears. My voice was almost gone; leaders in charge of such events understand. I was at my wit's end when I yelled for Emily to go back to The Learning Station and search for all the different CDs with our songs on them.

Clint worked for solutions, children squirmed, and the time ticked, Ms. Elizabeth talked to the children about what was going on and asked them to come forward and pray. I felt like a chicken with my head cut off, had thoughts of running away, and resorted to rebuking the enemy who was enjoying this testing time.

I headed to the foyer where parents were wondering why the doors were still closed. I was completely honest with them, telling them we had no sound and needed their prayers. I promised them the show would go on for the Lord would provide. Ms. Emily handed Clint a pile of CDs, giving him instructions as the curtain opened, children stood still, parents and guests applauded loudly, and I whispered, "Thank you, Father. I love you so much!"

Clint maneuvered the music; children and teachers made all the right moves, but I malfunctioned what I had worked to perfect for months. Our signature song was "Testify to Love." The lyrics seemed to tell the story of my life; I wanted to sing it for all the world to hear the power of love. As the program progressed, I put each dance, song, and child's part in God's hands; it was wonderful. When the music for my song began, I went to center stage and felt a rush of emotion as the children stood with smiles. I was humbled and honored that we could share a program testifying of our love for the Lord. I opened my mouth to sing as the music crept closer to my cue, but no words were coming to my mind. In a matter of seconds, I realized I had forgotten the words to the song. In times past, I would have failed that test—but not that night. I put my trust in God and knew I would sing my song for Him—no matter how foolish I looked or sounded.

I heard the last notes before I was to begin singing and said a prayer in my heart. God told me to sing—and I did. The words that came out of my mouth were not the lyrics I had memorized. I began singing about God's love and making up lines as I went. The girls had puzzled looks as they danced to what I was singing. They made movements to show the colors of the rainbow and voices of the wind. I sang of God loving you and me and seeing if we will be faithful in all that we do. Finally, at the beginning of the chorus, the right words came and I sang loud enough for all of heaven to hear.

I knew we had passed the test and the last laugh was on the devil. He had tried to steal our show and stop what God was doing through His little children to bring people into the Kingdom. When I laid me down to sleep that night, I prayed for all the little children so precious in His sight. I thanked Him for sending the music, the words, and all the people who helped us pass the test. Before I said amen, I sang my song again—just for Him. The performance was fabulous. I didn't miss a single word as I sang my song for Him.

Is the devil tormenting you and keeping you from passing the tests that can bring prosperity and pleasure over poverty and putdowns, triumph over tragedy, joy over sorrow, happiness over heartaches? Remember the faithful obedience of Abraham. His willingness to sacrifice his son showed his love for God. That act foreshadowed what our Father was willing to do for you and me. He gave His only Son so that we might know Him personally as our Savior and have life everlasting in heaven. Are you preparing for tests and placing your all in His hands? We pass the test when we accept God and give our best!

Never be afraid to sing His song—even when the words won't seem to come. We must rise up in faith and take the first step. He will do the rest! Give God your best and you will pass the tests.

Keep Love Flowing

HAVE YOU FELT THE FRUSTRATION of dealing with clogged drains or commodes? When something is stopped up and things can't flow, problems come when the mess won't go. Are you thinking of a time when something was stopped up at your house, causing headaches and hassle? Only months after we were married, a wolf rat decided to worry us with his presence in our home. Tim assured me we were fine, but that big rat teased us one time to many. One night I walked in our bathroom and he was on the rim of our commode. I screamed as I shut the lid, knocking him into the water. Tim rushed in; our attack began, and soon we were cleaning up from a clogged mess and a dead rat.

Children at The Learning Station have sparked multiple clean ups when clogged commodes made afternoons miserable. Who put paper towels inside the toilets? Who filled up the bowl with rolls of toilet tissue? "Who did it?" became the cry when commodes were out of commission and children couldn't wait.

This same problem affects our lives when we aren't attentive, allowing things to be stuffed inside our bodies and hearts that harm our physical and spiritual well-being. Taking care of our temple is important. When we neglect nutritional needs, fail to exercise and keep our minds and bodies in shape, we are headed for trouble. Our arteries easily become clogged just as the pipes underneath our sinks do. When we pour grease down the drain once or twice, things keep flowing. If we continue putting excess grease and grim in the drains, it won't be long before they are clogged and finally nothing will flow through the blockage. Hardening makes removal even more difficult.

Caring for our spiritual well-being is important. Allowing jealousy, hatred, unbelieving, lies, gossiping, scheming, busyness, or anything that will hinder our relationship with our Father to clog up our hearts are problems that only Christ can cure.

The children at The Learning Station do a daily cleaning before homework begins. We brush our hands across our chests, cleansing in faith. We ask God to take away anything that has seeped inside during the day that would clog up our hearts. When we're all cleaned out, we bow for prayer and feel His sweet, spirit settle in our hearts. Then, we're ready to do homework without hassle.

Proverbs 4:23 provides awesome advice as we strive to keep our hearts unclogged and open for our Lord's love and power to flow through freely. "Keep and guard your hearts for out of them flow life!"

If you're all clogged up, clean out your heart today. Don't delay; the sins will harden your heart and stop the flow of faith that keeps you close to Christ. Repent and rededicate your life to Him. He will clean up the mess and you'll be good to go.

Correction Without Condemnation

*D*O YOU CARE ENOUGH ABOUT those you love to correct them? Are you thinking about times when you've received correction and how it was given? Correction is good when given and received in the right spirit. Hateful correction can be harmful.

In fourth grade, my boyfriend was a handsome redhead with a charming personality. One spring morning, he knocked on our classroom door with a bunch of daffodils wrapped with wet paper towels. Our eyes met; I knew those flowers were for me. I can still see his smiling face as I clutched the beautiful bouquet that even FTD couldn't match. I quickly tucked them in my desk, but not before my teacher turned tyrant. She walked to my desk and demanded my yellow flowers. She took them from my hands and threw them into the trashcan, while giving a little lecture to the whole class. I will never forget how happy I was when those pretty daffodils were delivered to me and how humiliated I was when my teacher made this act of kindness seem silly. She thought critical correction would get her point across powerfully. Her lesson backfired. Criticizing or correcting in a mean spirit is not helpful. Jesus surely didn't do it that way.

The woman at the well needed correction, yet those who knew her steered clear and made no effort to help her rise above the sinful life she lived. She was the subject of gossip and ridicule. Perhaps that's why she found herself all alone while drawing water from the well. Then, along came Jesus. He stopped for water to quench His thirst. Striking up a conversation with this woman with a reputation was part of His plan that would cleanse her heart and change her life. He accepted a cup of water, sharing thankfulness for her kindness and generating conversation about things of interest. Jesus knew her lifestyle but didn't treat her like an outcast. He talked with her without being drawn into her world. She marveled at his kind heart and words of truth relating to her life. Jesus knew she needed correction, but He gave it without condemnation.

Can't you see Jesus's smiling face as He spoke words of correction that would change her life? He told her she wasn't condemned; to go and stop sinning. She did go and tell the Good News of this man named Jesus. What a difference it made when Jesus was willing to show humility for her act of kindness, talk with her openly when most people dared not go near her, and finally share words of correction that caused her to change her ways and win many people to Christ. How might we have handled that opportunity to correct without condemning?

Revelation 3:19 shares how we should change our minds and attitudes. Living our lives in amazement of God's gifts and glory is wise. Staying stirred up and in awe of the power of our personal Savior serves as a foundation to a strong faith and a fulfilling life. Through the seasons of our lives, there will be times when we are corrected and times when we must give correction. Being wise with our words and carrying out correction with an amicable attitude is what Jesus would do. Losing tempers, stewing in silence, correcting with condemnation, and hurling hateful remarks is devilish and destructive. How we handle giving advice, instruction, correcting loved ones, friends, or fellow colleagues powerfully affects our relationships. We might be surprised to know the number of people who have been wounded by our words. If only we would wait on the Lord before getting on our high horses and hurting people while thinking we are helping them.

However, there are times when corrective measures must be delivered with might. Jesus's humbleness must not be mistaken for weakness. When needed, He stood firm and corrected with power and purpose. Remember his pain when He saw the merchants making a mockery of God's house. His rage was real; He turned over tables and stopped the buying and selling, showing the people this was unacceptable in His Father's house. He stood firm—never compromising, backing down, or losing an opportunity to lovingly or forcefully give correction or teach a lesson of love and forgiveness, repentance and restoration.

Jesus modeled servant leadership and gave correction without condemnation. His sweet spirit settles inside when we allow Him to come into our hearts. God cares enough to correct us. This is a sign of His love. May we accept His correction, embrace His conviction, and model His example in our own lives.

Rightful Places

*W*HO IS SITTING IN YOUR daddy's chair? It's amazing how little things happen along our paths that impact us powerfully, like the stories from childhood and things children say and do. Who is sitting in your daddy's chair focuses on the faith we have in knowing our Father is always there, that no one can take His place—unless we allow it.

The story of Goldilocks and the Three Bears shows a little girl trying to find a chair, a bed, and food that's just right. She tries the big one, middle sized one, and finds her place in the little chair, sized just right for her. She is burned by the food that's too hot and finally finds peace in the little bed that's suited to her size. The ending of the story comes when the owners of the house come home and find someone has broken one of their chairs, eaten their porridge, and is actually sleeping in one of their beds. While the same question asked becomes the focal point of this children's classic, we know there is much more to the story when related to life.

My grandson, Connor, was the vessel God used to teach this powerful lesson, with him so unaware of his prophetic words. That reminds me of another lesson: being mindful of the power of our words. That's a story each of us could write with lots of chapters.

Connor begged to take home a big box of cereal as I prepared to leave work late one afternoon. We set the alarm and locked the door. I turned to see Connor slowly walking to the edge of The Learning Station. Just as he reached the corner of the building, Mrs. Sue (a teacher), drove past him. Since it was dusk, she couldn't see Connor. He stopped dead in his tracks when she whizzed by. Actually, he wasn't dead in his tracks, but he learned a lesson to prove it can happen when we aren't attentive to oncoming dangers.

Usually, when we stand there talking and locking up, he takes off running toward Tim's Gift to see his daddy. That day, the big box of Cheerios slowed him down and saved his life. Mrs. Sue never knew he was so close to the danger of being hit by her car. It would have crushed her. How often do we find ourselves in the same situation? We run toward destinations, out of God's timing, and can be hurt or even killed in our attempts. Wrong actions and words are harmful. Hurtful words haphazardly dished out can destroy happiness and healthy relationships. We should stop and think before speaking or acting.

Mrs. Beth and I seized the moment to teach the lesson of watching closely and waiting until the time is right. He listened and clutched the box of Cheerios even tighter. I kept reminding him never to rush ahead, to always look, and stopped mid-sentence. A flashback of Tim's own words when we would lecture our sons surfaced in my heart: *You've said enough, Becky. They get the message.*

I hushed and hugged him tightly, thanking God for being there to protect this little child—and all the little children of the world that He loves so much.

As I dumped my take home load into the back seat, I heard Connor's words that stirred this story. The big windows of Tim's Gift give full view of all that's going on inside.

Connor turned toward his daddy's office and said, "Who is that in my daddy's chair? He's not supposed to be there—that's not my daddy."

Connor took action, going inside to get the imposter out of his father's chair. Mr. Bill was sitting there while working on Cameron's computer. Cameron was amazed by Connor's passion for getting his daddy back in his rightful place.

We enjoyed a good laugh and learned lots of lessons that afternoon. Watch your words. Be watchful and alert wherever you're headed in life—even walking in your own yard. Make sure your Heavenly Father is in His rightful place in your life. The enemy would like to take His seat and reign, but we have the power over the devil when we keep God first. The enemy will flee when we remind him that we belong to Christ and we worship the Lord in our house.

Who is in your daddy's chair? God is glorified when He keeps His rightful place in our lives, but it's our choice to keep Him there. God is the greatest daddy. He will never hurt, neglect, take for granted, or leave His children. He stands His ground and honors His Word. He blesses and protects. He gives grace and keeps His promises. He loves us and is preparing a place where we will live with Him forever and ever. Keep Christ in His chair. If someone slips in and tries to take His place, be passionate about putting Him right back where He belongs and longs to be in your life.

Baby Bear did just that when she saw someone had been sleeping in her bed and was still there. Goldilocks was where she didn't belong and ran away when the bears came home. When the devil pushes his way into your heart or home, be brave like the bears, be passionate like Connor, speak words that tell him that's your daddy's chair and you're going to get things straight. The devil will flee as did Goldilocks and God will have a good laugh as did the three bears. Our Lord loves it when we keep Him in His rightful place in our lives—all the time!

The Power of Prayer

WHAT MOVES YOU TO PRAY? Is it the splendor of a sunset or watching that same sphere rise high above the ocean? Is it snowflakes lighting up the night sky or is it when your thoughts turn to the homeless who have no place to warm their hands or hearts? Is it when you behold your blessings or when you are broken before your Lord? Is it when a crisis comes your way or when nothing but sunshine fills your day? Is it when death knocks and takes your loved one away or when good comes from bad the enemy sent your way? We are drawn to prayer when we rest in the peace that victory is ours when we give our hearts to Him. A real desire to pray and enjoy a personal relationship with the Lord brings happiness.

Prayer is often reserved for special times and places. Jesus prayed wherever He went, whatever He faced, and whomever He was with; portraying a prayerful spirit that people noticed. He didn't need notes; He prayed boldly, fervently, and faithfully—always seeking the will of His Father. This season reminds me of His lonely time of prayer in the garden when drops of blood dripped from His brow. His time in prayer prepared Him for what was ahead. Are we praying passionately, purposefully, and persistently as He prepares us for our tomorrows? Prayer is powerful and puts our worries, woes, and what-should-we-dos in proper perspective. He promises to be with us—even when two or three are gathered together in His name, He hears our prayers. Praying is personal and precious. It sends you higher than you've ever been lifted before.

Saints We Call Mothers

*H*AVE YOU EVER WONDERED HOW mothers of handicapped children are chosen? My little sister, Mary Gaye, is truly a saint. God blessed her with two wonderful children. Her daughter, Katy, was born in 1995 with spinal bifida, causing complications and creating hardships she's bravely battled for sixteen years. She is a model student who brings home A's on her report cards, but hurdles physical disabilities daily that confine and confuse this precious little girl. Her story is one that breaks your heart and bolsters your faith. They have endured long painful nights when Katy begged for relief, shopping trips when no clothes would fit, wheelchairs, kneecaps constantly popping out of joint, operation after operation, back braces, knee braces, rods in spine, seasons of doubt, endless questions (Why me? When will the pain stop? What will I do?), sleepless nights, outbursts of anger, opportunities for praise, loneliness, being a poster child for Shriner's Hospital, awards for academic excellence, desire to play softball—reality and rejection, friends who don't understand or hang out, summer camps for special needs children, hope and help from a whole host of people who care . . . mostly from her mom—Katy's strength.

Two years ago, Mary Gaye and Katy came to Clinton for an overnight visit. Catching up on news and wrapping Christmas presents was heavenly until Katy reached for the tape and gasped in pain; her knee had popped out of joint. I witnessed the long nights of suffering they have shared since she was born. For hours, the pain brought tears, vomiting, and pleas for relief from a little girl who bravely fights what many will never experience or understand. A humble spirit and honor for all mothers who endure long, sleepless nights caring for ones they love settled in my heart.

We can never truly understand the triumphs and tragedies unless we've walked in the shoes of those who endure hardships, heartaches, boundaries, and blessings of being handicapped. Neglecting to file the old newspaper that paid tribute to Erma was a blessing. I wiped my tears and read the headline of one of Erma's classics, "A Saint We Call Mother!" Reading it twice was confirmation to send it to my sister and share it with my readers. May it bless you and open your eyes to the pain and daily stress—as well as the joy and blessings of raising a handicapped child. May God bless the hearts and homes of all women whom God has chosen as mothers for His special children.

> Somehow, I visualize God hovering over earth selecting his instruments for propagation with great care and deliberation. As He observes, He instructs his angels to make notes in a giant ledger.
>
> "Armstrong, Beth, son, patron saint, Matthew, Forrest, Marjorie, daughter, patron saint, Cecilia."
>
> Finally, he passes a name to an angel and smiles. "Give her a handicapped child." The angel is curious. "Why this one, God? She's so happy."
>
> "Exactly," says God. "Could I give a handicapped child a mother who does not know laughter? That would be cruel."
>
> "But has she patience?" asks the angel.
>
> "I don't want her to have too much patience or she will drown in a sea of self-pity and despair. Once the shock and resentment wear off, she'll handle it."
>
> "I watched her today. She has that feeling of self and independence that is so rare and so necessary in a mother. You see, the child I'm going to give her has his own world. She has to make it live in her world, and that's not going to be easy."
>
> "But, Lord, I don't think she even believes in you."
>
> God smiles. "No matter. I can fix that. This one is perfect. She has just enough selfishness."
>
> The angel gasps. "Selfishness? Is that a virtue?"

God nods. "If she can't separate herself from the child occasionally, she'll never survive. Yes, here is a woman whom I will bless with a child less than perfect."

"She doesn't realize it yet, but she is to be envied. She will never take for granted a 'spoken word.' She will never consider a 'step' ordinary. When her child says 'Momma' for the first time, she will be present at a miracle and know it. When she describes a tree or a sunset to her blind child, she will see it as few people ever see my creations.

"I will permit her to see clearly the things I see—ignorance, cruelty, prejudice—and allow her to rise above them. She will never be alone. I will be at her side every minute of every day of her life, because she is doing my work as surely as she is here by my side."

"And what about her patron saint?" asks the angel, pen poised in midair.

God smiles, "A mirror will suffice."

To my sister and all the other women God chose to be mothers and grandmothers of handicapped children: look in the mirror and see the saint your family and friends pray for and applaud. You are a saint we call "Mother!" May God bless you abundantly.

Cradle to Cross

*W*HAT IS THE GREATEST LOVE story of all time? Who so loved mankind that He died for us that we might be free from sin? Who looks beyond our faults, sees our needs, and loves us unconditionally? It's Jesus. This love story began when God so loved the world that He sent His Son. If we believe in Him, we will not perish but have everlasting life. How awesome is that storyline? Yet, we take this love story and He who created us for granted. Oh that we would cherish Christ and concentrate on sharing His love. I was taught this lesson of love powerfully during the holidays.

Windows at our business provide the perfect place to share the Good News. The white fences behind the gigantic windows have displayed messages to usher in new seasons, celebrate milestones, applaud community helpers, congratulate students, and share special events throughout our community for twenty-two years.

My mother loved to see the windows all dressed up and decked out for the season. She encouraged me to share the love of the Lord there. I couldn't wait for her to see new window displays, knowing I'd always get a nod of approval. In 2001, my mother died along with my desire to decorate my windows. I cut letters and tearfully stapled them as a tribute to the woman God chose to give me life: "Hats Off to My Mother." Silly as it seems, I couldn't force myself to change my windows. Mama was gone, yet I'd catch myself dialing her number and wishing she would answer.

A simple conversation with someone you love so much should never be taken for granted. Don't delay calling those you love; share messages that tell them how much they mean to you. Don't be stingy with your time or your love. Four seasons passed after mother went to heaven before I changed my windows. Tim allowed me to grieve, but when the time was right, he gave me a lesson on love to help me move forward. He told me how I could share her love for the windows by dressing them up and letting love shine for others to see. I learned tough lessons and made mistakes I hoped never to repeat. Once, we lined each window with real pumpkins to usher in autumn. The hot sun baked the plump pumpkins. The odor was unbearable for days, the carpet was drenched in pumpkin pulp, and I vowed to use fake pumpkins forever more. Through the years, seasons have come and gone—as have the many messages proclaimed in our windows.

Short messages with powerful presentation grab attention. Our lives are a presentation, always making a statement. We should look good and remember others are always reading us. The way we act, react, and present ourselves is a key indicator of who we are and what we stand for. If we greet each day with a grumble and grunt, we push people away. Wearing a smile and sharing sunshine, we are a billboard with a blazing message: life is good—God is great!

When we bow our heads for a silent prayer in restaurants, share a scripture with a friend, pray with a co-worker, or praise the Lord as we walk through the park, God will be glorified. Silencing the Christians can never happen unless we allow it. We may be denied the privilege of praying out loud, but no one can stop us from bowing our heads and honoring our Father in our hearts. Sometimes, that silent message is more powerful than one shouted out loud for all to hear. Do others see Jesus in how you live your life?

Thinking about a creative Christmas display for my windows collided with dead ends, until a dream showed me the message just right for the season of love. I dreamed of a huge cross and the words "Cradle to Cross." My kids helped me get the words and lights in place for the window display, "From the Cradle of Christmas to the Cross of Easter."

That title stayed in our windows for five months, sharing Jesus who came so humbly and died so horribly. He cried in the cradle where his mother comforted him. He cried in the garden where His Father comforted him. He conquered death and took the keys from the devil. He arose and showed His nail-scarred hands to Thomas who loved him but doubted what had happened. He ascended to heaven to sit by His Father's side. He did it all in the name of love!

Do we truly profess that Christmas has its cradle and Easter has its cross? When we witness His awesome love and accept Jesus as Lord and Savior, He washes away our sins and victory with Jesus begins. It's not just the splendor of Christmas morning or the sunrise service by the cross that shares God's message of eternal and everlasting love. It's day by day, storm and sunshine, valleys and mountains, good times and bad, from the day we accept Him until the day He takes us home—living our lives in love with the Lord and sharing that love through all our seasons—that makes us a child of the King. Believing and being His is a blessing!

He went from the cradle to the cross because of His love for you and me. He gave His best; He gave Himself. What will you sacrifice for Him? Take time to talk with the Lord and seek his will for your life. He orders the steps of those who love and serve Him. Let your little light shine for Him and cherish the greatest love story of all time.

Finding Missing Treasures

HAVE YOU EVER LOST SOMETHING so precious that you felt your world would crumble if you didn't find it? Most of us can list numerous possessions we've lost through the years. My diamond ring glistens as I type. It dangled from our Christmas tree in 1981, six years after we said, "I do!"

My husband was so excited when I pulled the tiny box from the top branch. He slipped the ring on my finger and sealed it with a kiss. Waiting for my ring made it even more special. That's why I was devastated a year later when I realized that the diamond was gone; my ring had a hollow hole in the center. My heart did too, but I never gave up hope that I would find my ring.

Three years later, Tim was on a business trip in Chicago when a miracle happened at home. I tucked our sons in bed and sat on the bottom bunk, talking with them after our prayers. The phone rang; the man God sent to protect and love us was on the line. The boys talked excitedly with their dad as I listened with joy. Then, something shiny caught my eye near the molding behind their bed. I reached down and came up with a ball of dust holding my long-lost diamond captive. Tim heard my screams; we all celebrated and I said good-bye to my husband and thank you to my Father. All of us have such stories of recovered treasures stored in our hearts.

Losing material possessions can't compare with losing a loved one. The hole in the hearts of those who have lost a loved one can only be filled when a miracle brings their treasure home. Clint and I experienced such a miracle when our black lab was lost. Clint's love and devotion to Harley brings to mind a message in Isaiah 20 about God caring for us as a mother cares for her young.

Once, Harley came home from a trip to a nearby pond. Her sleek body was covered in something awful, which smelled worse than it looked. Clint grabbed her and bathed her gently while scolding her for getting into this mess. I watched in admiration, thinking of the magnitude of love and care needed as mothers care for their young. This unconditional love assures us that we are so loved by someone who will always be there to help clean up our messes.

The Friday we lost Harley had been a great day. Clint left for Wilmington; I headed to church without taking time to secure our lab in her pen. When I returned, Harley was not waiting for me in the garage. A stirring in my spirit told me she was gone. After a sleepless night, dawn found me searching and screaming her name throughout our community. Neighbors joined the search; Clint came home. I cancelled plans to attend an East Carolina football game. Nothing mattered without Harley. I thought of how we take things for granted, thinking things and people we love will always be there. My broken heart throbbed; I could only wonder where she was and wish I had been more careful. Darkness stopped the search but not my prayers.

On Sunday morning, sunshine filled my bedroom. I ran outside to search again—but no Harley. Clint and I went to church. We ate lunch in our sunroom with a grieving silence. All afternoon we canvassed the neighborhood, handing out posters with Harley's picture and hoping a miracle would bring her home.

As dusk settled, our neighbor pulled into our driveway. Don and Willie sat in the front seat, grinning from ear to ear. Clint and I felt a surge of hope turn into tears of joy when Harley leaped from Don's seat back into our lives. Our miracle unfolded as Erika, a family friend, was running Sunday afternoon and stopped to tie her shoelace. She noticed a black lab resting beside the gravestone in the cemetery where she was running. Erika remembered hearing about Clint's missing dog and called Don to find out more details. She patted the dog and called her name. Harley responded; Erika kept a close watch until Don and Willie arrived and brought our missing dog home.

The moment we saw their smiling faces and heard Harley's happy barking will live in our hearts forever. We learn great lessons when we lose precious possessions. Take nothing for granted, live each day cherishing the things we hold dear to our hearts, get our priorities in order and our lives right with God, never lose hope, and believe in miracles. In Jeremiah 33, we are told to call to God and He will answer. May all who have lost a treasure, keep your heart's doors ajar so God's grace can enter and fill the darkness with the light of hope.

Lessons of Love from Mama's Bible

*W*HO WILL INHERIT YOUR BIBLE one day? Will it hold treasures for your family, be tattered and torn from years of use, or be a collector's item, crisp and clean—with no underlined scripture or notes in the margin?

I think of things in our lifetime guaranteed to bring big bucks—if we had held onto them long enough. Our family's collector's items included GI Joes and Cabbage Patch dolls we searched high and low for in the rush of many Christmas seasons. Our things never enticed collectors because we enjoyed using them through the years. Our family's greatest treasures are those trademarked with personal touches, handwriting from a loved one, handprints in cement, homemade presents and cards given in an unforgettable way. Bibles of loved ones filled with years of personal notations and tender hearts teach lessons of love and longevity.

I was taught this lesson several years ago when I removed my precious whatnots from my curio cabinet and placed books I seldom use on the bottom shelf. I almost missed one last lesson of love from our mother who had gone to heaven in 2001. My brother and two sisters were faced with the task of cleaning out her home and dividing treasures equally. When the devil began his job of dividing and frustrating loved ones, we realized just how much we needed prayer, protection, and peace as we proceeded with this heartbreaking job.

After months of working, weeping, and worrying, we finally finished this job no family is ever prepared to do. The house was empty, except for the kitchen table where we gathered one last time. Through the years, this is where we shared pancakes and homemade sausage, mashed potatoes and fried chicken, pound cake and ice cream on birthdays, conversations and celebrations that kept us close. For this last gathering, the old oak table held family Bibles and personal treasures that were near and dear to our hearts, our mama, daddy, and stepfather's special things. We recalled memories with laughter and love filling our hearts. Then, we drew numbers to divide the treasures on the table. With everything finished, the four of us held hands and prayed, holding one another close and crying tears of heartache and joy. Then, we left our home place and headed to our own homes. Our lives would never be the same, but the enemy had been defeated as we embraced forgiveness, family ties, and the future in unity.

For months, I sifted through stacks and plundered through boxes crowding our garage. How do you depart with one single thing—from old receipts with my daddy's handwritten notes to my mama's recipes with smudges left by her hardworking hands? Sorting through such treasures and clearing clutter is something we should do for ourselves and our families. Holding onto everything clutters every corner, making our hearts and homes a hazard. Refusing to prune our past and face the future prohibits growth as God intends. Hard as it is, we must hold to our memories and move forward in faith.

One year later, our garage was cleared and my task of finding a place for family keepsakes was complete. Late one night, I decided to look through the Bibles and books that had become mine by drawing a number when we divided things. I pulled a small brown Bible from the bottom shelf of my curio cabinet that had belonged to my stepfather. His companionship and compassion brought sunshine to my mama's cloudy days. I found a letter inside his Bible with my handwriting. Reading it brought back memories of their wedding and words from my heart.

Mr. Gurnie,

I am happy for you and mama. I respect you and remember many good times from my childhood when you would stop by our country store. When you and your wife did the flowers for my wedding, never did I dream you would marry my mother one day. You know how much I love my daddy. He was my hero. Even though you can never take his place, I thank God for bringing you and my mama together.

I love you,
Becky

Mother and Mr. Gurnie spent twelve wonderful years together before God called him home. How thankful I am that God sent a special stepfather to our family. Often, we resist and reject new things in our lives that God intends for goodness and growth. May we humble ourselves and be accepting. Trust God to bring good from the bad things that break our hearts and homes.

I pulled the Bible from the shelf that was protected by a zippered pouch. For hours, I sat on the floor, flabbergasted by what I found. Mama's old Bible was packed with newspaper clippings, pictures of her grandchildren, mints, tissues, and church bulletins bearing her handwritten notes. Newspaper keepsakes showed my family at Tim's grand opening, Cameron riding a tractor given to him by his papa in 1980, and a picture of him juggling a football and soccer ball his senior year in 1996. There were pictures of Clint at his prom and receiving the MVP award his junior year. My heart was tender as I thought of how happy my mama must have been when she clipped those articles and secured them in this sacred spot. As I zipped up the cover to her Bible, I left the treasures just as she had placed them between the pages. I thanked God for a mother who cherished her family and taught lessons of love and unity—even when we were unaware.

Growing tired, I almost missed the blessing God intended for me to find. The Bible she had been using when she passed away held a hidden treasure. I pulled it from the shelf and ran my fingers across the golden letters that spelled her name. I opened it to find only a heart-shaped golden clip that talked about how children will arise and call their mother blessed. I noticed a small slip of paper where mother had written, Gal. 6:1 and Corn. 1:10-12 and secured it safely under the clip. My heart stirred as my fingers fumbled through the pages of her Bible, searching for Galatians. I read the passage and the meaning sank deeply in my heart. It talked of not being overtaken in a fault, restoring one another in the spirit of meekness, and not being tempted. Mama was speaking to us through God's Word, telling us to stay united and overlook one another's faults and stick together in meekness.

Turning the pages as fast as my fingers would go, I found the verses in Corinthians with a neatly folded tissue between them. I read the scripture and thought of mama searching for just the right words to leave for her children. The words told us to speak the same thing and to have no divisions among us. My head dropped, my heart sank, and my mind drifted back to the difficulty of accepting their death, of dividing their belongings, and being joined together in the same mind and judgment with no divisions among us. I held the Bible close to my heart and wept, thanking God for my mother who knew her children well and stayed closely connected to us and to our Heavenly Father.

I thought of how her children had overlooked the greatest treasure she left: her Bible with words of love from God, to her, to us. Our task would have been much easier had we gone to her Bible first. We were so intent on dividing things while not being divided that our family unity was threatened. I realized the love for the Lord and spiritual discipline taught in our home had been deeply rooted all along. Mama just wanted to remind us to stay united and to reassure us of God's promise. I rushed to call my brother and sisters and shared the treasure that my mother had left for us. With a happy, humbled heart, I looked to heaven and told my Lord and loved ones how much I loved them.

Will someone you love cherish your collection of keepsakes one day? Are you building a treasure in the hearts and minds of those you love? Do you model love and unity in your family? Don't let the sun set with any divisions among you and those you love. A close, personal relationship with your Heavenly Father and your family is a treasure that touches eternity.

A Day at the Beach

*H*AVE YOU EVER LEARNED LESSONS about life while weeding your garden or dodging waves in the ocean? We can learn great truth from most anything we do when our hearts and minds are willing and in tune with our Father.

I inherited my love for flowers and gardening from my mother. Her green thumb was the envy of most anyone who admired her lovely yards and houseplants. She invested much time and hard work making her gardens grow; she even talked to her plants, declaring that they thrived on her loving words and caring hands. My weekly job was to polish every houseplant with baby oil. I hated this boring job, but I loved how shiny the plants looked when I was finished. Still, I declared no gardens for me when I moved into my own house. One lesson learned is to never say what we will not do. Another is that the older we get, the more like our parents we become. To my mother in heaven, I confess my love for gardening and appreciation for your example of working hard and loving passionately. Those lessons have transformed me into the person I am today. And yes, I do talk to my plants—and my Lord—all the time.

My flower gardens at Topsail Beach had been neglected all summer. Finally, I had some time to spend with my flowers that were waiting to be rescued from weeds. The cool ocean breeze made getting started easier. Usually the weeds and grass give up easily as I pull them loose, but that's when I keep a close eye and weed them out as soon as they start to show their ugly sprouts. Leaving my garden unattended and allowing the weeds to grow and gain ground gave me a fit. Sea grape, a plant brought to the island because of its beauty, was the toughest villain of all to remove. Its roots never stop; it takes over. What was meant to be a thing of beauty turns out to be a beast. Working until sweat blinded my eyes, I found rest and revelation in our swing. God showed how the weeds choked out my flowers the same way sin destroys lives.

One little weak sprout, growing and gaining strength with roots inching deeper into the ground is like sin in our hearts spreading relentless roots on a mission to steal, destroy, and take over our lives. Thoughts of quitting kept popping in my mind, but the more weeds I cleared, the more beautiful my garden became. I was reminded of how God cleanses our lives and cleans up our messes. When we accept Jesus, repent our sins, and follow Jesus, He removes every deep-rooted sin and makes our lives beautiful again. Much of my day was spent working on my knees, giving time for repentance, renewal, and respect for our Creator. Have you weeded your gardens and cleansed your heart lately? Don't delay. The enemy is ready to root and grow unless we weed sin out daily and nurture our hearts with God's love and mercy.

Giving a little loving care to my flowers came the next morning. My asparagus ferns weren't thriving, so I decided to repot them. What a job! After pulling and chopping the roots with all my might, I sought help from my neighbor, PaPa Fussell. He didn't just tell me what to do; he helped me with my tremendous task. With huge scissors, we cut through thick, tough roots. It looked as if my ferns were forever ruined, but a great lesson was being taught. Papa showed me his harvest of beautiful ferns that had come from one. When my work was done, I rejoiced at how my one fern had multiplied. God showed me that's how unforgiveness is in our lives. My ferns were root-bound and wouldn't grow and prosper.

When we refuse to forgive and keep tough, thick roots bound up inside, our lives are unproductive. We don't thrive and are unable to grow and go outside our root-bound selves. When we forgive and cleanse our hearts, we are released and ready to thrive again. Is there someone you need to forgive so that you can thrive again? Do it today. Root-bound sins in our hearts keep us out of heaven. Forgive and accept forgiveness before it chokes the life from you. Our ability to show mercy to others comes from the gift of God's mercy to us. We cut ourselves off from the flow of God's love and forgiveness when we harbor resentment toward others.

With our work done, Clint and Harley headed to the seashore for some fun. God loves to see our work completed, but He desires for

Rise Up, Recount Love

us to enjoy life and be happy. We had so much fun watching Harley retrieve the tennis ball and chasing her through the sand. She paddled past the waves; we joined her for a cool swim. I never intended to go so deep into the Atlantic. Riding the waves was awesome—until I let down my guard and a monstrous wave knocked me down. Reaching shore, inside out and upside down, my laughter turned to tears when Clint motioned that my sunglasses were gone. While we searched, I beat myself up for being so careless with something I treasured. Those sunglasses had been a Christmas gift from Clint. As I scanned the waters like a hunting hound, I remembered the smile on my son's face when I opened his present that Christmas morning. He was so proud to give his mom designer shades. It wasn't the name brand that made them so valuable to me; it was how Clint had saved his money and gave them in a spirit of love. Again, God showed me how Satan snatches us, our loved ones, and our possessions—anything we love dearly—and leaves us wiped out and lost.

Clint saw my sadness, but he forced me to give up the search. I knew it was useless, but I went back one more time to look. I thought of what Jesus told Paul when he asked what to do when people wouldn't listen and accept his preaching. Though it breaks our hearts, sometimes we must just dust off our feet and move on.

As we left footprints and paw prints in the sand, we held hands and walked home, soaking up the lessons learned that day. Losing things you love is never easy, but material possessions can be replaced. I thanked God that we were not calling off the search for a loved one lost at sea. I was humbled and hopeful. We should never stop searching for those lost in sin.

Are you lost? Jesus is softly and tenderly calling your name, ready to weed out all your sins, to make your garden bloom again, and to give you the promise of everlasting life.

Spending a Day with Mother

*M*OTHER'S DAY IS SET ASIDE to honor those we call mother. This day brings happiness and heartwarming memories for mothers and families to share. Mothers are placed on pedestals and pampered for an entire day. Flowers, perfume, and celebrations galore greet mothers as children spend time with the woman who gave them life.

Mothers are love. The relationship we share with the one who bore the pain and brought us into this world is one we should keep precious and pure. Our relationship with the One who bore the pain, died for our sins, and gives us eternal life is important for peace on earth and the promise for eternity in heaven. I can only imagine how awesome it will be when I see my mother standing on that heavenly shore, waiting to welcome me home. Keeping ourselves ready to meet the Maker, walking and talking with Jesus every single day, honoring God's gift of everlasting life and a mother's gift of life on earth all give peace and promise.

We can know and love our mothers but spend little time with them—or even take them for granted. Mothers love deeply and devotedly, yearning to be closely connected to their children. A personal relationship—one of trust and treasure, peace and purpose, understanding and acceptance, confidence and caring—comes from investing time and being true to the one you love. Mothers often grate on children's nerves and require care as they age, but when they are gone, so is your treasure. Spending time and money without being truly connected cannot fool your mother—or your Heavenly Father. Having a heart that beats with love, appreciation, and a desire to spend time and do things together makes your mother and your Maker happy.

Tim's mother shared a story about my eighth grade teacher, Mrs. Mila Faircloth, and her son, my high school teacher, Weldon. When Mrs. Mila went to be with Jesus, we were talking about what a wonderful woman she was. Mom pointed out what a mighty man her son was. Every morning, Weldon shared a cup of coffee and a conversation with the woman he adored. Do you spend time with your mother without her asking for this precious gift?

I remember the last day I spent on earth with my mother. God tugged my heart to call her from school, one hot August morning in 2001, and offer to take her to Duke Hospital to visit my sister. Mother was like a little girl as we made plans to leave on Wednesday at lunch from Tim's office. On Wednesday morning, I kissed my husband good-bye and started out the door. Something told me to go back inside and get the gift I had bought for my mother a week earlier and give it to her that day. I listened to that gentle voice, but I didn't obey it. I even picked up the pretty wrapped package, but I placed it back in the corner where I keep special gifts. I thought I'd save the gift for Grandparents Day. We should listen to the gentle nudging of the Holy Spirit in our hearts; Mother never received that last gift I bought for her.

Mother waited for me as I took care of the never-ending list of teacher duties facing me at the beginning of school. When I entered my husband's office, my attitude was not right; I felt compelled to be at work. I thought I had hidden my frustration well, but we don't hide anything from our mamas.

The day was a gift from God—a gift I almost missed, a gift the enemy tried to steal. Since childhood, mama had always packed picnics for her children to enjoy and to save money. Little did I know that we were sharing our last picnic on earth that summer day. I drove while she prepared the meal in her lap. She pulled a little jar of mayonnaise from the bag that held the loaf of bread she boasted was fresh off the bread truck that morning. Forgetting to put a knife in her bag didn't deter her mission to make her little girl a good lunch. She laughed and told me her finger was clean, then spread mayonnaise and broke off pieces of banana to complete my favorite sandwich. That memory is preserved and plays back often in my mind. What a sweet picture of sacrificial love God showered me with that day. We visited my sister Glenda before driving on to Greensboro to spend time with my sister Gaye and her family. Since my mother had never seen Gaye's classroom, we surprised her at school, spent the afternoon laughing and talking, and had a marvelous time at dinner with Gaye's family. After staying much longer than we had planned, we drove home on the busy interstate. Mother spoke of how the big trucks seemed as if they would run right over us. Throughout the day, Mama made many comments that foreshadowed the tragic day awaiting my family, but I didn't recognize the meaning of her words.

I kept thinking about what a happy day it had been, but how I would pay the price the next day for being away from work. My restless legs and bit of an attitude made me miserable. Mama sensed it and kept telling me how she appreciated me taking time for her that day and apologizing for being so much trouble. I assured her of my love and devotion to my mama—no matter what the future held for us. It was almost midnight when we made it home. I kissed her and told her I loved her for the very last time.

The next morning, a huge pile of work waited for me on my desk, but I couldn't get myself in motion. Something was tugging at my heart again. I headed down to our hall phones to call my mother, but she wasn't home. Little did I know she was on her way home to heaven. Two hours later, I was called to the guidance counselor's office where my husband, son, brother, a patrolman, and a whole host of friends stood somberly. The patrolman broke the silence with the news that no child ever wants to hear. My mother had been hit by a transfer truck while driving to Clinton that morning and had not survived. Tim reached out and held me close as I felt my world crumble. My mother was really gone. I thanked God for giving me a gift I will cherish forever, spending her last day on earth together. All my work mattered little in comparison to the treasure of being with my mother during her last hours before Jesus took her home forever.

Our mothers will not be with us on this earth forever. Cherish your time together and make sure the time and gifts you share with her are given with a sweet, loving spirit. If there is anything that keeps you from being closely connected to your mother or your Maker, clear it from your heart, repent, and reach out to spend time with Him and her. Praise God for your mother being with you here on earth or with Him in heaven.

Lost and Found Treasures

*H*AVE YOU EVER LOST SOMETHING so precious that you felt your world would crumble if you didn't find it? Most of us have lost plenty of possessions through the years.

My diamond ring glistens on my finger as I type, a reminder that once it was lost, but now it is found. Losing material possessions pales in comparison to losing a loved one. Amber Alerts and Silver Alerts send shivers down my spine. On March 21, 2006, I walked in the shoes of one who waits for a lost one to be found. My husband and I were staying in Chapel Hill while he received treatments for brain cancer. We were settled in our motel room when I realized I had forgotten our toothbrushes. I told him we'd get some at the front desk, but he insisted on driving to a nearby store. He told me to rest; he'd be back soon. Sensing danger, I insisted on going. He asked if we needed to bring in any other items from the car before we left. I reminded him our Bible was in the back seat. He brought it in our room, laid it on the bed, and announced it was time to go. He drove across the busy highway and stopped in front of CVS. He puffed on his sweet cigar and smiled, telling me he would fill up the car with gas while I shopped. I hesitated, but he insisted he would be fine. As our car slowly pulled away, I stood on the sidewalk with a fearful heart, watching his smile fade as he became lost in the five o'clock traffic.

Five minutes later, I waited on the sidewalk with the new toothbrushes. Two hours later, after pacing back and forth, waiting, looking at every vehicle that resembled ours, my hope dwindled. People passed by, glaring at my swollen eyes, but no one stopped to offer help. Finally, one Good Samaritan came to my rescue. He was on his way home but took time to ask, listen, and call the police. I resisted leaving that sidewalk, knowing he would come back for me, but the policewoman insisted we needed to go back to the motel to proceed with the paperwork. The missing person report was filed; some of the questions pierced my heart. I called my sons to tell them their dad was missing.

When the policewoman escorted me to our room, she offered to call a chaplain. I thanked her, assuring her I would be fine. The emptiness in that room and my heart was huge. Tim's flannel robe, cell phone, and our Bible stared at me from the bed. I kneeled and broke before my Lord. My time with God gave me strength to endure the next eight hours. I opened our Bible and read where God promises to take care of His children. I prayed, paced, and powered myself with scripture. Holding tight to scripture that encourages one not to let imaginations become thoughts, to resist the enemy, to think on things that are lovely, I prayed and pleaded to my Father.

My prayers were answered amazingly. By nine o clock, my room was filled with family and friends from our hometown, with prayer chains formed from Clinton to the coast. We prayed together in our motel room—and friends searched the streets of Chapel Hill and surrounding areas—while my family held and hugged me throughout the frightening ordeal.

Our minds were boggled, hearts were broken, and hands were tied as we waited. Calls to our credit card company came up with no activity on the card. I couldn't believe this was happening. God's Helper, sent to live and dwell in our hearts, was my comfort. He kept me grounded and flooded with peace when panic begged to plunge me to a pit of pity.

Hope came when the phone in our room rang in the wee hours of the morning. A manager of Holiday Inn in Whitsett, North Carolina, called. His news was good. Tim had stopped at his motel looking for me. When the manager realized Tim needed help, he took action.

Isn't that what Jesus expects us to do? The manager gave the phone to Tim. His weak voice was music to my ears. He told me he couldn't find me. Seeking the right words, I assured him I was waiting for him where he had left me—and his sons were on the way to where he was. Cheers, prayers, and praise filled our room; friends and family filled up cars and headed west to bring Tim home.

Hours later, a joyous celebration took place in the motel parking lot. Hugs and happiness brought light to the darkness that surrounded. Everyone headed home to Clinton. Tim and I held one another close and waved good-bye. Clint stayed. The three of us crawled into bed without asking for any explanation or seeking answers to the questions burning inside. We just held one another close and prayed, thanking God that the man we loved was not lost.

Cameron headed home that night with the convoy of family and friends who cared enough to come and look for a loved one who was lost. I prayed for each of them in the quiet of our room—with both arms wrapped around my man and thoughts of what could have happened. Those strongholds had no room in my heart; joy, thankfulness, and confirmation that God watches over us and answers our prayers overpowered any tempting or tormenting thoughts the enemy tried to plant.

I prayed for family and friends driving home in darkness, knowing a new day would soon be dawning and their tired bodies would be back at work. They would tell the story of how Tim had been lost and a faithful few kept looking and believing, while a whole host of people at home were praying and believing. I stayed awake the rest of that long night, soaking up the sweet spirit that rested in our room and thanking God over and over for bringing Tim home. I prayed for those who came to us in our time of need, who did as the Good Shepherd and Samaritan taught us to do. Go out and search for a lost one until he is found and get off your horse and help those in need. I will forever remember those who searched and helped us that night. Are you thinking of people who have stood by your side in times of trouble? God puts people in our paths at the right time for the right reason. Praise Him and thank them for sharing and caring about you and those you love.

Tim and I did not discuss what happened in Chapel Hill until two months later. It was difficult for me to wait; my heart ached to know every detail of him being lost and tell him how hard it was for me. God is teaching me to zip my lip and wait on His timing to talk. That's a lesson most of us need every day. How selfish I was; my agony paled in comparison to what Tim experienced that frightful March night.

It was a June afternoon when we recounted the story of him being lost and reaffirmed our love. Tim and I watched the sunset over the sound at Topsail and settled down on our daybed to listen to music while we cuddled. Good music and holding close the one you love is priceless. One of our favorites by the Eagles began to play. The lyrics told of lovers with question of why things happen as they do, losing the one you love, believing in angels and loving again, a place where the sun always shines. Tim turned the volume down and drew me closer to his body. We were still and quiet for a long time. His body showed signs of the battle he was fighting for survival. The brain cancer, chemotherapy, and radiation had taken a toll on the man of my dreams. His mustache tickled my face as I ran my fingers through his gray hair. Doctors said Tim would lose his hair; Tim told them differently. His faith was strong as the battle waged. Never did he complain or ask why—and he didn't lose his hair.

Tim smiled while I talked, telling him stories of our love that will live in my heart forever. The love song we sang to one another in the seventies still spoke the truth to lovers who had weathered seasons of trials and triumph and were still crazy in love today: "So in love are we two that we don't know what to do."

Tim and I did not know what to do when cancer came into our lives in 2006. We listened to doctors, friends, and family who wanted healing as much as we did. Finally, we listened to the still, small voice that brought peace to our hearts. We put our situation in God's hands and trusted Him for help and healing.

I rested my hand close to Tim's heart, watching his broad chest rise and fall with every beat of his heart. I felt safe and secure—just as I always have with the man God sent and I chose to spend my life with. Memories of dating days and three decades of marriage flooded my heart, reminding me that I was still crazy in love with my Lord and my husband. That peaceful, precious gift is pure and priceless.

Tim listened with a look of love in his tired eyes. Then, he held my hand in his and shared his stories. He recounted the nightmare he lived the night when he was lost. He told how he stopped at so many CVS stores and waited for me to come outside. He was hungry and needed to use the bathroom, but he had no money or cell phone, so he kept riding and looking for me.

He remembered we were staying at a Holiday Inn and stopped at several with no help in his search. He shared how one person at the front desk humiliated him when he told her he was looking for his wife. He gave his name, my name, and our room number. She shattered his hopes, hurting more than helping him when she offered no assistance and asked why he lost his wife. He needed a Good Samaritan—not a mean-spirited person who wouldn't help people put in her path, much like the priest and Pharisee who passed by a brother in need.

Tim found a Good Samaritan five hours later in a little town hundreds of miles from where he had left me. Tim charged gas at a station at I-40 and asked if there was a Holiday Inn nearby. The kind man helped Tim. He said he did not know which way to go and wondered if he would ever see me again, but he kept believing.

Hours later, he entered a Holiday Inn in Whitsett and told the man at the desk he was looking for his wife. This man was truly Tim's Good Samaritan. He spoke with a different accent, was of different color and culture, but showed the sweet spirit of love and humility to a stranger seeking help in the middle of the night.

The desk clerk realized Tim was sick and took action to help a brother in need. He calmed Tim's fears with assurances that he would find me and everything would be okay, without making Tim feel humiliated and helpless. The man made numerous calls, alerted officials, gave Tim food and drink, showed him where the bathroom was, and provided a comfortable chair where he told him to rest and wait while he found his wife. This gentleman gave graciously and got off his horse to help someone he didn't know and would probably never see again. He cared and shared the sweet spirit of love and showed the power of faith in action.

Tim said he thought that night would never end as he sat in the lobby of that hotel; he felt helpless but not hopeless. The man sat down and listened as Tim shared stories of our lives. This man knew that comforting Tim in his hour of need was important—just as the Good Samaritan showed when he went beyond the call of duty and gave graciously.

Tim talked openly about being lost and wondering what his family was doing and where we were. He kept telling the man he had to find his wife. Then, the door opened and Willie Hobbs stood there with open arms. He rushed to Tim and hugged him. Tim said the power of the love of a good friend was strong and sweet.

They thanked the Middle Eastern gentleman and Willie said, "Come on, Tim, let's go home."

My tears had soaked my shirt by the time Tim finished his story. My eyes were red, but my heart was happy and thankful as we knew the ending of that night could have been tragic instead of triumphant.

We wiped one another's tears. Then, Tim told one last detail of how he never found the bathroom and the dilemma he endured. We laughed until our tears came again and our spirits were lifted higher than they'd been lifted in a long time. We praised God for we were together and that mattered most of all.

In silence, we rested in one another's arms and watched the bright sunshine slip slowly out of sight. The orange ball of fire sank into the sound where we had sailed and shared our love for many seasons. Memories we had made in these tranquil waters would rise up and comfort me in years to come when I would watch the sun set without Tim by my side.

We didn't say it, but in our hearts we knew the sun would soon set and our season of listening to music and cuddling together would soon slip away. We didn't allow that to spoil the joy of the season. The beauty of being together was our praise; we thanked God for bringing Tim home and all the people who He was sending to help us on this journey. We loved and laughed and looked to tomorrow with hope for healing.

Tim lost his way a month later when he decided to visit his mother one Saturday afternoon. I was writing my weekly story while he watched television. I jumped up to go with him, but he insisted on making this trip and me staying home to finish my work. I called his mother as soon as his El Camino was out of sight, telling her Tim should be at her house in twenty minutes and to call me when he arrived. Two hours passed with no sign of Tim. I prayed. We prayed.

I waited and held to hope. Finally, the phone rang and Tim told me where he was. Several Good Samaritans helped us that day. My brother, Billy, had joined the search and rushed to the country crossroads far from Tim's mother's house where Tim's car had broken down. He waited with him, telling funny stories from family adventures and reassuring Tim everything would be okay. I drove to Piney Green Crossroads, praising God all the way for protecting Tim when he didn't know which way to go. Our friend at Spell's Body Shop came and towed Tim's car to my brother's store—and his mechanics took care of it. Neither of them would charge for their services of towing and fixing Tim's car and encouraging him in his time of distress. Good Samaritans are alive and well today—even in a world where many people turn their heads and look the other way when God provides opportunities to help people rise up from troubles and tough times.

Some may say it was coincidence that Tim's car broke down, but I believe it was God's favor. Our Father was watching over Tim and bringing people into our lives that would provide assistance in our time of need.

One year later, Tim left us again. This time, he went home to heaven. The joy of knowing the one you love is with the Lord in paradise gives peace and comfort—even when your heart is broken. God gives guidance as we walk lonely paths in faith.

We learn valuable lessons when we lose something or someone we love. Take nothing for granted, live each day cherishing the things we hold dear to our hearts, get priorities in order, live each day closely connected to the Lord and loved ones, and never lose hope. Reading Jeremiah 33:3 gives peace and promise.

May all who have lost a treasure remember to keep your heart's door ajar so God's grace can enter and fill the darkness with the light of hope.

The Love Story

*A*RE YOU ENJOYING WRITING YOUR love story? For too long, the enemy has heralded hate and caused people who truly love one another to imprison themselves in loneliness and lies. Failing to communicate honestly, connect with one another, and keep God in relationships has opened doors for the enemy to enter and crush beautiful love stories. Keeping Christ first and cherishing loved ones promotes long lives of peace, prosperity, and promise. We can't give up on love or life just because our love story didn't end the way we planned.

Many love stories never make it through the first chapter. Others become bored in the middle and give up way too soon. Some make it through the entire book only to walk out wearily and start a new book. A select few become classics—never-ending love stories that touch eternity. What kind of love story are you writing in this lifetime? You may be fortunate to be writing a classic—one that will live on in the hearts of all those you have touched on this earth. You could be the author of a love story with a plot filled with heartaches and headaches—one with more chapters about struggles than successes, more sadness than sunshine.

It's easy to give up on such stories, but what happens to the characters who have poured their lives into a love they truly believed would last forever—those who never thought they would grow tired of one another, who could never understand why their little child died, who never imagined they would be left alone night after night, who didn't plan on being abused, who never thought sickness would steal—and kill, who didn't plan on dementia robbing precious memories, who never believed their mate would cheat. Characters allowed selfish desires to override plans made together, became too busy to recognize what was happening, put God on a back burner, and the sweet love story He planned to be a bestseller became a failure.

Magnificent love stories have flopped for many different reasons. Some seemed to be doomed from the start. Others had everything needed to make them the best—even silver spoons that shouted success. Yet, when love isn't cherished and protected, treasured and shared from hearts pure in spirit and closely connected to one another and to Christ, it's easy to close the book and pack it away—out of sight, out of mind. That's when the enemy sets in for the kill—unless we allow the love of our Lord to rescue us from pits of sin that become places of refuge and retreat. God is love. His love story has been a bestseller for ages. It is filled with chapter after chapter of promise and precious stories that guide and give hope—even for those who feel their book will never make it.

God allows us to see stories from the beginning in the garden to the return of His Son. Every chapter captures the glory of a loving Father. His love story was to be perfect. Imagine His pain when Adam and Eve distorted the storyline from the very start.

Some of His children created more havoc and heartache than most chapters even begin to reveal. He saw His children turn their backs on Him, mock Him, wage war on one another, leave Him and come crawling back over and over, take blessings for granted, worship idols, kill family to receive birthrights, steal from one another, take things into their own hands, forget Him—even crucify His own Son.

God's Book had two parts. The Old Testament was filled with stories of history, commandments, legalism, love, war, and predictions of God's Son's birth, childhood, death, resurrection, ascension to His Father, and return to take home the saints who kept Him in their stories. His Good Book continues with The New Testament. These stories document the miraculous birth of Jesus, the Great Commission to share the Good News, the new wineskin granting us a direct line to our Father. The disciples spread the Word, the fulfillment of signs came from prophets of old, and salvation was made possible by Jesus drinking from the cup. There are signs of end times when God will gather His saints, prepare His army, build His church, come for His bride, destroy the devil and all the demons of hell, and finally proclaim victory over death, over evil, over the enemy forever. Finally, the devil will be cast into the lake of fire and will be no more.

Those who stand firm and keep writing love stories from pure hearts will find strength to hold on—to keep believing and being all they can be for God. Some of our stories will be finished before the conclusion of God's story unfolds. When will God send His Son and show the world the end is near? His Book of Revelation is real and unravels before our eyes as we read and pray, work and write endings to our own books. When will our book end? Let God's Word—His promise of love and life eternal—encourage you to write carefully and courageously, tenderly yet tough, continuing instead of quitting.

He will send signs, wonders, and miracles to confirm your climax. Your time to write here will one day end. If your love story includes Jesus Christ being your Lord and Savior, you will close your book and hear His voice calling you home where you will live happily ever after!

Hope

*D*O YOU HAVE HOPE? HOPE is something we believe in, but we must take action to help it happen. Do you remember the seventies song? Just wishing and hoping and thinking and praying won't get Him into your heart. You gotta show him that you care—just once more. Do the things you used to do; trust Him and love Him and He will be yours. Those words aren't exactly how the lyrics went, but the message is the same. You must take action and not sit around waiting for things to fall into your lap like manna fell from the sky for the Israelites. And when we get what we hoped for, we have to care and do things to show our love and honor. In other words, keep love alive and live out loud.

Waiting around for things to happen isn't wise and doesn't always work. While we should wait on His timing, we must be careful not to lag behind or rush ahead. And we can't use waiting on Him as an excuse not to do what we are called to do. The poor, sick fellow who waited by the pool for more than three decades to be healed, was hopeless He needed to engage and exercise faith. His miracle was so close, yet so far away. Still, he held to hope, believing that someone would happen by and help get him into the healing waters.

When cancer invaded my body in 2007, just two months after my husband lost his battle with cancer, I left the doctor's office in disbelief. Sitting in my car, I beat my steering wheel and asked why. Crying and carrying on like a woman of little faith is exactly what the enemy wanted, and I did for a while. Then, I dried my tears, said a prayer, praised God that my doctor found the cancer early, asked Him to take care of me, slipped my gearshift into forward, and drove back to work to tell my son.

Now, that is exactly what Jabez did. In the Old Testament, we read his simple, powerful prayer. Many might think that prayer is vain, but God heard Jabez and answered his prayer. I wanted God to help me and heal me from cancer. I wanted to feel the warm flowing of His Holy Spirit cover me from head to toe.

For three weeks, I waited. More doctor appointments and many prayers filled my days. The night before surgery, I drove down a little path to a home where Prayer Connection friends were meeting. They prayed over me. Mrs. Eloise prophesied I would come home the next day. The sweet spirit flowed mightily in that humble home and in my heart, but I drove home not fully believing the prayer warrior's words. I knew surgery was planned, but God can change plans in an instant. The next day, I was prepped for surgery, but doctors decided more tests were needed and sent me home. Mrs. Eloise's prayer empowered me to fight in renewed faith and claim my miracle.

While recovering from surgery weeks later, Prayer Connection friends sent a card with a love offering for my ministry. I was baffled; I had no ministry. Months later, I awoke in the middle of the night with a stirring to find that card and plant the seed offering. I didn't hesitate and sit around hoping and wishing for good things God had in store for my life. I headed to the bank the next day and opened an account with the seed money from my friends.

The miracle of Tim's Gift happened. How thankful I am that I didn't give up and get discouraged when God was waiting to send a miracle and ministry. Tim's Gift was in God's plans from the beginning. How humbling it is when we watch God's amazing power put all the pieces in place, propelling us to His plans.

The Love Ministry is a ministerial arm of Tim's Gift, offering spiritual support to cancer patients and their families. We are stepping in faith as God grows the ministry and enlarges our territories. Tuesdays are designated for early morning and noon prayer time, Bible Studies, New Beginnings, afternoon intercessory prayer, and Sunshine Kids ministry.

Cameron quit his job to come home and serve as executive director of Tim's Gift. This did not happen by coincidence. As the ministry began to grow, I worked by myself trying to take care of everything. I prayed and asked God for guidance. In a vivid dream in March 2009, God showed me my eldest son working alongside me at the ministry and helping my neighbor sell health insurance. It was three o'clock in the morning when I sat up in bed and talked to God like He was right there with me—and He was.

Cameron doing what I dreamed seemed impossible in that season of our lives. It would have been so easy to shake off that dream and go back to sleep with disbelief in my heart. I pulled on a warm robe and began praising God all over my house. I sipped coffee between prayers and watched the clock like a hawk. When six o'clock finally rolled around, I called my neighbor to come over quickly. Bobby was baffled at my early morning request but soon stood knocking at my side door. He listened as I poured out the details of my dream. It must have sounded ridiculous, but Bobby believed with me. We prayed together and agreed to be quiet about the dream and remain in prayer.

Waiting for the right time to release what God puts in our hearts is important. I am slowly learning this lesson, for I am anxious to tell things and get things done, a go-go, as my sons call me. Years ago, a lady I did not know told me God spoke something to her heart to share with me. She told me I was doing too much and should slow down, being still and knowing that He is God. Whoa! Those powerful words were true, but having a stranger speak them made an impact I would remember. Often, I start to speak, but a small voice reminds me to be still and shut up. It is important to share and speak—even be doers of the Word—at the right time. How sad that many Christians choose to sit on the fence and be silent. There is a time and a place for everything as we read in the Good Book. I believe the time to rise up and recount all that God has done for us, to honor Him, and put Him first in our lives is here. If each of us makes this commitment not to be silenced, our world would notice and winds of change would bring love and goodness where evil and sin have ruled for way too long. Waiting for the right time is crucial.

While we waited, the enemy was working too. Cameron and I were in a season when situations threatened to separate us. I prayed morning, noon, and night, asking God to keep me moving forward with the ministry and not to be offended when Cameron and I were at odds. I prayed for Cameron and praised God for the plans I knew He had for my son. I asked God to send the right people and dreams to guide Cameron. I waited on God, believing and actively seeking what I hoped for in my heart.

God's timing is perfect. Our Lord waits on us and watches how we handle the things He puts in our paths. I kept praying and waiting, but I continued to work diligently in the ministry and my afterschool care. In June 2010, Cameron became the director of Tim's Gift and a partner with Bobby in his insurance business. God is so good and His Word will not return void. God still speaks to His children—even in dreams. Working together to give help and hope to people in need is a gift I treasure. Learning to hold my horses and let God be God is bringing calm where chaos once controlled much of my life. It's precious when peace reigns and dreams come true.

Just wishing and hoping won't make our dreams and miracles come true. We've got to show God that we care, that we love and respect Him, and wait with active faith while He works out all things in His time. Watching things happen we hope for is a hint of heaven on earth.

Dealing with Death

*H*AS YOUR HEART BEEN BROKEN by the death of a loved one recently? Mine has. While writing stories about how we live and die, death claimed two more links in my family's chain. Today's story is written with tears flowing and God giving the last lesson to help us understand death.

Good Friday was the first story I shared from Morrie's lessons on dying. He told how we all must one day leave this life—dwelling on death isn't good for anyone—but being ready for it any given day is wise for all. The date of that story was April 22—the same date my daddy died in 1983 and my husband died in 2007. This year I was by my sister's side in High Point on April 22. Her husband died with loved ones surrounding his bedside. The sting of death pierced the depths of our souls.

Our family and friends gathered in their church on Easter Sunday to pay tribute to a mighty man who had loved deeply and given generously. My son preached at his Uncle Kurt's funeral, sharing a message that sounded much like the lessons from Morrie's book and the Good Book. He talked about the life Kurt lived, how he helped people and lived life with a quiet, gentle spirit, like Jesus did. He encouraged everyone to live each day closely connected to those they love and to God. He told how his dad and uncle's lives paralleled, about the void in our hearts and homes with them now living in heaven. I listened to Cameron's words and smiled through my tears. While we may not understand all the things of this world, especially death, God does! And He doesn't make mistakes—or put on us more than we can bear. He knows the plans for our lives and answers prayers. Cameron's prayer gave hope to people who filled that church to honor and remember his Uncle Kurt. I praised God and prayed for my son as words of life flowed from his heart. Death is not the end but the beginning. May the love of the Lord live in our hearts, take away fears, and dry our tears.

Death should not be feared. We should accept that death is coming and be prepared on any given day for our last storyline. We should love deeply and devotedly, making sure we never let anger rule before retiring. Before going to sleep, all should be well with our Lord and loved ones. Each day should be lived out loud in love. Being humble and honorable before God is good. Enjoying the journey is a gift we should cherish each day. Dealing with death is easier when we know we are headed to heaven.

Death knocked again and took Harley home. Yes, I believe God has a special place for the pets that enrich our lives and leave us with broken hearts when they go away. When I opened the door on Harley's house early Tuesday morning, my spirit stirred when I looked into her sad eyes. She headed for the flower garden and began digging furiously. Her loss of hearing deafened my cries. *What's wrong, baby?* She dug with a purpose, paying me no attention. She was preparing a place to lie down and die. She couldn't tell me, but my spirit stirred that our time together was about to end. I called Bobby and Rhonda, our neighbors who love us and Harley like family. We gathered around her with questions and tears swelling inside.

I called Cameron, who brought Harley into our lives eleven years earlier, seeking advice and comfort. He came quickly and scooped Harley up and gently laid her in my back seat. I longed to be with Harley but headed to The Learning Station to greet my children. As parents dropped off their precious cargo, I thought of how death had hit many of their homes too. I held back tears throughout the morning; the children reminded me that they were praying for Harley. Cameron and Rhonda headed to Raleigh where doctors were waiting for Harley at an animal hospital. Harley died five minutes before they arrived, but the doctors still tried to bring her back. Rhonda and Cameron were ushered to a room to wait and seek comfort, much like a chapel. They headed home with our Harley prepared for burial in a white coffin and a paw print in putty that would harden and remind us of our days together. God knew the day she would leave us and put all things in order. Cameron and Rhonda loved Harley with a deep, special love. It was right that they shared the last leg of our lab's journey, holding her paw and promising her peace from the pain that twisted her stomach.

They drove home to Clinton with lots of Harley stories bringing tears and laughter to their broken hearts.

That night, our families gathered together to celebrate Harley's life and bury her beautiful black body. First, I thought she should rest in the garden beside our dog, Alf. Cameron reminded me how much Harley loved us and the Spells next door; the little path between our houses would be a perfect resting place. That night we dug a grave, told stories, and remembered the dog that stole our hearts and gave us sunshine.

Harley wasn't a favorite of anyone's when she came into our family—except Cameron. When she was young, she barked, ate shoes, chewed furniture, jumped and slobbered on everyone, and destroyed everything in her path. Her night howls were especially disturbing to our neighbors. Instead of complaining or feuding over our barking dog, they bought a fan to cover her howls and allow them to sleep.

Years brought changes to our lives. Harley aged and mellowed, as did we. Our bond of love and commitment to one another grew through seasons of sorrow and sunshine. The day came when Harley had to leave us here. Each of us threw a shovel of dirt to cover the sweetheart who had stolen our hearts. We read words from one of God's good stories of life beyond death. Cameron prayed and each of us threw a rose petal from a birthday bouquet sent to me from Clint. Those petals on the fresh grave marked the spot where Harley's body rested in peace. Ironically, it was the place where she barked the night away many years ago, keeping us all awake and wondering if she would ever hush. Tonight, no barking filled the air, but the sweet spirit that settled in our hearts brought peace. Love was in the air and our hearts were right with our Lord, our loved ones, and our Harley.

I've lost my best friend, my dog who loved me unconditionally. I've learned the power of the words I've shared with you for many weeks about life and death. I've learned what really matters most in life—being committed to and crazy in love with the Lord and loved ones. Death comes to each of us, breaking the links from our family's chain. One day that chain will connect again; when we all get to heaven, what a day of rejoicing that will be. Let your love shine for Jesus and for your loved ones—whatever season you are in.

What Are You Called To Do?

*W*HAT IS GOD CALLING YOU to do? I've thought about my life, reflecting and asking, "Have I done what God called me to do? Is there more He desires for me to do? How many blessings have I missed by not obeying His call?"

How many times have we talked ourselves out of a blessing when we think too much about the wrong things? We all stand accused! God places something in our hearts and, by the time it reaches our heads, we've already thought of a dozen reasons why it won't work, why people will think we're crazy, or why we're not equipped—spiritually, physically, mentally, and financially—to do what God is calling us to do. We should embrace obedience the first time God calls. Step out in faith and trust God to lead us to do whatever is needed to help others know and love Jesus. Do we truly know Him personally and peacefully and are we doing what He has called us to do?

It seems like yesterday when He softly called my name in a classroom at Fayetteville State University. Actually, it was 1983 when I felt a powerful pull to drop out of graduate school. It made no sense then, but it does today. God called me to teach. Securing an administrative degree would have tempted me to leave the classroom.

Last week, I was reminded of how beautifully God has blessed what He called me to do as I taught children about His love and mercy. Little hands shot in the air, waiting to share prayer requests at the close of our morning devotion. I wrapped my arms around my children as they prayed. Times like this confirm we are doing what God called us to do. If you aren't happy in your job, have you asked why? Often, we look in other pastures thinking the grass is greener. Doing our best where we are planted means greater rewards in our work. There was a season in my life when I questioned my profession.

Serving on a task force for my state during my tenure as Regional TOY, I was blessed with opportunities to share my love for teaching.

One particular meeting etched a memory in my heart as people all across our nation stood to tell their educational background and job titles. The enemy filled my mind with thoughts that made me slump in my seat. *You're out of your element—just a little fish in a huge sea of more important and impressive creatures, your little voice can't be heard. You don't really matter.* He was winning the battle in my mind as I stood to share my story. In that weak moment, I told those important people just how unimportant I felt. "I'm Becky Spell from Clinton, North Carolina, and I'm just a teacher."

That year of telling others my view from the classroom made me realize my voice did count, my calling was teaching, and my Father was pleased with what I was doing. Never again will the enemy minimize my life, job, place, or influence in this world. I will shout it from the mountaintops—my name, my calling, and my love for my Lord.

Are you proud of who you are and what you are doing? Whatever job we have, we should give our best, asking God to bless us as we work and bless others. We should never put ourselves down—or stop dreaming and seeking God's will and call on our lives. The future belongs to those who believe in the beauty of their dreams. We should stand firm, take risks, be practical, put God first, and enjoy the journey.

When it seems our world is caving in, hope looks dim, jobs are scarce, and times appear troublesome, we must call on God. He is our only peace and promise. In the late nineties, a storm struck my business that caused me to consider throwing in the towel. Enrolling in programs, which offered parents assistance in child care costs, seemed to be the solution for growth. I was ready to jump on the lucrative offer, paperwork and all, in order to secure my dream.

I remember vividly the night I got on my knees in front of Tim's big recliner, buried my head on his lap, and cried tears of frustration and fear. I told him I was tired of dealing with the hassle of running a business, begged him to let me incorporate the new program, and tearfully threw out words I never believed I would say. *Please, let's just sell out!* At that moment, Tim took the authority as head of our home as instructed by God in His Word.

He let me have my pity party, allowing me to empty my burdens as I sat at his feet. Then, he lifted me to his lap and wrapped his arms around me, giving me comfort and courage to face his words of truth.

"Becky, we will be just fine. God will take care of us!"

And He did! It didn't happen overnight; we plowed through several years of suffering. My mother was killed in a car accident, my right hand teacher and friend took another job, enrollment kept declining, my sister died, our sons were seeking His will in their lives—and then God called Tim home. All in one season, yet God was gently calling through it all.

At my time of brokenness, I fell to my knees and sat at Jesus's feet. God lifted me up and guided me to higher ground, where I could see clearly the plan and purpose He had in place all along. His gentle spirit spoke powerfully to my broken heart to keep Him first in all things and we would be okay! When I finally listened and put my eyes totally on Him, He guided me with ease and excitement to blessed and beautiful days in my personal and professional life. He revealed my obsession of trying to please everyone—family, kids, parents, and employees—on and on the list goes for most of us who try to fix things and keep everyone happy and hopping! We're on fire, working our fingers to the bone for our family and friends, our jobs, our church, our community; in reality, we are burning out and are not much good to anyone—especially our Father. God stirred my heart to please Him and all things would fall into place. And it has.

With prayer and a step of faith, my life is precious and purposeful. The fruit is sweet and satisfying. Are you doing what God has called you to do? Listen to His voice and He will lead you to happiness here and in heaven when He calls you home.

Open the Eyes of Your Heart

*D*O YOU BELIEVE PRAYERS BRING us closer to one another and to God? As spring ushered in new life, Lent reminded us of sacrifice, Easter encouraged reflection and spiritual renewal—believing in God, praying for guidance, and His glory growing, as do the flowers in our gardens. Believing and being closer to our Lord and loved ones bolsters our growing faith. End time seasons tether on turbulence at every turn, yet peace and promise propel us onward and upward. Tough as times are, Christians who stand firm will persevere; it is proof that what God promises, He delivers. The cross is a reminder of His suffering and sacrifice. He arose, triumphed over His foes, and reigns with His Father forever. His greatest sacrificial gift should never be taken for granted.

A recent Tuesday morning after prayer partners left Tim's Gift, I began working on card ministry. As I wrote notes to people on our prayer list and others in my heart, Donald Honeycutt's smiling face was like a pop up on my computer . . . he wouldn't go away. This dear man impacted my life when I was a little girl working in our country store. Playing with rolling cans made from empty oil cans and pumping gas was my cup of tea. I loved greeting customers outside, seeing people coming and going, and pumping gas.

I remember watching Mr. Donald walking slowly on the side of the winding highway past our store many days. I'd yell at him and hear his friendly voice echo blessings—with his trustworthy walking cane and keen senses keeping him safe. Sometimes, he would stop for a little Coca-Cola and a chat with folks who loved hearing his stories. The few times I visited his home were treats this little girl loved. He played the piano like a pro, giving toe-tapping performances. His piano renditions were no match for his lively conversations. Mr. Donald knew facts and figures, Bible trivia and current events, names and notorious dates from our little community happenings to worldwide news. He spoke kindly and intelligently to all who took time to spin a yarn with him. Five decades have passed since those days; many things in our lives have changed.

Today, he is on my mind so strongly; I leave my letters and head to visit him in his new home. Entering the doors at Mary Gran Nursing Center, I was already blessed by smiling faces of residents and caregivers. I said prayers for the nurses, assistants, and all those who give hope and help to these precious people whose home away from home keeps them safe and secure from all alarm.

Mr. Donald's curtain was pulled, so I waited near the door. Donald heard my voice and said, "Hello, Becky. It's good to see you again. You haven't been in a while; it was Thursday, two weeks ago when you were here, right?" His sharp mind still spits out information like a computer. Once again, I was in awe of the memory, integrity, and dignity of this mighty man whose sunset ebbs closer each day. He continues to treat people like royalty, rarely talking about his condition—and always telling tales of happy times.

When the nurse finished, I pulled the curtain to see his smiling face and feel his firm handshake. For a fleeting moment, I flashed back to the days we talked in front of Daddy's country store. Don rattled off remembrances from those years gone by, when the world was like a fairytale waiting to be written for this little girl who believed—and still does! His memory was sharp as an ax; his stories played back blessings both of us praised the Lord for. I thought of the scripture I had read at Tim's Gift that morning where we are told to keep our ax sharpened, always prepared and ready for what comes our way. Visiting Donald inspired me to sharpen my ax and refrain from complaining. I wiped my tears, held his frail hand, and we prayed.

I told him about the gift I brought, reading words from the ribbon that declared this was his special day. He thanked me over and over, requesting I bring the kids again. Promising to come back real soon, I left his room with greater blessings than I had given. Praising God for Donald's faithfulness, his choice to embrace happiness and hope amidst the handicap that could have made him sorrowful and secluded throughout his lifetime, uplifted me.

Donald didn't get one of the gifts most of us take for granted: sight! I remembered the tap, tap, tap of his walking stick as he went forth in faith on that winding highway fifty years earlier. Today, I walk the halls to visit other dear friends, wiping tears that tell a tale of humility, hurt, but most of all, hope. Donald's blindness made him even more beautiful and blessed in my sight. His wonderful witness draws me closer to God—with a humbled and thankful heart that I can see. Walking from the nursing center, I hummed the words to the old hymn about once being blind but now I see, while beholding the wonders of His wonderful world all around me.

Sitting in my car, regaining my composure before heading back to Tim's Gift, brought the ending God intended for this story. The doors opened wide; a nurse pushed Donald into the crisp morning air where sunshine struggled to shine through the clouds. She positioned him so he could see people coming in and going out of the nursing center. I rested my head on my steering wheel and wailed, "He can't see anything, Lord!"

And God spoke to my heart through what my eyes could see. This dear man sees more than many people blessed with 20/20 vision! Donald sat in his wheelchair with a smile that lit up the cloudy day, and he prayed. For the longest time, I watched him witness and reach more souls than any preacher or teacher could with a ten-foot pole. Donald prayed aloud, softly and tenderly, boldly and beautifully; he was telling a tale of tremendous faith, a love story about his Lord for all who would open the eyes of their hearts to hear.

Are you listening? Are you sure you're listening? Yes, Preacher Jones, I listened and learned lessons of love from my friend and my Father. How thankful I am that I listened to Him calling me to stop what I was doing—even though it seemed so important to write those letters. God had another plan for my morning. He opened my eyes even wider to the needs for ministry in our own community, to the blessings He gives when we go, to the times we pass up being doers of His Word, to the day we will answer for when we didn't listen and didn't do, to the judgment when we will wish we had believed and been all we could be for God. Jesus is waiting to enter your heart; won't you let Him come in as Lord and Savior. If once you were lost, you can be found; if blinded and bound by busyness or burdens, He can open the eyes of your heart and color your world with hope and happiness.

Do you believe the beginning of the way to heaven is to feel that we are on the way to hell? Hebrews 9:27 tells us, "And as it is appointed for men to die once, but after this the judgment." We must remember that we aren't living the life God created us to live. Adam and Eve changed all that when they sinned (Genesis 3).

No change is bigger than death. We were made by our Father to live eternally. That eternal life will be interrupted by death, followed by resurrection to eternal life. The big question is where one's eternal life will be spent. The Bible gives two options for eternal life: with God in heaven or not with God in hell!

Jesus explained in John 3:18 that if we fail to believe in God's plan for saving us from sin, we face spending eternity apart from God. It seems so simple, almost too easy, but the only way to our Father is through His Son. When we believe in God's plan, we are saved from condemnation and will have everlasting life.

Reading John 3:16 or repeating it from memory plants that promise deep inside our hearts. We will always have questions, but when we stay connected to the Lord, trust and obey, and keep our eyes on Jesus, we will have everlasting life in heaven with God.

The sun 'rising up' at Topsail Island, North Carolina, a favorite place where Becky loves to spend time with family and friends, read, write, and watch the sun rise over the Atlantic Ocean.

Mr. and Mrs. Timothy Cameron Spell greet the world with a smile just after saying "I Do" to a covenant of love with God and one another. Union Grove Baptist Church is where their story began.

Tim Spell's family poses for a picture in 1959. Pictured left to right- younger brother, Michael; father, Odell; mother, Agnes; Timothy, and older brother, Dwight.

Tim and Becky loved dressing up for the Centenial Celebration at their church in 1978.

The Spell household was blessed with two sons. Cameron Odell, back, and Clinton Harold, front, are the apples of their parent's eyes.

Becky's family gathers for a picture after Clint's baby dedication service outside First Baptist Church in 1983. Back Row L to R- Tim, Mary Gaye, Billy, Wyman; second row L to R Becky, her mother-Mary Dean holding Clint, LeAnne, front row, proud big brother, Cameron.

Father and sons dress up and show off happy smiles for their picture in the church directory.

Tim and his sons enjoy time together watching the sun set on the west coast.

Tim and his Aunt Emy share gifts of love at Christmas time in 1996.

Becky and Tim celebrating twenty five years of marriage in 2000.

The men in the Spell family proudly pose with their newest gift of love, Cameron and Angel's baby boy. Proud 'Poppy' holds Cameron O'Connor Spell, Uncle Clint and Cameron-Proud Daddy- beam with joy.

Connor Spell and his NaNa share the look of love that all grandparents and grandchildren understand.

Proud Nana hugs her grandchildren, Corie and Connor,

Becky and Tim enjoyed sailing the waters near Topsail Island. They raised up their sails and set to sea, where many stories were born.

Becky raises the torch high at her hometown Relay for Life Celebration, where thousands of people rise up to remember those who lost battles with cancer and to honor survivors. People walk in faith while watching HOPE burn brightly in Relay events across our nation every year.

This verse and serene setting reminds us to slow down and smell the roses, to recognize that God will direct our steps, protect and bless, but we must be still and listen.

Becky and Timothy pose for a picture taken by their good friend Ed Jordan. Sons, Cameron and Clint, and daughter in law, Angel, were in the studio making faces and memories as one big happy family endured a photo shoot.

Elanor Bradshaw, friend and prayer partner at Tim's Gift, and Becky enjoy sharing good times and the good news of our Lord wherever they go.

Connor, Becky's grandson, shares a cup of water in HIs name -a case of water, actually- with Ms. Rosie, who lost her husband and almost lost her life in a car crash. She lives to tell her miracle of survival.

Becky and her family pose for their first holiday picture with the family circle being broken, Tim's first Christmas in heaven.

Becky enjoys a day at Topsail Beach with her sons, Cameron and Clint, and their black lab, Harley. Jamie, Clint's fiance snapped the picture and framed it with a special message . . . "It's Better When We're Together".
Family time is a treasure!

Tim snaps a picture of a Colorado sunset. Each sunset reminds us of the splendor of God's creation.

The rainbow is God's promise to mankind. Tim snapped this picture as he and Becky stood on their porch at Topsail Island, only months before he would go home to heaven . . . somewhere over the rainbow.

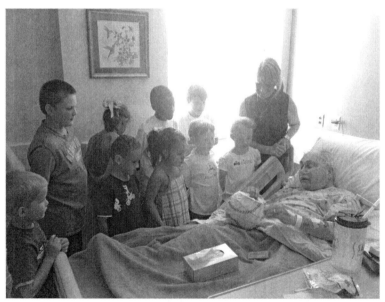

Children from The Learning Station share sunshine with Mr. Chuck Tryon, a volunteer at Tim's Gift who reads with the children each week.

Becky and children from The Learning Station prepare a good will package to be shared with a local ministry.

The Learning Station is an afterschool and summercare Tim and Becky opened for school age children in 1990. His insurance office was next door. They worked side by side and raised their sons to understand the power of pulling together in all things. Becky continues to operate The Learning Station. Her husband's insurance office is now Tim's Gift Inc., a ministry giving help and hope to those in need.

Cameron, the author's elder son, snapped this picture at Topsail Island. He and his wife, Angel and son, Connor were making memories and catching fish on an Autumn afternoon. The message Cameron attached to his picture is priceless, words of truth from a Father who loves and looks after His children.

Clint, the author's younger son, drew this picture of his father and mother only weeks after his Dad went to heaven. He captured the beauty of each of them at a time in their lives when love peaked. Clint sketched his dad as an angel, drawing a cross on the tuxedo worn when he entered a covenant of love with Becky. Clint's drawing was a gift to his Mom on the first Mother's Day without his Dad here on earth. Clint's choice of scripture shares a powerful message, for his parents did love with an everlasting love, as does our Father God.

Christ the Creator and Caretaker

*D*O YOU FEEL ONE MUST travel to a foreign country to do mission work and make a difference in people's lives? Recent earthquakes have raised an awareness level of the tremendous impact of missionaries in action. Watching devastated people gather to praise and worship God sends one into mission-minded mode. But why do we wait for disasters to strike to take mission work seriously? We should take action to do mission-minded acts of kindness every day.

A foreign mission trip changed my life. The impact of facing poverty firsthand, the imprint of children's faces in my mind, and the irresistible urge to go again and get more than you give sticks with you long after returning home. It's easy to understand the bonding when we help others and watch our actions making a difference, but we don't have to travel abroad to do mission work and impact people's lives. There are countless opportunities to be missionaries right here at home. When we sow seeds to help others, we will see the benefits of God's blessings firsthand. Whether we share sunshine and sow seeds of missionary work at home or abroad, we are lining ourselves up to receive blessings and beginnings that will enrich our lives at home and in heaven. We should never be discouraged from sowing good seeds as missionaries of Christ—no matter where we roam. Serving Him, locally or globally, sets us up for God's favor and fabulous stories of bounty and blessings to share with others.

I am reminded of the verse in Galatians that speaks to us of sowing and harvest connection. "Do not be deceived, God is not mocked; for whatever a man sows, that he will also reap." In all of life, spiritually and physically, we reap according to how and what we have sown. It's so important to sow what we desire to reap. If a farmer sows corn, he will harvest corn, not watermelons. This relates to our lives also. If we sow frugally, we reap very little. If we put off sowing, then our harvest and blessings will be postponed also.

While we might be unable to visit other countries and share our gifts of ministry, we can send donations and offer support to those who are blessed to make such pilgrimages. Often, the cries of those in need fall on deaf ears. We plan to offer help, have good intentions of sending a check, think about organizing a fundraiser, but put it off. Others take the lead and lend helping hands to their brothers and sisters in Christ. When we fail to sow seeds in due season, our harvest of blessings will be scarce and come slowly. That same concept applies to the way we live our lives daily. Sowing to the flesh reaps destruction, but sowing to the Spirit reaps life. When we think of the harvest we want, our desire to sow accordingly should be a constant reminder of what Jesus taught.

God stirred many hearts showing unlimited opportunities to sow seeds of ministry in our own community on the day after the earthquake shook Haiti from its foundation. Early that Tuesday morning, we gathered at Tim's Gift for prayer. Throughout the day, a steady stream of people came in for prayer and praise, but a gentleman's plea for help opened a door to share the Good News of Jesus in a most unexpected way. We heard the front door open as we finished praying for the earthquake victims. A rugged, older gentleman poked his head in my office and flashed a smile that lit the room like sunshine. I greeted the gentleman who wasted no time sharing his need.

He said, "Excuse me, but could I please have seventy-five cents to buy a cup of coffee?"

Often, we resist when people hit us for money, but a sense of peace flooded my heart that day. I replied, "I'll be happy to help you . . . if we can pray."

He put down his cane and a bag of empty soda cans. I surveyed this man of fifty-plus years, realizing how hard those years must have been. He looked tired and weary as he told his story of sickness, loss of job, and fight for survival. I knew David's heart was right even though his life seemed all wrong. We held hands and prayed. His rough, dry hands were like pieces of ice, but his story was heartwarming. An unexplainable feeling gripped my heart; entertaining angels unaware stuck in my mind. I gave him money for coffee—and then we walked next door to the Learning Station where I introduced our visitor to the children. His rough appearance and tender story touched them too. He leaned on his cane, holding his bag of cans securely, as two children came forward to pray before homework.

David's determination to get out and pick up cans for money taught my students a powerful lesson. The next day, David stuck his head inside, as I worked at Tim's Gift. Immediately, I thought he was back for money. He smiled and said, "I just wanted to stop and say God bless you."

I asked God to forgive me for assuming the worst. The next night at choir practice, Jean asked if anyone had experienced a God moment that week. I shared the story about David. After our prayer, a fellow choir member tapped my shoulder and placed a ten dollar bill in my hand. Her tears told me his story had touched her also. She asked me to give it to David if he returned. Driving home, I was in awe of how one shared act of kindness keeps on giving and of God's goodness.

The next day, I drove to work talking to myself and my Lord. It's amazing how close we get to Jesus when we have a little talk with Him throughout the day. I prayed for David, repeating, "Not *if* he will come back, but *when* he'll come back, Lord." At closing time, the door creaked open and David limped in. He'd stopped to warm himself and bless us again. I clapped my hands and headed next door to retrieve the money waiting for David in my desk. The children joined me in telling the story of my friend who wanted David to have this gift. He grinned and held the money close to his heart. He left holding his bag of cans and leaning on his cane for support. He said he was headed to McDonald's to eat a meal fit for a king.

I smiled as he walked away with a song rising in my spirit about leaning on the everlasting arms, safe and secure from all alarm. The seasons of our lives when we feel our world has crumbled beneath us, we can feel safe and secure when we lean on our Father's everlasting arms—and we can be mighty missionaries right here at home!

The next morning, I sat in my beautician's chair watching an older gentleman carefully remove a lady from a van and wheel her into the salon. He made sure she was settled and lovingly assured her he'd be back to take her home to Mary Gran Nursing Center. I was touched deeply by his kindness. Rose, my beautician, unfolded a story of sowing and reaping that left me in tears. Mrs. Strickland had lost her husband, her health, and her home and had to go to a nursing center. The man who helped her was a longtime friend of the couple. Many years ago, he had endured hard times and went to them for help. They opened their hearts and did good deeds according to his needs.

He repaid their goodness and began helping them with odd jobs; they developed a relationship that kept them closely connected through the years. Mrs. Strickland taught my sons in Sunday School, was active in church functions, and was always by her husband's side. They never had children, but God knew that wouldn't be a problem in her time of need. By sowing seeds of kindness and helping this man, she was being cared for by him. He takes time to visit and take her places outside the nursing home that she'd never be able to go without his help. The good seeds he sowed long ago are blessing him today too. How awesome that God knows our needs and takes care of them—even before they happen. I prayed right there in Rose's chair for all people who open their hearts and sow seeds of love and unity. I whispered, "Thank you for being our Creator and Caretaker."

We should never stop supporting and praying for missionaries in foreign countries. We are given never-ending opportunities to sow good seeds, helping those in need. I hope that this story has prompted you to be mission-minded, helping people abroad and right here at home. Think of the harvest you desire, then go out and sow accordingly—in His love!

Writing Your Story

RECENTLY, STORIES WERE SPEWING FROM my heart one right after another. I was on a roll—until the enemy began reeling me into a pit of pity. Feeling forgotten and forlorn overshadowed my words of joy to the world. My writing became a never-ending story. We don't know the ending of our stories, but God does. That's why He dwells in our hearts and desires for us to live closely connected to Him and to those we love. Our storylines won't always be sweet, satisfying, and succulent. Staying closely connected to the vine, our story will be easier to write and have a happily ever after ending! He keeps us lifted through the valleys and moves the mountains.

Faith footnotes the ending of God's story. The Book of Revelation is filled with wonders to behold and prophecies—many we are seeing unfold. His story ends with a promise: "Surely I am coming quickly. Amen, even so, come, Lord Jesus! The grace of our Lord Jesus Christ be with you all."

His story starts with, "In the beginning God created the heavens and the earth." No matter how we read the story, beginning or ending first—He gave us life and all that we have. He is coming soon. If we have accepted Him and believe, He will take us home. If we have neglected Him and His promise, we will be left behind. How will your story end?

Have you learned lessons from your Heavenly Father that brought you to your knees and left you in awe of God? More importantly, what does it take to bring us to our knees and be thankful for what the Master Teacher imparts to His children over and over and over again?

To better understand how we handle learning lessons, we only need to look at how we teach and reach our own children. It's refreshing when children react kindly, showing they practice the Golden Rule. Kids are honest in how they represent what we are to them. Teaching and training a child in the way they should go is a tough job that takes lots of time. We think those tough years will never end—and then they grow up and go away. Our lonely hearts and empty nests ache for yesteryears while embracing a new season of our stories. Often, we don't remember the very lessons we taught.

Recently, I endured a difficult week when my emotions emerged, ruling me like a child. I failed lessons that had been mastered long ago. My miserable mess finally became untangled when God got my attention and handed down remediation lessons for the umpteenth time. You'd think we'd learn, retain, and be cautious, instead of learn, forget, and become callous. That's why going to our knees is always the best place to receive His instruction. It keeps us humbled and in honor of our great responsibility as His children—and to our children. Let us never think we can do it on our own. It truly takes a village to raise a child. When we are united in love for our Father and follow the universal Golden Rule, we won't fail Him or our children.

The week after Christmas can be a sad season. One would think we'd learn that holidays aren't always a perfect greeting card. Holidays are difficult to endure for many people, especially those missing loved ones. My week was wonderful; I made the mess all by myself. God had checked off gifts given to me even without my asking. My blessings were bountiful, but my actions didn't show appreciation to the Giver. Surely, He frowned with me, taking His gifts for granted: comfortable home, soft, warm bed, healthy family, food galore, good job, growing ministry, fabulous friends, abilities to read, write, and enjoy life with more gifts than I could even list. Ironically, instead of glorifying Him; I grumbled for troubles and things I didn't want to be given. Self-pity settled in when it seemed everything around the house would take a holiday from working. My car battery died, the fluorescent light bulbs burned out in my garage one day, my bathroom the next, my Learning Station van's taillight broke and the fence bent when I backed into it, the fan on our gas logs stopped working, my best friend was gone for the week, my microwave wouldn't respond when I hit start, my garage doors stopped working, and the real kicker was when my sons didn't respond to my e-mail about attending our annual Smith Reunion that Saturday. I was recovering from a flu bug that invaded my body and left me coughing and crying over the least little thing. Been there, right? So, I stewed and sank in self pity.

Immediately, the door was opened for the enemy to do his miserable thing he has mastered with most of us. It was my choice—my actions—that magnified the predicaments I faced, making molehills seem like mountains. I was wrong, but you couldn't tell me that—even though I knew it in my heart. I continued my little walk to the pity party, primed and ready to take center stage. The enemy filled my mind with thoughts that should have been discerned and done away with immediately. Then, the rascal would have had no power over me—making my days dismal and week wretched.

I kept telling myself what a wonderful mother I was, how good I was doing with the load on my shoulders, how hard I worked, how I went the extra mile for my family, how they could always count on me to be there for them, how they should spend more time with me and do things together that meant so much to their mama, how Tim and I looked after them when they were little and I'm still doing everything in my power to make sure they are protected and doing well in this world and ready for the next.

In the middle of my pouting, a telemarketer called. His aggressive sales pitch was not music to my ears, so I gave him something to think about besides that pitch for me to receive a dream vacation for two, no cost, just call the number and come. He insisted on speaking with Timothy Spell. Previous calls with requests for Tim left me crying—or being rude to the person on the other end of the line. Not today. I was way too pitiful to be mean-spirited. More importantly, my heart beats peace that Tim is out of pain—living in paradise.

I said, "Sir, Timothy can't come to the phone; he is in heaven." There was dead silence for the longest time, and I didn't dare rescue the poor guy who had called the wrong woman at the wrong time.

Finally, he said, "I am so sorry for your loss."

I didn't stop there though. I told him Mr. Spell is happily living in paradise forever and ever! The caller softly said good-bye.

I sat in silence, being still and knowing God was right beside me—as He is for all of His children. I was reminded that it's not about me or what I'm going through that should determine my mood, my happiness; it's all about my relationship with my Father who loves me unconditionally—just as I love my children. My thoughts turned to the cross; I tried to imagine the pain He endured while watching His Son suffer and die for me—for you! My Heavenly Father was teaching his child lessons about love, sacrifice, and feeling forgotten, especially on holidays we celebrate concerning His own Son—the day He was born and the day He died! My pity turned to praise for my Lord who never forgets to show His love to His children and longs for us to show ours for Him. My long week wasn't over—and neither were His lessons that would bring me closer to Him and my family.

God brings His children to a place of brokenness before bringing blessings. Ironically, the things I desire from my children are what He desires from His. Whatever season we are writing, let us stop sulking and start soaring to new levels in our love for the Lord.

Blessings from Brokenness

*H*AVE YOU EVER MOPED IN misery—even when God was giving lessons of His amazing love and leadership? Amidst the bleak, bad, broken times, He brings blessings.

The Lord knew I needed immediate attention, and I got it while grumbling before heading to a family reunion. Oh, that we would embrace mastering lessons of love, compassion, endurance, and enjoying the journey as strongly as we do passing tests and reaching plateaus. God gives tests every day. Often, we indulge in pity and fail to receive the blessings He has as our reward. He teaches accepting responsibilities in life while not losing our relationship with Him and those we love. Are we too busy to do the things that matter most and keep in close relationship with our Father and our families?

Driving to the reunion, God tendered my heart. He revealed my frustration with my own children for not attending the family reunion, for not giving the attention I felt I needed, for quick visits, for putting their desires before mine, for taking me and the things I do for them for granted. I was in total agreement with Him. I stopped by my parents' and sister's graves at Union Grove Church. It was there that He finished the lesson. Surely, our parents had felt the same way about us. I remembered how mother would beg us to come visit when we didn't have to rush home; how Tim's mother was eager for even a five-minute visit, how we wanted to stay longer, but there was always so much to do that kept us on the go. Becoming too busy to be with our Lord and loved ones is dangerous.

God cleverly climaxed His lesson. *Now, you understand how I feel, my child. I get left out, leftovers, and looked over for things of the world, when my children mean well, but are too busy to spend time with Me.* My sadness shifted to my Savior, who doesn't get the honor and glory He deserves. He didn't have to stir this old girl's heart anymore; lesson learned.

I thanked Him for two good sons who love the Lord and honor Him, who live their lives in accordance to His Word and will, who treat others as they would like to be treated, who watch one another's backs and love me with all their hearts. My red eyes were not a pretty sight, but my broken heart was on the mend. His final elaboration gave guided practice to my homework ahead. It was as if a picture show had revealed His heart to mine in living color. His heart is broken over and over when we take Him for granted, say we'll do something for Him and seldom follow through, give His house quick visits and pray selfishly and shortly, love Him—but put other things ahead of Him, mean to do more for Him but get busy. The list could have gone on and on, but I stopped the show and spent some needed time with Him—on my knees. My brokenness brought blessings.

Your Last Day on Earth

*D*O YOU DELETE FORWARDING E-MAILS that take your time, but leave you wondering if you missed a blessing from a friend? It's hard to do, but it's necessary if we hope to get our work done. Today, I began my delete routine but stopped when my brother typed a please read plea beside his. The title inspired me to open instead of delete. While I read, tears rained on my keyboard and sunshine flooded my soul.

My thoughts turned to my last day on earth. When will it be? What will happen on that day? Will I go quickly or will sickness slowly steal my tomorrows? Will my family be with me or will I go alone? Will there be time to think about my life or will it happen in the blink of an eye? The last day is something we don't dwell on, but we should remember it is coming. Are we ready? My early morning e-mail made me think strongly about this day and the questions God won't ask. Think of your last day as you meditate on this powerful message. "The last day of our life when we meet our Lord, God won't ask:

1. What kind of car you drove but how many people you drove who didn't have transportation.
2. The square footage of your house, but the many people you welcomed into your home.
3. The clothes you had in your closet, but how many you helped clothe.
4. What was your highest salary, but if you compromised your character to obtain it.
5. What your job title was but if you performed your job to the best of your ability.
6. How many friends you had but how many people to whom you were a friend.

7. What neighborhood you lived in, but how you treated your neighbor.
8. The color of your skin, but the content of your character.
9. Why it took so long for you to seek salvation?

He will lovingly take you to your mansion in heaven and not to the gates of hell.

What takes most of our time and attention in this world will have no value in our Kingdom bank account. When our last day comes, what matters most is our relationship with our Father. Our last day will be a celebration in heaven and here on earth if we have professed Christ as our Savior and asked Him into our hearts.

Are you thinking of the last day on earth for someone you love? It's like memories frozen in our minds that we repress and relive from time to time. My mother's last day was difficult because it was so unexpected. You go to work and think your world is sunshine and roses. Then, you are called to a room where your husband, son, friends, and a patrolman wait to bear the bad news. Shock grips your body and sends you into denial. Friends you haven't heard from in ages show up at your front door. Food begins to pour in. Your pastor comes. Flowers and plants arrive with cards from faraway friends and close buddies. Reality sets in; you realize the one you love is really gone and isn't calling you on the phone ever again—nor coming home. Oh, the sting of death. Yet, our sadness is no match for the celebration in heaven for those who are ready to meet their Savior on their last day. They have gone home and will forever live in our hearts.

Those who have spent days and nights by a loved one's bedside and watched them slowly slip away—or lost them without warning—understand severe heartbreak. Do you remember your last day together? Tim was unable to talk the last few weeks he was with us. On a warm Sunday morning in April 2007, our home filled with family and friends. I felt a Martha spirit needing to keep things done, but chose to be a Mary for our time together would soon end.

The pain we bear, when one we love leaves us, can't be explained or surmised—only endured. Yet, when we know they are in the arms of Jesus, we can embrace peace and promise. Jesus gives strength and supplies our every need as we carry on and embrace His promise of eternity with Him and them. Our time here is but a mist. Take time to invest in heavenly things, to seek salvation, and to prepare for your last day!

God's Plan

*D*O YOU ALLOW GOD TO teach and lead you in the way you should go? Those words are His own, found in Psalm 32. God has a plan for our lives. He doesn't want part-time or lukewarm anything from His children; He desires having us on board—ready, willing, and fully engaged in sharing His love and spreading His Word. Last week I typed until my eyes closed, staring at my computer in the darkness of early morning. His message was strong on my heart but slow to come forth from my heart.

Early Sunday morning, I awoke my hibernating computer and continued my story, hoping to finish it before church. When the ending wouldn't come, I closed down and dressed for church. The temptation to stay home and finish was strong; Clint, Jamie, and I had early church around our kitchen table before they headed out for a day on the beach.

My love for Jesus and my parents' example make going to church on Sunday special, securing that indescribable, good feeling deep down inside your soul all week long! While I packed a picnic lunch and tucked a love note in Clint's cooler, I thought of the sermon Cameron preached earlier that week. Jamie and Clint listened as I recounted Cameron's message:

> God wants us in our assigned and aligned place. He is calling us in order to show the flow of authority, blessings, and protection. He is aware we need focused vision to get in order; we must protect the presence of God. His structure is seen in 1 Peter 2:5—we read of building a house and us being the lively stones. In Ephesians 2 19:22, we find that Jesus is the chief cornerstone. When the building is fitted right together,

> you grow! We are the stones; we're a brick that's alive. We are building material. This means relationships. Many of us are complacent; some are tired, scared to move forward, or in denial. This causes us to justify our actions. Being accountable will seal us with God.

Clint, Jamie, and I joined hands to pray, and then I headed to church. Greeting brothers and sisters with hugs and handshakes is a sure sign His love and spirit hovers in His house. A wave of silence moved across the overflowing chapel as the service began. What I love most about our church at Topsail is the variety of preachers and the profound witness and love shared by the body. Something good is going on all the time at Emma Anderson.

I sat with Francis, a friend from Belize, and knew from the start that the service was going to be awesome. Our responsive reading hit home immediately. While the hand bell ringers brought a joyful noise, I read the reading titled Teaching Children:

> Take heed to yourself, and diligently keep yourself, lest you forget the things your eyes have seen, and lest they depart from your heart all the days of your life. And teach them to your children and your grandchildren. Fear the Lord your God; keep all His statutes and His commandments which I command you. Teach these words diligently to your children, and talk of them when you sit in your house, when you walk by the way, when you lie down and when you rise up. You shall write them on the doorposts of your house and on your gates. Train up a child in the way he should go, and when he is old he will not depart from it. And you, fathers, do not provoke your children to wrath, but bring them up in the training and admonition of the Lord.

Okay, Lord, I'm listening and learning more and more how important it is to teach our children to love and honor their Maker, Creator, Father, Friend, Daddy, Lord, Savior, Emmanuel, Christ. God! He is Lord of our lives and loves the little children of the world. Our duty is defined clearly in His Word: teach and train the children and they will not depart when they are grown and on their own. What peace this passage has brought many praying parents through the years.

As the choir sang, I rested my eyes on my favorite thing in our chapel: the breathtaking painting on the wall behind the pulpit. A huge cross looms in fluffy clouds surrounded by angels. Tim and I stayed late after many services to pray and ponder as we looked to that cross. We didn't know the plans God had for us, but He did. Our lives were under attack by cancer, but God was in our corner and healing would come—of that we were sure.

I smiled from my heart, knowing my husband is among the angels, enjoying heaven and happiness that I can only imagine. I was in tears and shouting hallelujah in my heart by the time the sermon started. The preacher's scripture reading was only one verse: "I will instruct you and teach you in the way you should go; I will guide you with My eye" (Psalm 32:8).

He preached from his heart and touched mine. He told how God has a plan for all of us; we decide if we will allow Him to guide us. Application made his message come alive as he told how he tried to parallel park on a busy street in Raleigh. After several attempts, his wife offered to help. She stood on the sidewalk and instructed him which way to go, but he kept looking for the safety net in his side mirrors.

Finally, she said, "Time out. Stop trying to do it yourself. Keep your eyes on me and I will help you." He was parked perfectly within minutes by keeping his eye on her. He shared how his little girl was afraid to jump in the water. After months of desperate pleas for her to trust her daddy to catch her, she finally jumped into his arms where she was safe and secure.

He compared this to God always being there to catch us when we leap in faith as Peter did when he stepped out of the boat into the water. He walked until he took his eyes off of Jesus. What a message of confirmation to what God stirred inside my heart for weeks before writing about following His calling on our lives.

I listened intently as the preacher pointed out the personal touch in this scripture. God says He will instruct you, teach you in the way you should go, and He will guide you with His eye!

This assures that God will determine our path; He has the plan. He gives us free will to choose our path, but when we are connected personally to our Father, it's much easier to detect His lead. We must keep in touch and trust Him or we will become disconnected and unable to follow where He leads. When we walk in obedience to our Father, we keep that personal relationship with Him precious and prepared for whatever crosses our paths. Knowing and serving Him doesn't mean we are exempt from troubles and trials; it's knowing we can cast those burdens on Him and He will supernaturally lift the load and light the way.

Cameron's sermon sums up this story well. Keeping Jesus as our chief cornerstone means our foundation is on solid ground. When we are fitted together in right relationship and following His calling, we will grow!

Psalm 32:8 teaches us that God's promise to guide us is personal and precise. He will not leave us in the dark, wondering which direction we should go—as long as we make staying close to Him and in a right relationship with Him top priority. He is the light that shines and shows us the way, especially during those tough times when troubles threaten to drain love and light from our lives, leaving us to wander in darkness.

He is the light and the way. We can only go to the Father through His Son. Keep your eyes on Jesus, trust His calling, and you will always grow and go in peace and prosperity.

Following God's Will

DO YOU STRIVE TO FOLLOW God's will for your life? The choices we make show if we are willing to walk in faith and truly follow God's plan.

Philippians 2:12 says, "It is God who works in you to will and to act according to his good purpose." If we listen to God, He will lead us and provide protective covering. Often, we read the Bible and think it was so easy for those characters of long ago to follow God's will. Imagine how hard it would have been when Joshua and the Israelites stood at the edge of the Jordan River. Instead of its normal size of about a hundred feet wide, the river was flooded and the water was moving fast. It looked very difficult to cross. How could Joshua get all the people over to the other side? And if he could get them across, what direction should they go? We know God has a perfect plan. He led them across, but not until the priests were willing to get their feet wet. The priests followed instructions to walk in the water until their feet were wet—then the waters split apart, the same way the Red Sea opened up for Moses.

We read this in awe of such a miraculous happening. God is still in the miracle-making business; good things are happening all around us. He promises good things to those who obey him and follow His will for their lives. How sad that most of the good news in our world is shadowed by evil events and the media's preference to report the bad instead of the good. I believe people are tired of hearing the doom and gloom that dominates every avenue of news coverage. We've been saturated in sad news far too long. It's time we take a stand for the Good News from our Father and seek His will in our lives.

No matter how desperate, devastating, or dismal things look in our situations, our homes, our jobs or loss of jobs, our nation, or our world, God is greater than anything that comes against us! That's much easier to believe when everything is coming up roses, but when weeds threaten to take over, we must work fast and furiously to remove them and keep our lives clean. Joshua faced such a time when he wondered what to do about the river in front of him. Think of all the other people in the Bible who faced fear and overcame it with faith. Our walk of faith is no different than those of other eras who endured hardships and heavy loads. We must follow God's will and get our feet wet. Many times, we choose to cozy ourselves in comfort. It's fearful to step out, get off the fence, get out of the box, go against the grain, be politically incorrect, or do it differently that it's been done before. So, we carry on business as usual, playing it safe and refusing to wade in the waters where He leads.

This is why we miss many of God's greatest blessings. We won't get our feet wet and we fail to follow His will for our lives. We ask how we can know what His will is for our lives. Prayer is an important part of finding out what God wants us to do. When we ask him for directions and listen to what He tells us through His Word, we will find it much easier to go where He leads and do what He would have us do. Yet, we may not know just where to step if we don't wait on the Lord.

My favorite verse in the Bible has helped me control my go-go spirit while embracing a slow-slow it down and listen to His calling. These words caution us about moving too fast and forgetting who is in charge of all things.

"Be still, and know that I am God" (Psalm 46:10). We may have to wait a while for God's answer to our prayers and pleas for His will, but He always comes through with flying colors. When we least expect it, a blessing, an answer, will come out of the blue—straight from our Maker to me and you. We must be patient as we persevere. The Helper He sent will guide and direct when we are facing the giants. When we are willing to engage with Him leading the way, we will live in victory every day.

The Power of Pentecost

*D*O YOU UNDERSTAND THE POWER of Pentecost? It's clearly felt when that quiet voice whispers softly to your heart—as it did to mine this morning.

Pentecost was the first baptism of men with the Holy Spirit. In Acts 2, we learn how it happened:

> And when the day of Pentecost was fully come, they were all with one accord in one place. And suddenly there came a sound from heaven as of a rushing mighty wind, and it filled all the house where they were sitting. And there appeared unto them cloven tongues like as of fire, and it sat upon each of them. And they were all filled with the Holy Ghost, and began to speak with other tongues, as the Spirit gave them utterance. And there were dwelling at Jerusalem Jews, devout men, out of every nation under heaven. Now when this was noised abroad, the multitude came together, and were confounded, because that every man heard them speak in his own language. And they were all amazed and marveled.

Witnessing the powerful movement of the Holy Spirit is amazing, but have you also doubted as did those who witnessed Pentecost? Some who were there were moved; others mocked and thought the people had consumed too much wine.

The noise of the thunder and the sound of the rushing wind brought the people of the city running to the temple; they found the disciples full of the Spirit and speaking in foreign languages. Peter stood to preach from the inspiration of the Spirit, but in his own tongue so they could understand. He boldly told the people they were not drunk, for it was only the third hour of the day. In Paul's first apostolic sermon, he shared how the prophet Joel prophesied what had happened and that it would be fulfilled again in the last days.

While everyone has their own interpretations of God's Word, often we shy away from things we don't understand. Understanding comes when we become close to our Father. It's as if He lifts a veil so we can read and see the message and meaning clearly. You become hungry for time with God; His sweet Holy Spirit fills you with love, satisfaction, and happiness that the world cannot give—and the world cannot take away. This closer walk with Jesus and understanding of the power of the Holy Spirit comes by choice. We must first *love* the Lord our God with all our heart, mind, and soul.

We must believe and have faith. The hardest part for most of us is being obedient to our Father's will and His Word. We want it all—a close relationship with God and the world. It just doesn't work that way. If you wonder why you aren't feeling deeply the sweet Spirit tugging in your heart, it simply means you aren't in tune with Jesus. His Spirit comforts and consoles. Those who jeer or just don't believe try to discount the power of the Holy Spirit today as they did at the first Pentecost. Those who were filled with His Spirit were accused of being drunk. While we may not understand how the Holy Spirit moves, we should never grieve it, take it lightly, or make fun of it.

Have I questioned? Sure, I have. I remember watching certain preachers on television as a little girl. My brother and I would take turns knocking one another in the head and falling on the floor, mocking what we saw on their broadcasts. We were wrong, but we didn't understand.

I believe many people make fun or discount the power of the Holy Spirit because of ignorance and isolation. It is real or it wouldn't be in God's Word. One of my most memorable dates as a teenager was attending a revival. It was a wonderful service, but at the end I stood shaking in my shoes and holding to the back of the pew for dear life. I felt afraid and foolish, being the only person who hadn't moved to the front of the church in celebration of the Holy Spirit. I watched and wondered without understanding, but seldom had experienced teaching about this great power in my own church. Ironically, ten years later, I attended another revival in the same church. At the end of the service, I made my own choice to move to the altar for prayer and praise to our Lord. I wasn't consumed with what others were doing or thinking; it became a personal time with God and me!

The evangelist laid hands on me and prophesied that my husband would visit a foreign country as a missionary. I soaked up the sweet Spirit like a sponge. It's so amazing and awesome. Those who have Holy Ghost goose bumps truly understand this powerful and precious movement of the Holy Spirit. It compares to the refreshing wind from heaven that blows through our hearts—healing, helping, and honoring our Lord powerfully and purposefully. Some will never understand!

Imagine my husband's reaction to the words spoken over his life at the revival meeting when I rushed home to tell him the good news. He was watching the Dolphins win another Monday Night Football game in the fall of 1975. Not deleting a single detail, he listened to me and held me close as another touchdown secured the victory for Miami. We talked about that night often—never truly understanding until we moved home to Clinton in 1979. God brought us to First Baptist; Bill Jones became Tim's Christian father and mentor. In the early eighties, Tim joined men from our church on a mission trip to Venezuela where they helped build a church. What had been prophesied became reality; we were on board and believing in the power of knowing, loving, and believing Jesus Christ, Father, Son, and Holy Ghost.

How do we find freedom from sin and comfort from His Spirit? Romans 8 clearly maps the way. Sin in the flesh is condemned. Living in the Spirit is pleasing to God and brings His favor and blessings.

There you have it clearly explained in God's Word. The Spirit of life sets us free from sin. Paul spent his days (after he was transformed and came to understand the love and power of Jesus Christ) directing people to the Holy Spirit. Paul didn't build a reliance on himself; he pointed his people in the direction of God. Christian mentors do that. We must be careful of where and from whom we seek navigation in our Christian walk. We may not understand it all, but we can't go wrong when we go to Jesus for direction and discernment to guide us and give us the freedom from sin and abundant blessings. The Holy Spirit navigates life for us. In Romans, John, and Corinthians, we read where he intercedes for us, directs and testifies to us, empowers and anoints us for service, searches and enables us to discern, and confirms and bears witness with us.

"Likewise the Spirit also helps in our weaknesses and we know all things work together for good to those who love God, to those who are called according to His purpose. What then shall we say to these things? If God is for us who can be against us?" (Romans 8:28).

An old hymn we love to sing sums up this message and sends chills down my spine. The words talk about the Holy Ghost with light divine shining upon this heart of mine, chasing the shades of night away and turning my darkness into day. He is the light and the love of my life. If He does not live in your heart, invite Him in today. He will always stay!

A Lesson from the Eagle

*S*PRINGTIME BRINGS BEAUTY TO BEHOLD as we watch flowers burst into bloom, trees dress themselves for a new season, and the animal kingdom spring into action.

We would be wise to learn lessons from the wonderful world of nature. The eagle majestically shows the beauty of building a home and emptying the nest when it's time for the birdies to fly away.

"As an eagle stirreth up her nest, fluttereth over her young, spreadeth abroad her wings, taketh them, beareth them on her wings" (Deuteronomy 32:11).

Mama Eagle and Daddy Eagle work together to build their nest. Daddy Eagle brings home lots of things to make the nest bigger and better. Mama must get rid of some of these things Daddy brings home when the nest gets too heavy. The baby eagles grow and must go; they are taught to fly. Many times they try and fail, and must return to the nest. Mama Eagle and Daddy Eagle love them and put them back out to fly again. It's not easy leaving the safety of the nest—for any of us!

This scripture and story of the eagle teaches a great lesson for families. Parents spend their lives accumulating things and making the home a comfortable, cozy nest. We get rid of things to keep our nest cleaned and prepare our children to leave home and make it on their own. Often, they fly but fail. We encourage them to try again and spend our lives helping them when at home and when they build their own nests.

The Bible notes how the scripture relates to Israel and the Holy Spirit. We are told how we are stirred up to leave comfortable situations and find our calling in life. The eagle flies over the world, watching all things below. His graceful movements remind us of his majestic power and ability to build a nest for his loved ones, providing safety until they are ready to fly on their own. God is watching and waiting for His children to leave the safety nets that keep them bound. He provides all we need to freely fly and follow our dreams. Protection, favor, and blessings are abundant for those who keep God first in their lives.

Let us remember the lessons of nature that touch our own lives. The greatest lesson we will ever learn is listening to the lead of God's Holy Spirit in our lives. His Spirit sends us soaring here; when it's time to leave our nest and fly away, Jesus will be waiting to welcome us home.

We Can Pray

How many would give John Hancock a high five for his bravery and bold stand for a free nation? What an awesome act when he took the quill pen and proclaimed his patriotic support. He wasn't wimpy as he wrote his name large enough that even the king of England could read it without his glasses. Signing the Constitution was a step of faith toward freedom from a group of men who believed and brought action to their faith.

Would you be willing to sign your name to a proclamation of faith to save God's blessing on our nation? Think about these things and you just might be ready to pull out your pen and place your name alongside names of fellow citizens who believe that America should continue our support of the nation of Israel.

God's Word is the foundation and guidance as we seek understanding of all that is happening in our world today. Our nation has been blessed through many trials and troubles, joys and jubilees. Psalm 33:12 says, "Blessed is the nation whose God is the Lord."

God has been our guiding light for centuries; are we still seeking Him or hiding Him under a bushel? If we let our little lights shine, we will be seen and heard and blessed by our Father who is watching our faithfulness flourish or falter. Do we fade into the background, hoping and waiting for others to take a stand? God will honor our faith as we walk in wisdom and the leading of the Holy Spirit. Righteousness exalts a nation and an individual. We cannot sit idly and silently. We must get ourselves right with God first. Uniting in prayer and purpose, placing our trust in God and putting Him first, while petitioning Him for protective covering will bring favor from our Lord who loves us so much that He sent His only Son to die for our sins. When we seek the Lord's way and stand strong in love, our voices will be heard.

Irving Berlin, an immigrant, wrote many songs that touch our hearts, including "White Christmas" and "God Bless America." While many of us dream of a white Christmas like the ones we used to know, we also dream of a united America, one nation, under God, like the one we used to know. We embrace Berlin's beautiful words with boldness as our nation is under attack and moral decay from within and without. America is a land that we love with God standing beside us and guiding us with His light from above. How much longer will He shine His love and protection on our land?

Genesis 12:1-3 proclaims, "I will make you a great nation; I will bless you and make your name great; and you shall be a blessing. I will bless those who bless you, and I will curse him who curses you."

God is saying He will bless those who support Israel and His chosen people and curse those who do not. History has provided many moments when our support for Israel was challenged. Praise God for people who propelled into action and powerfully positioned themselves to stand up for righteousness and support for Israel.

Israel's story begins in Genesis; God made a binding covenant with Abraham, who was to be the father of the Jewish nation. In Genesis 12:1-3, God promised to bless Abraham, to bring out of Abraham a great nation, to make Abraham a blessing to many, and to bless those who blessed Israel and to curse those who cursed her. He has kept that promise faithfully.

Today, countries less friendly to Israel are gaining influence in the United States. Could we be in danger as we watch and wait for decisions our leaders are making today concerning Israel? If we believe in the Bible, the answer is yes. The bond of God's covenant is real and must be taken seriously by all nations of the world.

The strong connection to the land and God's covenant with Abraham has held the Jewish people together throughout the ages. What a journey! Moses told the people before they entered the Promised Land that a time was coming when they would be driven from the land because of their idolatry. In Deuteronomy 4, we read God's words of warning; throughout history the Jewish people have suffered. They were scattered by the Assyrians, Babylonians, and Romans like the chaff in the wind to the four corners of the earth. The Jews suffered immensely before and during World War II.

Moses prophesied their misery to come in Deuteronomy 28:65: "And among those nations you shall find no rest, nor shall the sole of your foot have a resting place; but there the Lord will give you a trembling heart, failing eyes, and anguish of soul."

And He did!

Think of the pictures in our minds of the concentration camps and stories from Anne Frank's diary that portray what Moses prophesied. The Jews suffered, but God kept His hand on His people and brought them home. Ordinary people were put in place and their obedience to God was instrumental in Israel becoming a nation in 1948. President Harry Truman was to cast the deciding vote of whether or not to recognize the state of Israel. His Secretary of State, George Marshall, was against Israel. Yet, President Harry Truman followed his heart, gave support, and kept God's blessing upon America.

God uses people today just as He did in the Bible to bring about His promises to His people. The miraculous survival of God's chosen people shows He will accomplish His purpose—even when it seems impossible to us. The future of Israel, our world, our nation, as well as your future and mine, will be fulfilled. The best blessing we can receive from the history of the Jews is the reality of God. He is all powerful, keeps His promises, really does exist, is calling us urgently, and has claim on our very being. What we do individually and as a nation determines if we are blessed or cursed. What will our stand be?

The story of the Jews is not over yet. Our president and advisors are faced with difficult decisions concerning Israel's future—and our own. Will we remain a blessed nation as we continue to support and befriend Israel—or will we be pressured to go against her and lose the blessing God promised? While we may think there is nothing we can do, there really is. We can pray.

Finding by Faith

*H*AVE YOU EVER DUG YOUR heels in and stood firm in faith when the situation seemed hopeless? Hebrews 10 speaks boldly about faith in tough times: "Let us draw near to God with a sincere heart in full assurance of faith. Let us hold unswervingly to the hope we profess, for He who promised is faithful."

Hebrews 11 reminds us of Biblical characters who held to their faith:

> By faith, Abel offered God a better sacrifice than Cain did. By faith, Enoch was taken from this life, so that he didn't experience death. By faith Noah in holy fear built an ark to save his family. By faith Abraham when called to go to a place he would later receive as his inheritance, obeyed and went, even though he didn't know where he was going. By faith, he offered Isaac as a sacrifice. By faith, Moses's parents hid him for three months. By faith, Moses led the people through the Red Sea as on dry land. By faith the walls of Jericho fell after the people marched around them seven times.

These are only a few of the faithful people and encounters we read about in the Bible. Hebrews 11:1 tells us the magnitude of faith. "Now faith is being sure of what we hope for and certain of what we do not see. This is what the ancients were commended for."

We read Bible stories and realize those were real people who didn't know the outcomes in their situations any more than you or I do in ours. We must seek His will and make decisions in faith. Will we always get it right? We only need to look at King David to find that answer. He loved the Lord with all his heart and was favored by God, but he made mistakes and found himself in a pickle more than once in his lifetime. What God loved so much was King David's willingness to admit he was wrong, seek forgiveness, and get back on track in faithful service. We will make mistakes and find ourselves broken before the Lord as we walk in faith. Yet, in our brokenness, we come closer to Christ—just as King David did. We're talking sincerity, not sinning and saying sorry without remorse. He still gives signs, wonders, and miracles as He did in the Bible. When we stick close to our Father and stand firm in faith, we will hear His voice within and see signs of confirmation in our lives.

Reading the fourth chapter of James shows how God aches for our fellowship. He yearns to be close to His children but never forces Himself on us. He wants us to learn how to hear His voice. We must first be broken and submit to God. Then we resist the devil and he flees. Finally, we get close to God, drawing nigh to Him as He does to us. We must clean up our messes and purify our hearts, stop being double-minded, remain humble before our Lord and He will lift us up and come to us. We must stop judging, boasting about tomorrow, and do what we are called to do.

The sin of omission hurts deeply, while we justify not doing with every excuse under the sun. In order to be close to our Father God, to hear His voice, to feel that gentle tug on our heartstrings that aids us in making decisions and moving forward in faith, we must have things right between us and Jesus. It's the same as being close and connected with your loved ones. Think of how your loved one can walk in a room and not say a word—just give you a look that says a thousand words and you both understand the message. How profound that in a multitude of people, you can hear your loved one's heart speaking directly to you without speaking a word. That's the way it is with God's love when you know Him intimately, obey Him earnestly, and respect Him ultimately.

His sheep know his voice! And He speaks to His children today as He did to the characters we read about in the Bible. How does He speak? You may never have a burning bush encounter or audibly hear Him speak, but you can be assured He does speak. Are we listening when He speaks? Our lifestyles have become so hectic that we barely listen to our loved ones. Communication is vital for families to stay connected and close. Couples, families, communities, and the whole wide world must start listening and speaking to one another in love. We must spend time together in order to recognize the voice. You will hear it when you stay close in spirit. Yes, God's sheep do hear His voice. His gentle stirring leads and lets us know He is with us.

The week before Thanksgiving, I decided to retrieve Christmas decorations from the little shed behind the Learning Station before our kids arrived. The timing was terrible, but the urge compelled me to do the task right then. Mrs. Angel begged me to stop, for I was making a huge mess with little time to complete my mission. A childlike desire to keep digging through old treasures took over. I felt a warm sensation flood my soul—like a silent cheerleader screaming in my heart. *Dig a little deeper*! For more than an hour, I dug deeper and deeper until one last box sat in the far corner, completely out of my reach. Dig deeper pounded, sweat poured, legs ached, heart raced, and I obeyed. Lifting the lid on the old box revealed treasures we thought had been lost in moving. I lifted the French phone Tim gave me for our tenth anniversary and my eyes nearly popped out of my head. There they were . . . the praying hands! I screamed, shouted, and praised God long and loud in the midst of the mess. I held the praying hands close to my heart. The kids heard the commotion and thought something had me in that old building. Something did have me—the joy of hearing my Father's voice!

Sharing the story with the children later that afternoon, they understood my excitement and listened intently to the lesson I had learned that day. Teaching those little children parables of Jesus's love is the sweetest thing this side of heaven. May what God taught me help you in your relationship with those you love and with your Savior. Jesus never gives up on us, even when we are lost. Even if we wander or stay packed up where we shouldn't be for a long time, He is still our gentle Shepherd who rejoices when we are found.

We must continually dig deeper for our calling and His plan for our lives. When we humble ourselves and follow the Shepherd, we will always recognize His voice—even without a word being spoken or no one else understanding. When He speaks, His faithful children hear.

Hearing His Voice Within

*D*O YOU BELIEVE THINGS HAPPEN by coincidence? I choose to believe that our steps are ordered and all things happen for a reason. Psalm 104:24 tells us that the Lord's works are varied and He wrought them all in wisdom. In other words, He's got the whole world in His hands. We must believe and bring honor and glory back to our Creator. Instead of looking to other sources for direction, we should always go to God.

People ask what the difference is for Christians. Those who follow Christ—who love and accept Him as Savior—share a personal relationship with the One who is the Alpha and Omega. Jesus becomes your best friend when you walk with Him and talk with Him and tell Him you are His. What a friend we have in Jesus—the one who bore all our sins and strife. It truly is a privilege to take all our troubles and triumphs to Him in prayer. Jesus came to earth and died to pay the price for our sins. The personal relationship we have with our Father God lives inside our hearts because He loved us enough to give His Son. When we honor and obey and stay closely connected to God, He speaks to us from the voice within. How can this stirring in our hearts possibly be God speaking to us? It's so simple; our efforts to analyze and explain the wonders of our Lord make it complicated. Jesus lives in our hearts when we open the door and accept Him. The more time we spend with Him in prayer, studying His Word, talking with Him, doing good things in His name, the closer we come to Christ. If we fall victim to busyness that keeps us from connecting to Him, our relationship suffers. When we leave Him out of our daily walk, we struggle to hear the voice within. It's easy to become hardhearted and wonder why we don't hear from Him. It happens so quickly—like missing church. The more you miss, the easier it is to stay away. When we wonder why we aren't hearing from Him, we should survey our schedules and see where He is penciled in. Time with God comes first. He is a jealous God who desires to be front and center in our lives.

Jesus loves us and longs to have close relationships with all His children. Imagine how it hurts to see the dreadful things happening all over the world He created, and to feel isolated, forgotten by the children He made in His image. God knows our sinful nature. He sent Jesus so that we could be free from our sins and share a close relationship with Him. Even when we battle storms that threaten to take us down and we can't hear His voice, He is still there. Some seasons He may seem silent, but He speaks in His time and His way. Often, we rush things and grow impatient when we don't get an answer to our prayers or hear His voice within. We don't fool God. He knows our hearts and plans. When we leave Him out and try squeezing Him in when we need Him, we know He's there but can't connect. The same thing happens with loved ones. Keeping covenants and staying close builds bonds of love that keep the lines of communication open. When we stay so busy and spend little time with loved ones, that precious, personal bond can easily be tainted and warm, loving relationships turn cold quickly. Our relationship with our Father is no different. We must nurture our relationship with Him just as we do our loved ones. We must keep covenants and care deeply. Then, we will easily discern the voice from within.

Keeping journals of my life experiences is something I've done since I was a teen. It is amazing to read and realize how God has worked His plan in my life. What seemed to be a burden one year turned to a blessing the next. His voice within has been my built-in GPS long before they were even thought of. How do you explain hearing from Him? I've never had a Moses experience hearing God's voice from a burning bush, but I have felt strong stirrings in my heart that could only be His voice within. Reading through old journals reminds me of things He orchestrated that many might call coincidence.

In 1972, my college roommate, Laura Younts, gave Tim and me a gift that would become a family treasure. The beautiful praying hands were always visible in our home. In 2007, Clint had a dream about strangers trying to lure him into a car. He thought they were his friends, but every time he edged near the vehicle, a dark force overcame him. A voice within screamed to stay away. He turned to see his dad and the praying hands he remembered in our home. He called the next day to tell me about his dream and ask if he could have the praying hands. I couldn't wait to hang up the phone and look for the praying hands. My search was unsuccessful. For two years, I looked and longed to find the set of praying hands so cherished by my family. Clint kept asking for them—and I kept saying I would find them. I would lie awake at night and wonder where they could be. How agonizing to lose something and know it's got to be somewhere close by, but you feel so helpless in your search. I never stopped believing I would find the praying hands. If you encounter signs and wonders this week that you declare mere coincidences, think again. Listen to your heart; hear and heed that little voice within. God gently speaks and shows He is the great "I Am!"

Eternal Sunshine

*D*O YOU BELIEVE DIVINE GRACE is flowing beneath all your need? Looking to the scriptures, 2 Corinthians 4:17 gives light to times when we must seek God's grace in grief. "For our light affliction, which is but for a moment, is working for us a far more exceeding and eternal weight of glory."

This verse reminds us that adversity and anguish actually strengthen and bring blessings to our lives. The trials, tests, and tough times that knock on our doors and seem to settle over our homes will only last a season. Those seasons that bring deep sorrow and sadness usher in His compassion and love to keep us lifted. When our hearts are broken, He is there to pick up the pieces and put them back together. Thus, love grows and divine grace flows. If love is to grow, it requires a proper climate. Love, if it is to be given, must also be received. When we are in need, in despair, in anguish, we are so ready to receive His love. The trials and tests we will endure in seasons of our lives do not have to be damaging. They will bring hurt and heartache, but the blessings that follow will mend our wounds and make our worries a thing of the past. The memories will always be there, but His mercy and grace erase the tragedies and accentuate the triumphs.

Are you allowing God's grace to flow beneath your need and ease the grief that can keep you in winter season? Changes, loss, and disappointment come to us in seasons when it would be so easy to waste away—withered and worn. We cannot allow a season of mourning to turn into a lifetime of mourning. A new season is coming with opportunities and blessings we never imagined possible. We must stay in an attitude of faith in order to come into a new season in our lives. You only have to look in your own yard to see this phenomenal truth. The green grass that graces summer lawns one day turns brown, appearing to be dead throughout the winter season. But winter doesn't last forever! New life cometh with a new season. The winters we must endure while overcoming discouragement are crucial. It is in these desolate seasons that we are being prepared.

Just as the brown grass does not flourish in winter, for it's not in season, so it is with us. In due season, we will reap—but we must not give up. God is working in us, preparing us for a new season when we will be all God made us to be. God lifts us—as He said He would do in Psalm 40—and puts a new song in our hearts. He will lift us from unfair situations and give beauty to our lives. He promises that joy is coming. We must accept our winters as times when He is working in us, bringing about good to glorify His name. As the sun rises on our season of blessings, our grass grows green and glorious. Where we are is not where God wants us to stay. He has new seasons of happiness and hope awaiting those who will accept Him and all the good things He is about to do in our lives. His plan isn't always our plan. We must remind ourselves in difficult seasons that even though the grass looks dead, it will turn green again. Just because a good season is over doesn't mean God doesn't have another good season waiting for us.

God was preparing me for a new season while working out recently at the Center for Health and Wellness. I went through my routine right on schedule—until He placed two people in my path who touched my life and tendered my heart to write this story.

The first person He sent my way was a gentleman with a love story that spoke volumes of the Christian spirit he and his wife live daily. They care for their daughter who died and came back to life—against all odds, and is dependent on them for all her needs. Her husband lovingly cared for her until he died a few years after her own brush with death. Then, she and her son moved in with her parents. I listened and wiped tears that wouldn't stop. Yet, his smile told me there was more to the story. The tough times they face only make their faith bolder, their family ties stronger, and their love sweeter as their winter season is preparing them for the miracle of healing he believes will come to his daughter when she will tell the world of God's wonderful love and grace. I believe too, for his faith shines like the sun in the summer season. I asked his name again and thanked him for sharing his story. While I showered, I wept and wondered why things happen as they do. I prayed for John's family—and for all families who are in winter seasons hoping for springtime to come soon.

Dressed and ready to head to Tim's Gift, I dropped my towels in the hamper, bid the ladies at the desk a good day, and hurried down the sidewalk—only to hear someone call my name. I was already off schedule and thought of keeping on keeping on, but that wasn't the right thing to do. I knew better than to let the imagination of that thought enter my mind. I turned to a lady's voice asking if I knew what Friday was. I stood still and listened.

She shared that Friday would make thirty years her son, Steve, had been in heaven. We stood in the morning sun and remembered the events of his last day as if it was yesterday. Those red letter days, when we lose a loved one, never fade.

I remembered Steve entering my seventh grade classroom that September morning in 1980. He buzzed with excitement over the bag of ink pens he was selling for his church. He showed me how the Lord's Prayer became visible as the ink rose in the pen and asked me to buy one. I was so busy that morning. All the stuff that must be done took priority; I told him I would buy a pen the next day.

Tomorrow never came for Steve. School was almost over when the secretary sent word for Steve to ride the bus home. The next five hours were the makings of a nightmare. Steve's bag of ink pens were nowhere to be found as he packed his books and panicked. I assured him we would find them the next day. I would buy one—and everything would be okay. He left my room, rode the bus home, hopped on his bike, was hit by a car, and entered heaven—just like that!

The next morning, several of his friends came to my desk with his bag of ink pens. They told how they were just joking around when they hid them on top of a classroom cabinet and planned to give them back to him the next day. I wanted to scold them but wrapped my arms around them instead. We cried and felt the cruel sting of death, the pain of putting off doing what your heart says do—but you didn't do it—the grief of hurting a friend and never having the chance to say sorry and make things right, and the tragic mistake of thinking we are assured of a tomorrow here. Then, we prayed for Steve and his family. That night, Wayne, my team teacher, and I visited Steve's family. I handed her the bag of ink pens and a radio that Steve had brought to class. He loved listening to music while we wrote stories. I could only cry and say, "I'm so sorry."

His mother's faith was a fortress; she was strong and sure of Steve's salvation and his new home in heaven. She asked me to take the radio back to my class—for Steve would want that. Then, she handed me an ink pen from his little bag. Then, I did cry! But the helplessness inside me turned to hopefulness. Surely, this family who loves the Lord with all their hearts will triumph over this tragedy. And they have.

Steve's funeral was a lasting testimony as people shared stories of his love for life and the Lord. His friends wrote a poem, a tribute to Steve, and read it at his funeral. God touched many lives and brought them into the Kingdom through Steve's life and death. He touched me and taught me to embrace each day with enthusiasm and eagerness to share His love—as Steve did! I remember Steve when I think of putting off until tomorrow what my heart tells me to do today. I learned that our winter seasons seem to last forever, but eventually springtime comes and the grass turns green again.

Steve's mother smiled as the sun came out from behind the clouds. I was reminded of a song about the sun coming out tomorrow—you can bet your bottom dollar. Mrs. Eileen and I held hands and prayed right there on the sidewalk. His spirit warmed our hearts with the joy of knowing our loved ones are in that place of eternal sunshine. We hugged and headed our separate ways with a song of summer season in our hearts.

When I opened the door at Tim's Gift, I felt refreshed and ready to share the love of my Lord and my loved ones with the entire world. If one person comes into His Kingdom, if one person sees sunshine beyond the clouds, if one person holds to the hope that winter will turn to springtime, then our work here is a gift to God.

Winters will keep coming, green grass will turn brown, but Christians can smile instead of frown. Psalm 30 promises, "Joy will come in the morning," even though the night seems oh so long. A river of divine grace flows beneath all our needs.

Doing Delightful Deeds

*D*O YOU DELIGHT IN YOUR service to God? Reading 2 Corinthians 9:7-10 gives reason to be a cheerful giver and doer of the Word. "The godly man gives generously to the poor. His good deeds will be an honor to him forever." Reading to the end of chapter 10, we are taught not to boast about our good deeds. "If anyone is going to boast, let him boast about what the Lord has done and not about himself. When someone boasts about himself and how well he has done, it doesn't count for much. When the Lord commends him, that's different."

Are you thinking of good deed doers who go tell it on the mountain, over the hills, and everywhere? Doing good deeds in humbleness is pleasing to God; boasting isn't. Do you know people who do brotherly acts of love in humility? I'm thinking of a man who never toots his horn but helps people keep their own horns tooting for a living. This story began one year ago when a cold front brought freezing temperatures to town. Driving home from work, I realized I wasn't prepared for such frigid weather. Little things can grow into giant headaches if one is faced with doing them alone. One of my favorite songs came to mind, "It's Better When We're Together." This is a powerful message for most anything we do in life. Our work is easier, play is happier, and loads are lighter when they are shared with someone who understands and helps us along life's way. That cold November night, I needed help. My sons and neighbors were busy, but I called Robby Malpass's home number when no one answered at his business. He answered on the first ring, heard my desperate cry, and was at my door within the hour. Never expecting a house call, I felt embarrassed and frustrated!

I could teach never-ending lessons on cherishing family and friends who share loads—making life better by being together. When I hear

Rise Up, Recount Love

people belittle or take those they love for granted, my heart aches. If only they could realize what a blessing they're neglecting! Love and appreciate them while you have them here to have and to hold! Don't allow things of this world to make your hearts grow cold. Prepare for frigid, tough times before they hit. Keep relationships right; stay closely connected to one another and to God, and you'll stay tuned up forever with a lifetime guarantee in eternity.

Robby graciously helped me that frigid night, assuring me he did what he hoped someone would do for his own mother. When my cars were doctored up, he came inside to give me directions for the rest of the cold season. Offering him homemade soup for his family's dinner seemed small in comparison to his kind deed. He accepted it with a sadness that stirred my heart. God opened a door that night as he shared concerns about his son's unhappiness at school. We talked about family and faith—and how God always works things out for those who love Him. Then, we prayed. When Robby left, I thanked God for a friend who loves his neighbors as himself and does deeds with a humble spirit.

Robby's family has always been a blessing to mine. His mother was a faithful prayer warrior for Tim. They often sat together in worship while Bobby and I settled in the choir loft for songs and sermons. Carolyn always complimented Tim's creative neckties and commented on his compassionate spirit. Her cards brought sunshine to our hearts, making us feel that we mattered—that we were favorites! It is awesome to know our faith and actions make us a favorite to God, family, and friends. Are you a favorite to someone? Are you one of God's favorites? Can He count on you to stay in tune and in service to Him—no matter what kind of storms threaten to destroy your life?

Robby's wife shared a story that tells how small miracles impact our lives. Their son left his book bag on a fence at Royal Lane Park while he practiced soccer. Later that night, he panicked when his bag was nowhere to be found. Such late-night encounters take a toll on families, but not the Malpass household.

Robby gave instructions for his son to prepare for bed, his wife to stay home with Robert, and he would go out and bring home the lost bag. With flashlight in hand, Robby searched every inch of fence at Royal Lane to no avail. Ready to give up and head home, he noticed a tennis ball near his car. He threw it over the fence to the family playing tennis. Something stirred inside his heart. He walked over and asked if they had seen a book bag. The mother didn't speak English but beckoned her son to help her understand the stranger's request. She motioned for her young son to go to their car. Robby watched as the boy lifted the hatch and pulled out a book bag. He handed it to his mother who graciously gave it to Robby.

While all this was happening at the park, mom and son were at home praying together. Dad returned home . . . a hero with book bag. Robby did homework—and the family thanked God and headed to bed with praise and precious memories of a miracle. Robby's last words to his son that night encouraged him to pray for the family who had found the bag and given it back to the rightful owner. This family time gave an open door to teach how God loves all His children, red and yellow, black and white, all precious in His sight. Even though we can't communicate with all people, our hearts beat to the same language of loving the Lord and doing what is right and good in His sight. God bless this family who did the right thing and Robby who practices Good Samaritan acts every day without boasting.

God wasn't finished with the book bag miracle. He touched my heart to change the message I was planning to share at Robert's school that week. Looking back on the events that transpired throughout the past year, God was bestowing blessings and answering prayers. The message stirring in my heart was powerful. Let your light shine for Jesus in whatever you are doing—being called out to help a friend on a cold night, at a tennis court with your family, in all daily endeavors.

When you do the right thing, people notice—and so does Jesus. If your batteries are burned out, get charged up and let your light shine again. God is watching and waiting. He sees what we do and how we do it. His Holy Spirit keeps us shining and sharing His love and light wherever we go—if we allow Him to live in our hearts and homes.

Be Ready

DO YOU SHARE BROTHERLY LOVE with the sweet spirit Jesus taught? A recent funeral for a good friend made me think long and hard about brotherly love and death. During the service, I thought of my own brother. Remembering our good times growing up warmed my heart. I could see us securing a rope around the huge tree where Daddy parked his witch weed truck. We'd jump off the top of the cab, soaring through the air and around the tree like flying squirrels.

Billy and I were daring and determined; some things never change, praise God! Family time, playing and working together, and a strong faith strengthened the deep roots of love planted by our parents. Having our fields prepared for tough times kept us connected when silly squabbles could have severed our close family ties. How I thank God for my brother, for forgiveness and restoration, for the happiness and love we enjoy daily. Nothing in this world is worth being separated or staying puffed up and pouty at those you love.

From the back pew, I watched as heads bowed in prayer and caught a glimpse of Cameron near the front of the chapel. I thanked God for the close relationship he and Clint share. My heart raced with passion remembering some of Tim's last words to his sons: "Give a firm handshake to all people and watch your brother's back!" As the preacher prayed, I wondered how many people in the congregation were thinking about their own brothers, sisters, children, or parents. If you are reading this and hold offense in your heart against a loved one—or you take them for granted as if they'll always be here—go to them before the sun goes down and make things right. A phone call, an e-mail, a visit—whatever it takes to mend and unite—just do it!

Sam's favorite song, "My Way," echoed through the room. I could see his smiling face and friendly hand waving from his beloved pick-up truck. I thought of the many kind deeds he had done in his lifetime. He knew how to do just about anything well. The preacher talked about close relationships, encouraging others to cherish their brothers and sisters. Sam's brother, Willie, had always been for him. Even when death knocked, **he** fell to his knees to help save his brother's life. God worked a miracle that day. The nurses called Sam a Lazarus, for he came back to life and shared a few more precious days with those he loved so much.

I thought of the week before Sam died. I had been in such a hurry when I stopped at McDonald's for breakfast. Willie and Sam were sitting in a booth enjoying coffee and brotherly conversation. I hadn't seen Sam in months; something stirred my heart to sit and talk for a spell. Sam's smile lit the room. I asked his permission to use his name in a friendship story I was writing for my column. He grinned and said, "It'll cost you!"

The story wasn't supposed to run until the end of October, but God had other plans. It was in the paper one week before Sam went to heaven. His wife said that he was so excited when they read the story together. Our tears flowed. Once again, I was reminded of the glory and grandeur of the great God we serve. It certainly wasn't a coincidence as many might claim. God works mighty and mini miracles every day to strengthen our faith and sweeten our relationship with Him. Our busyness and unbelief—attempts to analyze all things—keeps us unaware, ungrateful, and unworthy of the mighty miracle working power of Christ, our Lord.

God worked that miracle in His perfect timing, knowing the plan for Sam's entry into heaven was coming soon. He taught me another lesson of trusting, believing, being a doer of His Word, and being obedient when He stirs our hearts. When writing that story about friendship, Sam's face kept popping up in my mind. I stared at my computer, remembering that Sam and Tim worked side by side, night after night preparing the Learning Station for opening day. His faithful friendship and talented craftsmanship were God-given gifts.

"Write about him," my heart said.

I wrote but deleted several things without understanding why. Reading over the story, I finally followed my heart and put the part about Sam helping our family back where it was supposed to be because God wanted it there. I believe He stirs our hearts and minds; we would be wise to listen to that stirring, nudge, inkling, feeling—and follow what He puts on our hearts for us to do! Amen.

The preacher's prayer ended, the family stood to follow the casket to the cemetery, and I thought of Sam in heaven celebrating with His Father, family, and friends gone onto glory. Surely, he smiled and waved his hand high in the air as Tim rushed to greet his good friend. What a time it must be in that land in the sky with celebrations welcoming those who've told us good-bye. I thought of the many people in our community who had said good-bye to loved ones recently. Some had died suddenly, but others had suffered long and hard—is there any good way to leave this world? Ready! We should live each day as if it's our last one here, hearts packed with love, faith, trust, obedience, and belief . . . with no unforgiveness or unbelief finding even one little spot to settle. Pure hearts believing and trusting Jesus, ready and waiting when He calls our name—that's our ticket to heaven, my friends.

When will death come? We know not the hour or the day but are wise to be prepared for the Master may call us any hour, any day. There is a story of a man who was told death would visit his home soon. The man hurried home, shared the story with his family, packed his bags, and left for a nearby town in Samaria. The man was petrified by the words from death and didn't want to be there when death came calling. A family member hurried to the village, saw death still there, and asked death about visiting their home. Death relayed a message that stung the loved one's heart. The message was that death had another appointment in Samaria that night and would not visit his home. Death came to the man in Samaria where he sought safety. What the man feared had found him. Death is coming to all of us, suddenly or slowly—maybe sooner than we think.

Are we ready? Are we walking with Jesus in faith and treating one another in brotherly love daily? Are we enjoying the journey? Are we living close to Christ and those we love? Don't delay; put this book down and go to your knees to make things right with your Lord and loved ones. You never know when death will come knocking at your door. Be ready!

Until our day comes to tell this world good-bye, let us live our lives in service to our Lord and do it in love. Let God lead and light our paths so that we can shine brightly for Him. Psalm 73:24 says, "You guide me with your counsel, and afterward you will take me into glory." Today, ask God to guide, guard, and go with you as you live to magnify His name.

Words to Live By

*W*HAT COULD ONE POSSIBLY DO in a bookstore for three hours? Bless and be blessed! Spending an entire afternoon browsing and buttering up my heart was the best blessing—no hurry, no worry, no one to wonder where I was, no place to be, just enjoying my time with me and Thee.

Do you enjoy time with you—time alone—just you and the Lord? I'm not talking about get-away time with the television, the guys, the girls, shopping, or surfing the Internet. Do you take time for you—taking a walk, meditating, journaling, reading, writing, praying, or studying the Word of God? Do you desire to do that? Amazingly, many people have a hard time admitting they don't like or don't allow me time. I encourage you to take time to do things by yourself, for yourself—just you and God! He likes to get you all to Himself sometimes; it's easier to listen with our hearts and unload in our heads what He is trying to tell us. Being still and listening is wise. Life is a mere mist; let us live it loud and lovely each and every day.

The card nook captivated me. I pulled my pocket pal from my purse and began writing some of my favorite verses on greeting cards. A coffee refill and special spot at a corner table gave me fuel to read and write to my heart's content. May I share with you some of the wonderful words that touched my heart that day? I believe you too will be blessed.

Friendship is when people know all about you and like you anyway is a one-liner I read every time I open my pocket calendar. This really makes one think about oneself! There are those who beam with generosity and sunshine; people are drawn to them like a magnet. Do we dare ask if people like us anyway?

Good friends are like stars: you don't always see them—but you know they're always there. These lines brought many friends to mind that afternoon. I thought of what is most important in our lives, what matters most when our time here is done—friendships, relationships. Be thankful for all your friends; for even when you don't see them, you can count on them being there in a flash in your time of need.

May you always have enough happiness to keep you sweet, enough trials to keep you strong, enough success to keep you eager, enough faith to give you courage, enough determination to make each day a good day. When I wrote these words, people dealing with sickness or situations that cause them to seek enough determination to make each day a good day came to mind. May all who have any need find enough faith to press forward. Know that you are loved and lifted in prayer by friends close to your hearts and those you don't even know. You may not always see them, but you feel the prayers and know they're there. Living in a community where the focus is faith and family are gifts many of us take for granted. How blessed we are to have enough to make all our days good days!

Be the change you wish to see in the world. The power of this hits hearts hard. We crave changes; let us be those changes so we can understand the courage needed to bring winds of change to a world dictated by traditions. Most are quick to grumble and growl but slow to believe and be the change they claim to seek. We must be willing to risk and reach out when all we have is our faith.

Just when the caterpillar thought the world was over, it became a butterfly. Can't you just see that ugly covering break loose and a colorful butterfly flittering to freedom? God will do the same for you and me. When things look bleak, we feel ugly and unwanted in a world that vibrates being beautiful. When we would rather quit than keep on, this reminds us to hold onto hope. Our world will be colored with beauty and blessings in His time and His way.

When one door of happiness closes, another one opens, but often we look so long at the closed door that we don't see the one that has been opened for us. We should dwell on thoughts of how blessed and fortunate we are, but we grumble and gravitate to the past. When it seems that others get the worm, we should stop and review our track record. Often, we do much more talking about being happy and having opportunities than we do working to make things happen. We navigate to negative thoughts or mistakes from our past and it becomes like poison deep inside. When God open doors, we are often occupied with pity, plowing through tough times and being plagued by our past. Therefore, we miss the grand and glorious gifts God had planned for us all along. We've had so many doors of happiness opened for us that we've become selfish and satisfied.

Dwelling on predicaments and people from our past—lost loved ones, bad business deals, storms that wrecked our homes and hearts, sickness, death, poor choices—imprisons and kills hope in believing we can be beautifully blessed. To watch a butterfly delicately and delightfully fly in freedom is a reminder to respect our past while restoring our future. Look to each new day, believing and rebuking what has kept you from walking through open doors from your Father. Step in faith.

It's not the years in your life that count. It is the life in your years. Abe Lincoln penned these words; his life and unexpected death are witnesses of this truth. Each of us is given the same gift of time—twenty-four hours each day, seven days each week, fifty-two weeks each year—but the number of years we have is uncertain. Every day should find us giving and going, doing and dreaming, playing and planning, working and waiting for a new day to dive into and make marvelous memories. Don't be a drag—be a doer!

My story ends with a beautiful quote from Emerson. *To laugh often and much—To win the respect of intelligent people and affection of children—To earn the appreciation of honest critics and endure the betrayal of false friends—to appreciate beauty—to find the best in others—to leave the world a bit better, whether by a healthy child, a garden patch—to know even one life has breathed easier because you have lived. This is to have succeeded.*

I took my last sip of coffee, closed my journal, cleaned the corner where I had written witty sayings for hours, and headed home. Emerson's words stuck mightily in my mind while riding my bike beside the ocean and listening to the sounds of the sea. Do we have the respect of others and the affection of children? Do we appreciate honesty, especially from critics? Do we look for the best in others? Will we leave the world a bit better? Have we made a difference in even one person's life? Are we succeeding in what we want to be remembered for? To have loved the Lord deeply and devotedly, to have shared close relationships with those we love, to have enjoyed living each day wide open while preparing for eternal life—it is then that our eyes will close and our heart will say "I did." And when that door of happiness closes on earth, we will enter the open door to heaven and hear words of welcome and a pat on the back for being a faithful servant. I can't wait! How about you?

Believe

WHAT DOES BELIEVE MEAN TO you? Where do I begin to tell the stories of a word so brave, so bold that it boosts the best of us in bad times—a beacon that lights the way to good times? All we have to do is believe! It sounds so simple, even silly. Some jeer or boil with jealousy when friends believe so strongly and live so happily. I believe that most folks are just about as happy as they set out to be! When we have a positive attitude of Christian living, we can make a difference—one by one.

We can live happily in a world infected by sin and sadness. Jesus doesn't desire for us to live in depression and defeat, frowning and fussing at home, at work, even at church. He wants us to spread sunshine, especially on cloudy days, to believe in Him and who He made us to be. We are spiritual sparks that can fuel a fire for Christ. A fire of love, a movement of His Holy Spirit shall sweep the land and settle in hearts and homes, teaching that we truly can live in peace and harmony—all brothers and sisters who believe and love the Lord.

I believe a great revival is coming soon to a place near you. Do you have your heart ready and your seat reserved? I believe one day our churches will be overflowing, standing-room only for spirit-led services. People will beg to get inside to hear the Word of God. Hearts will be hungry, lives will be saved, and serving Jesus will be top priority. I believe God is starting a revival in hearts of ordinary people standing up extraordinarily to get the fire going.

I believe we will see events and happenings that will take our breath away, supernatural things that broadcasters are unable to explain on the nightly news. I believe things will be exposed that bring light to the darkness and despair in our world. I believe God is getting us ready for a great revival and His Son's second coming to take His children home.

Rise Up, Recount Love

Do you believe? Don't despair! Think of all the people who didn't believe in Jesus's first coming. Mary believed, Joseph did with a little supernatural help, the shepherds and Wise Men did. God spoke to Mary's heart; she accepted her calling and rejoiced that she was chosen to be the mother of Jesus, the Son of God. Did everyone rejoice with her and believe her farfetched story of God speaking to her, of a virgin birth, of her baby—God's Son—who would save the world from sin? Few believed, but many were ready to gossip, gawk, and stone Mary. She remained true to what she believed; God took care of all the rest. He will do the same for you and me when we stand with courage and believe with all our hearts. Our calling may seem insignificant in comparison to Mary's, but Jesus blesses everything we do for Him. He tells us the first shall be last and the last first; He sees and knows everything—even the number of hairs on our head—and is overjoyed when we follow our calling from Him.

Many people will come to believers asking what they must do to be saved. In Acts, the Philippian jailer asked Paul that very question. Paul told him to believe in Jesus! That summarizes the teachings of the New Testament. Believing, living for Jesus, and being ready when He calls us home is simple. We make it complicated and cloudy. Things work out in our lives according to how we believe, the choices we make, and how we live day by day. We can't live recklessly with little regard for Christ or others and expect peace and joy to flood our hearts and homes. When you leave Jesus out, the enemy comes in to set up camp, to steal, kill, and destroy everything. He wants it all. He laughs, leaving all who let him in miserably sinking in sin far from the Master's hand. The joy of believing is in knowing that Jesus can hear the faintest cry—even when nothing else can help. Love lifts me and you—even murderers, thieves, and those we can't imagine Jesus loving. Believe in the Lord Jesus who loves all His children!

Many people don't believe and don't care to hear about a loving God who can take away all sorrow and soak hearts in perfect peace and promise. If we don't practice believing and doing things to ensure victory, how can we expect to win? Do you believe and practice what you believe?

The story of the little engine who tried so hard to climb the mountain proves that what we believe and practice, we can do. I close my eyes and see those wheels turning in the book I read to our sons so many times while teaching them to believe. "I think I can. I think I can." Do you think you can? Nothing is impossible when we put our trust in God and believe!

When I felt led to write a column in our local paper, I prayed and waited on the Lord. I visited *The Sampson Independent* and shared my dream. I told them I believed people wanted to read stories of inspiration and encouragement. When I felt ready to give up, God opened the door for this column to become a reality. Oh how God has blessed me. I haven't missed a week of writing since that December day in 2006. I give God all the glory and do not put myself on a pedestal. When we believe we do things on our own, we can get ready for a great fall. My column is for God and from God. I appreciate faithful readers giving me encouragement to keep writing.

Jesus told a parable about a widow and a judge (Luke 18) to show us we should always pray and not give up. The desperate situation of believers in the last times is made clear in verse 7 of Luke 18. In Matthew 24, Jesus tells us that "because of the increase of wickedness, the love of most will grow cold." Circumstances may look so bleak and hopeless that believers will be tempted to give up hope. But Jesus encourages us by promising that those who stand firm until the end will be saved.

Do you believe we are living in last days? No one knows when the end time will come—or even when our last day on earth will come—but wickedness is rampant, hearts are cold, and our time will run out one day. We may not understand and wonder what in the world is going on. We don't have to worry when Jesus is our Father. We believe!

The Perfect Story

WHAT IS THE PERFECT STORY to write to honor Jesus's birthday? My heart overflows with Christmas messages and memories I long to share. Waiting on the Lord works; this Christmas story is written in love—a gift I pray will give you joy and peace as we celebrate the birth of our Lord and Savior.

When Jesus was born, love lit the world in a brightness that would never be diminished or destroyed. Satan had other plans—to stop love in the name of hate. Love against hate: this is the great struggle of mankind, the one we've got to win. Our world is filled with ideological conflicts and moral conflicts, with getting and grabbing, giving and serving, desperate longing and total despair. If we look beyond this world of appearances, we can see the eternal struggle between love and hate. Which one is winning in your life? If hate exceeds the amount of love in our hearts, life stinks. How can we hate more than we can love? Love is pleasant, pure, and pleasurable. Hate is miserable, malicious, and maddening. Why would anyone chose hate instead of love?

The Christmas story resonates with love, but hate was on the heels of those gathered around God's Son in that manger. The enemy was busy lining up people that would hurt, hinder, and hate Jesus and the Good News He brought to mankind. His parents and His Father provided love and leadership as He faced struggles throughout his lifetime. Most of the Pharisees despised Him, family members disregarded him, friends ditched him, Satan deceived him and never gave up trying to destroy him—all in the name of jealousy and hate.

Jesus brought love and light. His teachings, parables, and lifestyle were different, daring, and definitely not accepted by those in authority—those who professed to be leaders. Even family members questioned Him and His ministry, saying He was just the son of a carpenter. While that's hard to imagine, hate slithers in and separates us, keeping us grounded in cycles of sin and sadness far from the good life intended by God. God's love was so powerful that He sent His Son to save us and give eternal life. He was King of Kings and could do mighty things, even when tempted in the desert. Yet, He chose humility, loving us enough to go all the way to the cross. Jesus died on that cross to restore that which was lost. He was human and hated what He would endure to ensure victory. He didn't want to drink from the cup, but knew there was no other way.

Jesus was not self-centered. What about us? Have we given up childish self-centeredness? We can't stand opposition, temptation, or tough times. Our vision is limited and love wanes when we don't get our way. What we need most is to give and receive love. We can't fully love others when our main concern is for ourselves.

Is your soul sick or healthy? The sick soul is all about self; the healthy soul revolves around its life task in the service of other people. Can we not see why this is the first and most important commandment? God is love! No matter what we do on this earth—how good we are, how many degrees we acquire, how much we suffer in our service to our Lord and to those we love, how wealthy and influential we are, how successful we are—if we do all these things without love, they mean nothing to our Father. "Love in any language straight from the heart brings us all together—never apart." These words from my favorite song support the gift of love God gave.

Tim watched from the front row as Cameron stood shyly. Clint, only four years old, was perched on a stool beside me. With my arms around my sons, we sang, "Love sent from Thee for all the world to see, love in any language is meant for you and me." We practiced the song for weeks, with my sons begging to bail out, hating the thought of singing with me in front of all those people. The enemy tried every trick in the book to stop us; but our love for one another and the Lord was stronger than the hate and insecurity he used to discourage us. What the boys thought they hated, generated such love, strength, unity, and a memory we will never forget. Tim beamed with pride to see his wife and children singing about love—something we honored and cherished intimately.

We can't fully love others when our main concern is for ourselves—even in the little things. Our attitude toward giving, loving through thick and thin, and sharing love reflects what's in our hearts and homes. I continually seek forgiveness when self-centeredness knocks on my heart. Do you remember times when selfishness spoiled sunshine for you and your loved ones? My mother gave our family a trampoline for Christmas in 1985. Her gift brought us lots of laughter and good times together, along with unexpected ups and downs.

The boys grew up, the mat rotted, and the insurance inspector frowned on this round risk in our backyard. Deciding the destiny of this gift from my mama, now in heaven, was not easy for Tim and me. My emotional ties tugged to keep it—even if we didn't use it now. Tim thought we should give it to our neighbors so their three little children could enjoy it. My self-centeredness won. One summer afternoon, we disassembled mama's gift, growing hotter and more hateful by the minute. Tim's gentle nature and notion that we should give this gift away settled in my heart; I knew he was right but refused to back down. We stuffed the springs in huge bags with me reassuring Tim one day we would have grandchildren who would love bouncing up and down on a gift from their great-grandmother. I could see mama smiling down saying, "That's my girl." How foolish—how selfish I was! We stashed the small parts in our little storage room; the huge silver circle and four legs of the trampoline remained dormant under piles of pine straw until last month. My son and grandson played and plundered in my backyard, a gift this mama cherishes. We walked past the gift MeMa gave Cameron and Clint; he asked if he could take it home for his family.

Lo and behold, I was right, Lord! Our grandchildren would enjoy this gift from long ago. Excitement mounted as we gathered parts of the trampoline. The legs were lost. Finally, Cameron found them buried in the ground where we staked them twenty years earlier. Three legs were there; one was gone. We searched long and hard, but it was lost like the little lamb the shepherd looked for high and low. We never found the lost leg; Cameron bought his family a new trampoline for Christmas, and I was reminded how self-centeredness blocks blessings and beauty of giving generously and graciously. I repented again as I loaded the remains of the trampoline and left them by the roadside with the trash. I did it with a heart full of love. I thanked him for helping me see the love and goodness in giving from the heart and the heartache and hatefulness in holding on to things selfishly.

Tim smiled and said, "I tried to tell her, Father!"

Is someone trying to tell you things that you just don't want to hear? Listen to your heart, to those who care about you, to God who loves you and gave the greatest gift so that you can be free and restore that which was lost. He gave His Son—a Christmas gift that keeps on giving when we let Him live in our hearts and homes. Stop being self-centered, stomp out all the hate and hurt from your heart, accept Jesus and live your life in love with Him and all that He is. Live love out loud.

When we learn how to give love to each other, we will be able to send forth good will in all directions and make the world a better place where we really can live in peace and harmony—in tune with our Father who loves us so. Let us embrace love in any language—straight from our hearts—and share it in the name of Jesus. Then, the great struggle of mankind will end. Love will win!

The Perfect Gift

*I*S THE BURDEN OF GIVING the perfect gifts stealing the sweet spirit of Christmas at your house? My heart has been flooded with so many awesome stories to share with you during this season of love. Every scripture, each card, encounters with folks at work, at church, shopping, and especially my quiet time with God, all give countless messages. Each are relevant and real to our lives, yet the message of worrying over money and giving gifts keeps coming front and center in my mind. May this story be a gift to help you find peace and joy amid the turmoil and troubles of these tough times. Read it with a heart that adores and honors Jesus as Savior. Realize what is really stealing our joy, our money, our everything. Recognize, refuse, and resist the enemy. Rest in the promise and peace of God's grace and gift of salvation. Christmas is about love, hope, peace, and joy—not debt, despair, depression, and doubt. Are you seeking Christ and celebrating life with a humble heart and sweet spirit? May this story refresh your faith and rekindle your fire to share gifts of love in honor of Christ who loves us so.

Matthew 6: 19-21 shows what the love of money can do. "Do not store up riches for yourselves here on earth, where moths and rust destroy, and robbers break in and steal. Instead, store up riches for yourselves in heaven, For your heart will always be where your riches are." People have different ideas about how money and possessions should be handled. Some store money in the bank—others spend it before it ever hits their pockets. Some spend conservatively and give the same way—others spend sensibly and give generously. Some tithe and give beyond the 10 percent required by God—others let God's portion become absorbed in bills and belongings. Many people hide money matters from those they love, thinking they've got it under control. How sad that we are bombarded with credit card companies begging us to spend what we don't have. Yes, the love of money—whether we store it up or spend what we don't have—is wrong and will eventually bring devastation to individuals, families, and nations. Oh that we would see where we are headed and turn to God before it's too late.

Being good stewards of our money is biblical. May we sit down with our families, plan and practice smart spending, pray and ask God to protect us from the pressures of financial burdens. Let us give God His portion first. Instead of increasing debt loads that bring January blues, let's change the way we do Christmas. Let's embrace the beauty of gift-giving so wonderfully shown by our Father God. His gift was love. In Corinthians 13:8, we find peace and promise to satisfy our minds and sooth our spirits. "Love never fails!"

How awesome to realize that love is an action directed to another person that is motivated by our relationship to Jesus Christ. It is given freely without a personal reward in mind. Wow! There's our answer to gift-giving that keeps us out of debt and in tune to our Father's example. Give gifts of love.

Monk and Bo Fussell, our neighbors at Topsail, recently celebrated sixty-two years of marriage and challenging health problems that have halted their shopping this year. Yet, their smiling faces and loving hearts prevail. PaPa Fussell endured back surgery in October, yet he stood in their kitchen to bake dozens of pound cakes this Christmas for friends and family—delicious gifts of love. Their family, like many others, has vowed to spend less on gifts that are often not needed and give gifts of love.

My extended family celebrates Christmas at Thanksgiving. We love gift-giving, often going overboard. So, this year we opted to have food and fellowship without any gifts. The morning of our family gathering, I awoke early with a stirring in my spirit. God impressed upon my heart that we were to have gifts. Wondering how I could pull this off in just a few hours didn't stop the stirring. When God speaks, we are smart to listen. So I waited; He will direct our steps if we tune out negativism and turn to faith. I settled on the side of the bed, writing notes of love and direction on twenty-two cards, with instructions being downloaded quicker than I could write. After a delicious meal, the men and kids headed to the den for football games and fun; the women washed dishes and settled down to relax. I prayed that God would bless what He put on my heart, fearing my family would call me a fuddydud and it would fizzle.

Turning off the TV brought dirty looks as each person accepted a long white envelope. We gathered in Billy and Helen Raye's living room—the first time we had all been together since Tim went to heaven. What happened the next two hours was witness to the power and grace of a loving God. Each person read their card and responded in ways that blessed them and the rest of us too. Then they picked a package from the gift pile, with surprises like a bowl from my mama Smith passed down to my mama, to me, and now Jessica, who held the aged, cracked bowl close to her heart as we told stories of Mama Smith's cooking days for twelve children. She knew she had picked a treasure.

Family members shared a time in their life when God did something awesome, told the story of Christmas, recited verses and prayers, shared stories of sickness and heartache and how Jesus brought them through. Several cards held money and asked the person to collect and put the bounty in a basket in the middle of the floor. When we finished, we knew the sweet, sweet spirit in that room was the Spirit of the Lord. Through tears and giggles, giving and receiving, we all witnessed miracles of love that tendered our hearts and helped us deal with things of the past that had toughened our hearts.

God was in charge; the gifts we received changed our hearts, healed our wounds, and helped others. We collected $200 and split it between two worthy charities and two families in need. Driving home, I sang loudly with the CD of the Christmas musical that our choir would present with Holly Grove this year. "Kings and kingdoms will all pass away, but there's just something about that name. Jesus."

I thanked Jesus for stirring my heart that morning and for the miracle of Christmas my family had shared—things that wouldn't pass away. It's not too late for your family to enjoy this same sweet spirit at your Christmas gatherings. Stick to your guns on stopping the excessive spending, gift-giving, planning and doing. Stand up for sharing time together with peace, joy, and gifts of the spirit. Giving the gift of time is always one to be cherished.

Recently, Connor and I entered the Gift Basket at Topsail. We climbed the stairs and found paradise, a toy nook packed with treasures that brought delight to my blue-eyed, red-haired gift from God. Connor picked up every toy within his reach and asked tons of questions. My plans were to be in and out within a few minutes, headed home to decorate. My pleas to hurry didn't matter; his mission to find the perfect toy mesmerized him. I learned lessons of how we rush and regulate everything we do—missing hidden blessings that can't come when we aren't willing to wait on the Lord and get out of the box that binds us. Jesus is not in a box!

I sat down on the floor beside Connor, answered every question meaningfully, read books with him on my lap, played games we made up with balls of all sorts, pretended to be good guys rescuing the bad pirates he found in brightly colored boxes, raced little cars that zipped across the floor, told tales of family ties to familiar toys, and became lost in time. His favorite book told a story about Jesus. Connor told me he was a king.

When he saw tears rolling down my cheeks, he said, "Kings don't cry, Nana!" He squeezed me and opened his arms wide saying, "I love you this much, Nana!"

Then, a motorcycle, the one toy he hadn't played with, caught his eye and away he went. I watched his every move with a prayer of thanksgiving in my heart. It took me a while to unfold my legs and stand again. Ninety minutes had passed, but it didn't matter for I had received a gift from my grandson that would bless me over and over again. When Connor realized we really were leaving, he stood guard at the door, begging to look just one more time. He couldn't decide, so we left without a toy. He wasn't happy, but he honored his Nana!

We are guilty of wanting things and having so much that we don't even know what to put on our Christmas lists. When we don't get our way, we often act ugly and unbecoming to our Father and our family. As we walked down the stairs, I was proud of Connor for behaving like a king. He didn't get a toy, but he did put treasures in my heart and in heaven that day. The time we spent playing together didn't cost a penny, but is more precious than gold or silver.

Christmas is coming soon. Don't let the burden of money and gift-giving steal your blessings. Get in touch with God. "Wait on the Lord, be of good courage, and He shall strengthen thine heart." Take time to soak up the joys of Christmas—of life.

Seek Him with all your heart, remembering that love never fails and He is our only hope. He gave the perfect gift: Jesus! Ask Him into your heart today, follow His example, and give gifts of love that will keep on giving. That's when we'll get the best blessing of all and truly understand the reason for the season! Amen!

Protect and Cherish

*H*AS YOUR COMPUTER EVER CRASHED and caused you to cry? Computers usually aren't the creator of our crisis; we cause confusion and chaos when we don't know what to do and keep digging deeper into technology trauma. Recently, my computer died with me sitting in front of it, touching the keys that formed words unfolding a story on my screen. I mourned my loss out loud, begging my computer to come back to life. It didn't. *Why won't you work right? Why did I put off saving my stuff to a thumb drive? Why didn't I listen to my heart's tug to save daily—even when I was rushed and compromised to do it tomorrow?*

My day became a time for God's message to settle in my heart, giving me an attitude of gratitude, teaching me lessons and telling me to pass them on to you. It's funny how God orchestrates events in our lives, how burdens become blessings, how bad things are turned to good when we wait on the Lord. Be of good courage and believe!

I believe all things happen for a reason—hard as that is to digest during disgusting days, tough trials, and heartbreaking happenings. Losing my computer was painful, but the real problem was losing the treasures stored inside. The computer could be replaced; the contents couldn't.

God was teaching lessons I had learned as a little girl playing school on our side porch. My mother said "Don't put off till tomorrow what you should do today." I remember her using any opportunity to tell me the importance of doing my work first—play later and don't put off doing things. I sat at my desk, staring at my computer and replaying a memory of long ago in my mind. Mama hung out clothes while I wrote on my little chalkboard. She smiled in the morning sunshine as she clipped clothes to the line. I can see her face. Today, I understand her smile. She heard me teaching my little doll baby students the same lessons she was planting in my life—lessons that never leave us even when those who taught them do. I smiled and accepted this refresher lesson on the perils of procrastination.

My heart ached as I waited for a local PC expert to diagnose my problem. Other computers were in line awaiting attention; selfishly, I wanted mine taken care of right then. I waited, went back to Tim's Gift, and wailed at my desk, thinking of the hundreds of hours spent writing and saving stories that would be shared in this book. Writing ahead of deadlines is part of my work ethic, my desire to get my work done, and have time to play. Taking time to save my work to a source other than my hard drive seemed less important, something I could do the next day, or the next. Then, the day came when it was lost, leaving me to wonder if it would be found; my crying continued. Finally, Cameron came out of his office, held his mother and let me cry. Then, he wiped my tears and told me it would be okay.

My faith mounted up like eagle's wings. I cleaned my face and wiped the worry from my heart. I drove to Hargrove to pick up our students, talking to Jesus all the way there. *This test is tough, yet I will stand firm and trust you, Lord. I know that writing can be replaced, Father, but how can I remember all the messages you sent, the joy of seeing stories safely stored in folders on my PC desktop. I am sorry I wasn't more careful with the treasures in my care; please don't let my writings be gone.*

The children filed in the van and buckled up, asking why I'd been crying. Another lesson is that we don't fool our kids. I told them the story of my computer dying and my awful day. My little Zoie smiled with such innocence and assured me Jesus would take care of it. My spirits were lifted as the children shared stories about school. They listened as I encouraged them to clean out their hearts of the little stuff that can grow inside and cause heartaches. Mine needed cleaning the most. Rhylee prayed. I watched from the rearview mirror. With their little heads bowed and a sweet prayer penetrating their hearts, you could feel the presence of the Lord in our van.

I pulled into my parking place, told the kids how much I loved them, and headed inside to help get homework done. My prayer wasn't nearly as selfish as it had sounded to God a few hours earlier. I still wanted to know my work would be saved, but now it was completely in His hands.

Have you lost precious things too? Learning to truly trust Jesus in times like this grows faith and gives lessons on being more careful with things we cherish.

Lost and Found

*L*OSING THE TREASURES IN MY computer taught lessons that would never be deleted from my mind. I loaded up my computer and grandson and headed to the store where my son had purchased my computer years earlier. Connor was filled with questions as we drove to the nearby town. I told him a Geek Squad would take care of our troubles as we entered the store and headed to the service desk.

Prayers were about to be answered. While we waited, Connor asked a million questions: *What is a geek? Why do computers die? When are we eating?* By the time the young geek said, "Next please," I was ready to get this over and done with. He politely listened to my sob story, and began retrieving information from his register. Within minutes, he shared news that sent me into praise mode right there in the store. "Mrs. Spell, your son purchased a three-year extended warranty. Your computer is covered."

Connor joined the celebration as did several new friends we made while waiting in line. I left my computer in Geek Squad care, knowing it would be revived and good as new when I came back to pick it up.

Keeping promises, especially to God and grandchildren is important. All three of us enjoyed a good time at McDonalds's inside playground. Connor prayed before we enjoyed food, fun, and a history lesson about the pictures featuring Ft. Bragg painted around the room. We didn't rush to eat or speak harshly to one another, as did many people seated near us. When a father actually hit his crying daughter, Connor squeezed my hand in fear. We talked all the way home about things that trouble little children. He worried about the little girl and wondered why some daddies do bad things. We agreed that our Heavenly Father is the best and would never hurt His children.

One week later, my teachers were gathered in my office for a quick meeting. My phone rang. A lady with broken English began talking. I didn't take time to listen, assuming she was a telemarketer. I told I wasn't interested. Minutes later, the phone rang again. The same lady told me my computer was ready to be picked up. I quickly apologized for hanging up on her earlier and thanked her. Sometimes we act in haste and hatefulness when we should take time to listen. Our assumptions aren't always right, and blessings come to us that we could easily miss.

That afternoon, Connor and I waited in line again for my computer. A miracle was about to happen before my eyes. They opened my computer and there was the small golden cross shining in the top left corner. I had pulled the cross from a welcome bulletin at Emma Anderson Chapel two years earlier and had attached it to my computer. Today, it reminded me of God's love. Then, I saw my screen light up and everything was there—nothing was lost. I cried tears of joy, thinking of the long nights I spent writing instead of sleeping. What was lost was found; *thank you, Lord*. We left with a computer that had been revived, restored, and was ready to be used again.

That's how it is with God's love once we've experienced it. We can easily become lost, appearing to be dead, losing the treasures our Lord and loved ones have sacrificed to give us. When we think all hope is gone, our miracle comes when we put our trust in Him. He revives us, restores us, and is ready to use us again to share the unconditional love of a God who longs for us to stay closely connected to Him. For when we cut ourselves off from the vine, we wither and die. Life flows when we are connected to Jesus. Every time I turn on my computer, that golden cross reminds me of His love, of the miracle of my treasures being saved, of people who help us along our path, of believing and being all we can be for God.

Connor and I celebrated at Chick-fil-A. After a good meal and watching him play, we pulled on our coats and headed to a corner of the restaurant where a fundraiser was going on for children suffering from MS. I handed Connor some money and explained that we were helping people by giving. When Connor dropped coins in the container, I was reminded how we need to help others more.

Driving home, he talked of how good it feels to help people. He held to his certificates he would redeem on our next visit and recalled the excitement when he won and bells rang. He asked if they would help his cousin, Katy, who suffers from spinal bifida. He asked why some get sick and some stay well. He talked about things that bother little children. He looked in the sky and asked how God made the stars. He talked about galaxies and where God lives.

"Nana, I can't wait to see God. I can't wait to get to heaven. I want to be good and see God."

My heart was tendered by his precious words and the love and joy he brings to my life. God knows our needs and sends blessings—even through a little child whose love and faith is big and bold.

When I kneeled beside my bed that night, I had much to tell my Lord. He listened as I talked on and on as Connor had on our way home. I thanked Him for teaching me many lessons through my computer experience, for making sure my stuff was saved but more importantly that I am saved though once I was lost, for connecting me with people who could help, for the cross where He gave His Son so that we might be saved, for my grandson who loves deeply and yearns to live his life for Jesus, for the blessings overflowing in our lives, for freedom, for good to reign over evil in our land, and for the day when I get to heaven. *I can't wait to see You, God.*

How about you? Do you download your heart each night before the Lord? Are you ready for heaven? If you are lost, may you seek Him today and experience the joy of being found.

Loving Children Unconditionally

*H*AVE YOU WONDERED WHY CHILDREN sometimes seem ungrateful, unconcerned, and unable to realize just how much we love them? How can those we love the most in this world often take that love for granted? This is a most difficult story to write. It is not natural to speak negatively about those whom we gave life to, those created in God's own image, those precious children we would give our own life in order to save. We might speak words of correction—even condemnation to them—but if others come against them, look out. We'll be right there to protect and provide. The little bundles of joy that came into our lives bringing more happiness and hopefulness than we could have imagined can also be bearers of heartaches.

Children and parents make choices that keep them closely connected or sadly separated. It's the little things the enemy taunts us to employ against one another that can bring division, eventually death to relationships between parent and child, friends, husband and wife, brother and sister, even our Heavenly Father and his children. There is much truth in the old saying that the family that prays together, stays together. Satan saturates our society with negativism and nasty tricks intended to divide families, destroy faith, and distance us from our Father. The good news is that the enemy has no power over us when we put our faith and trust in God. The devil cannot divide families that stick together through thick and thin with hope and help coming from our Father God, our very best friend. Trouble is, we can be hardheaded and hold back when we should be humble and seeking His will and way. I pray this message will help many people come closer to Christ and to their loved ones.

The intent of this writing is not to cast judgment on our children. Children will be children. Some children create challenges that cause heartaches and headaches; others deal with the same challenges, never losing the close connection to their loved ones. Children act and react differently. Children stay and stray. Children are wise and foolish. Children need love and understanding—even when we feel they are so far away. How do we explain the bond of love we share with our children and the frustration we feel when they are off track? Hard as it is when things aren't quite right with our loved ones, we must look to how God deals with His children for a clear understanding of unconditional love.

Recently, I learned some powerful lessons of love and forgiveness in my big happy family. Our family is tightly woven like an heirloom quilt. The squares sewn together showcase seasons of growing up and giving, loving and learning, sticking it out and standing up for one another and for God. Times we shared became treasures, especially when our nest emptied and we sensed the pain of separation. When our heart aches, we hurt all over. The cure is staying close to Christ through all our seasons. Then, separation doesn't drag us down. It propels us to new heights where we help others who have fallen and can't get up. We must stick together and stay connected to the vine in order to enjoy the fruit of a big happy family.

My oldest son started this story when he hurt my feelings at work. Mind you, I've toughened up through the years, yet being tenderhearted brings tears when I declare I will not cry. When I wanted my sons to attend a family gathering and they had other places to go and things to do, I commenced lecturing about the importance of family. My feelings were hurt; I cried and got mad. I don't even know why, except sometimes we get angry about our situations and take it out on loved ones. So, I did what we women do well—I pouted. That made my sons not want to be anywhere near their pitiful little mama. I prayed that God would help me understand my feelings and give guidance in dealing with my children.

A dear friend was put in my path within hours of my prayer. She stopped her shopping cart near mine to tell me how Cameron had blessed her and what a kind, loving person he is. Her words carried a message God wanted me to hear and share with you. Driving back to work, I knew God had sent that person to help me when I thought it was my children who needed someone to set them straight. Isn't it ironic how we see the faults in others while overlooking our own? I sat in my car in front of Tim's Gift and thanked Him for sending a godly person to me who shared words of love and life, reminding me to see the good in my children and not accentuate the bad.

How different that little episode could have turned out if an unbelieving person happened by and had heaped negative words about my son on my pitiful self. That's happened to all of us, with people playing on our emotions: *you do so much your children, they take you for granted, they should appreciate you more!* Truth is we should all appreciate one another more and never take one another for granted, but we do. Who understands this better than our Heavenly Father? I hopped out of my car renewed and ready to embrace my son with a humble hug, after repenting to the One who loves me, my children, your children, all His children with a love that touches eternity, with the willingness to give His life that we might be saved, with unconditional love that forgives, forgets, and frees us to love one another with peace and promise.

God understands His children. He is able to help us when we feel unappreciated or taken for granted, forgotten on special days or forsaken in times of need, rejected or misunderstood, overwhelmed with busyness or lazy and apathetic. He feels the same frustrations for He is Father to all the children of the world. Can you imagine the pain He feels when you and I take Him for granted and go to Him only when we need something? Do we forget Him until tough times come or go to worship Him only on special days? Do we lash out at Him when things don't go our way—or as we prayed? Do we reject Him before man and deny knowing Him as did Peter? Are we so busy that we seldom take time to just sit down and have a little talk with Him? Do we wonder why He does things as He does and blame Him for bad situations in our lives? Do we claim to know and serve Him, but never spend with Him? Wow! The light suddenly came on inside my mind and lit up my heart. God really does understand. Yet, He always handles us just right. His example is his best lesson on how a loving Father acts and reacts toward His children.

God is fair and just. He doesn't mark us off his list just because we don't attend events when He really wants us there, or stay away from church for seasons and distance ourselves from Him. He waits while we wander. He nudges us to stay close to Him when we choose to stray. Our choices come with consequences. When we realize that staying connected to the vine really is the only way to be happy and have a home in heaven, He never turns His back on his children. When we ask for forgiveness, He marks our slate clean. Not only does He forgive, He forgets and never brings up the silly, sinful things we did to hurt Him. His unconditional love is truly amazing. He loves all His little children. No matter what we do or don't do, how good or bad we are, how far we stray—He is always there with open arms to welcome us back into the big happy family of God.

The next time you wonder how your children could be ungrateful or unconcerned, stop and remember that God sometimes wonders the same thing about you and me. Let us strive to stay closely connected to our Father and to those He gave us to love on this earth. It's an awesome feeling being part of the family of God—washed in His spirit and cleansed by His blood. If there are divisions or disputes that have distanced you from family members, friends, or Father God, take the first step to repent and reconcile, lose the bitterness that binds and God will replace the brokenness with blessings. You will live in peace and promise as one big happy family!

Live and Love Passionately

*D*O YOU PROTECT PASSIONATELY WHAT God has entrusted in your care? This story swelled in my heart last fall as I walked the beach two days after Thanksgiving. The day was warm and sunny with a brisk wind ushering in a season of cold weather and warm hearts for the holidays. Harley and I walked as I talked aloud to the One who made the sunshine and sea sparkle before my eyes. The glistening sun cast shadows of fishermen's poles and beach walkers. I wondered what stories the people I met would write during this season of thanksgiving and who would read them. I thanked God for the opportunity to write and share His stories that are downloaded in my heart. I thought of my family and prayed for our friends who had become parents on Thanksgiving and our friends whose precious little one went to heaven the same day.

I looked across the ocean and wondered what stories would be written by His children in countries where the freedoms and blessings we enjoy are endangered. I thought of my friend whose son celebrated Thanksgiving in Morocco while serving in the Peace Corps. Dear friends who had empty chairs around their table this year came to my mind. Whatever season we are in, spending time with precious family and friends should be protected passionately. I thought of how difficult it is for families to schedule gatherings and holiday celebrations, how doing stuff (vague word with little meaning, which is exactly why I used it here) has replaced valuing time together, and how complacent, apathetic attitudes have endangered the passionate, personal protection that keeps families and friends closely connected to one another and to God. I walked in silence, praying for my own family—for all families—to feel protected and passionate about life, love, and living out loud for the Lord.

Harley broke the silence with a whimper and attempt to walk right up under me. A pint-sized dog stood on top of a sand dune like a monster with his barking and fierce behavior. Harley didn't do a thing to protect me from the little dog. Harley towered over this intruder whose size was no indication of his ability to stir fear and friction. I wondered if the little dog would attack from behind, paused to calm Harley, and continued walking and talking louder than ever. I thought of Goliath, so big and bold against attackers, until the little shepherd boy hurled stones and sent him crashing to the ground. It wasn't David's size that mattered; his passion for what he was called to do made the difference. A poem in our seventh grade literature book came to my mind about a robin that protected her young. The lyrics tell of a baby bird that fell from the nest and a mother who took immediate action to save her little one. Danger approached when dogs headed their way, but the mother robin kept them away. She flapped her wings continuously and protected her baby passionately. The dogs recognized the determination in her eyes and left the baby bird because of the mother's cries. This short poem teaches a huge lesson about protecting those we love, protecting people who need help, and protecting the power of passionate love in a world where there's just too little of it. That's why my students spent time learning the lyrics and discussing the meaning of this profound piece of literature. It proves that size doesn't matter nearly as much as does passion and believing in your cause.

We may be small, but our efforts and enthusiasm, our spirit of fight and freedom, our determination and creativity, our faith and force to stay passionate and persistent is big and bold when we stand firm and refuse to give up, give in, or give out. We will fight to the end for faith, family, and friends. The intriguing factor is how good triumphs over evil. *Star Wars* showed moviegoers the winning power of the good force. The Bible is filled with people who lived their faith passionately and saw good come from the bad for those who loved God. Good guys really do win in the end.

The best part of this story comes when those who stand strong through the tests and trials taste the sweet rewards of victory over the giants of the enemy that threaten to steal, kill, and destroy everything. The devil blows up the little things that can kill passion and divide families and friends forever. Each of you knows sad stories of people who have allowed love and laughter to die in their hearts and homes over stuff that won't matter at all one day.

What in this world could be important enough to cause people to stay away from loved ones and fail to protect them with passion? Could it be feuding over land boundaries or things left behind by parents whose passionate love for their children was lost in settling an estate? Could passionate love be poisoned by family members who allow the enemy to work schemes and enhance sins that divide and destroy? Could people stand by, cowering in fear over little things that come against family and friends, without offering protection?

What can we do to promote love in our world today? Why not read the story again that tells how little David defeated big Goliath? The details show how David went against the grain; people laughed and looked for his quick defeat. He was a victim of scorn and ridicule, but that didn't deter him. David was totally committed to protecting and proving that his God was an awesome God. David knew the secret for sweet victory over anything that tried to steal his joy or go against his God. He believed strongly, loved passionately, and protected what was precious and priceless to Him—without allowing anything to stand in his way or steal his blessing. The mother robin proved that size was no match for sizzling love. She never left her loved one—even when the enemy seemed bigger than life and death looked her in the face. She stood firm, fluttered her little wings, focused on saving her baby, faced the enemy with no fear, and forbade him to devour her family. When the enemy tries to enter, we must be alert to keep him out. What begins as little sins or situations can grow into gigantic problems and predicaments that can cause love to be lost. Keeping passion alive and faith firmly rooted, the enemy can be defeated and love will rule the roost. Stand your ground and grow your love with passion and praise. Give God the glory and you'll be happy in love for all your days!

A Special Friend

*I*SN'T IT AMAZING HOW SPECIAL friends come into our lives and we are forever changed? A recent Tuesday morning at Tim's Gift, I settled in front of my computer when prayer time ended and everyone left. It would be a morning when little was accomplished with my computer work, but what God had in store kept me busy and blessed.

The front door opened and one of Tim's faithful customers walked inside. Mr. Willie's smile lit up the room like sunshine. We talked about work, the world, and the times he had come here for insurance. The story Mr. Willie shared sent chills down my spine. He talked about his son with a twinkle and a tear in his eyes. I listened and learned a lesson about friendship that I pray will bless you as it did me.

While Mr. Willie's story unfolded, I kept thanking God in my heart for this ministry where giving help and hope remains our mission. Today, I was helped and filled with hope for tomorrow. Mr. Willie told how his seventeen-year-old son had been killed in a tragic car accident in 1993 on his way home from school. He recounted the details of Anthony's death as if it had happened a day earlier, sharing how Anthony told his dad only weeks before he went to heaven that he wrote an essay in school about a special friend. He told him he would have written about his dad being his best friend, but he had to write about someone else. It was weeks after Anthony's death that his dad would read the writing that told a story about his son and his special friend. It revealed where Anthony would spend all his tomorrows.

Mr. Willie and I talked about how children are a gift from God. Knowing they love the Lord and are ready to meet Him gives us such peace in our hearts. He recalled painful memories of that season when God called his son home. He and his wife have moved forward in faith. Missing Anthony will never cease, but knowing he is in heaven brings sunshine to their days. They have no doubts of where their son is spending his tomorrows, for God touched his dad and told him that Anthony was with him. As Mr. Willie unfolded his story, I was reminded of what a friend we have in Jesus. Two days later, I found a copy of Anthony's essay on my desk at Tim's Gift. Mr. Willie knew it would touch my life. I read the introduction and thought of Anthony and the multitude of people who would come to know Jesus as Savior and friend, through his writing—his short life—his huge witness for the Lord.

> On January 15, 1993, we lost a very dear friend. Anthony Quinn Tyndall was only seventeen when he was involved in a tragic car accident. The Lord saw fit to take Anthony to be with Him. We know he is in a much better place now and we are thankful for the memories we have of him worshipping and praising the Lord in our local church. Anthony truly loved the Lord and he was a great witness to everyone he came in contact with. Here is an essay he wrote in school, not knowing that two months later he would be gone to live with the Lord. We pray that this will touch some soul who may have strayed from God.
>
> This person is not one to be picky about race or nationality. He is the type of person that has "no respect of persons." He is one who feels that each person "should love thy neighbor as thyself." This man feels that "you would that men should do to you, do ye even so to them." In other words he feels that "you should do unto others as you would have them do unto you.'
>
> Not only is this person loving, but he is very forgiving. He feels that a person should forgive someone "seventy times seven." This person "is longsuffering, and of great mercy, forgiving iniquity and transgression."
>
> This person, however, is selfish. He wants me to love him "with all thy heart, and with all thy soul, and with all thy mind, and with all thy mind, and with all

thy strength." He wants my full attention so that he can lead me in the right direction to keep me safe from harm.

I am one of the lucky many that knows this man. I got to know this man about five years ago; however, I also walked away from this special friend about five years ago. Yet, because of His forgiving spirit, He forgave me and allowed me to get close to Him again. This man says that he "will never leave thee, nor forsake thee." Not only is He my friend, but He can be anyone's friend who is willing to accept Him. This person that I am talking about is Jesus Christ. He is the only person that anyone needs to know, and I am glad that I know this man.—Anthony Tyndall

No words are needed to end this story; Anthony says it all as he shares the love of his life, Jesus! I thank God for sending Mr. Willie to Tim's Gift where we talked and prayed, giving one another help and hope. God spoke to my heart that this is what knowing, loving, and serving Him is all about—one person at a time or thousands gathered to hear the sweetest story ever told—Jesus desires to be our best friend.

Do you know Him? He is waiting to enter your heart; won't you let him come in? He's the special friend who will stick with you through thick and thin and take you to heaven to spend eternity with Him—when your life on earth ends. I'm so glad Jesus is my best friend.

Adjusting Attitudes

HAVE YOU EVER TOLD SOMEONE that he or she needed an attitude adjustment? Have you faced someone who relayed that same message to you? Adjusting an attitude can make life sweet or sour, happy or harried, blessed or beastly. Yet, many people live with little regard for the importance of making changes in how they act and react. Some folks proudly proclaim their right to have an attitude. In order to appreciate those with positive attitudes, think of times that people with rotten attitudes spoiled your day. Living with, working with, serving with, and dealing with people who have bad attitudes can spoil a lifetime. Life is too short to allow attitudes that aren't awesome to surface and sour precious memories.

Learning to control and create positive attitudes takes preparation, patience, and practice. We can't fly off the handle or look at daily encounters with pessimism. We must seek control of our actions and thoughts while embracing a positive outlook. We either learn to control our attitude or it will consume and control us. Reading an old essay by an unknown author brings revelation to this issue of attitude:

> The longer I live, the more I realize the impact of attitude on my life. Attitude to me is more important than the past, than education, than money, than circumstance, than failures, than successes, than what other people think, say, or do. It is more important than appearance, giftedness, or skill. It will make or break a company, a church, a home.
>
> The remarkable thing is we have a choice every day regarding the attitude we will embrace for that day. We cannot change our past—we cannot change the fact that people will act in a certain way. We cannot

change the inevitable. The only thing we can do is play on the one thing we have—and that is our attitude.

I am convinced that life is 10 percent what happens to me and 90 percent how I react to it. And so it is with you—we are in charge of our attitudes.

These words ring loud and clear a message of truth to our hearts. We have seen homes break, churches split, and companies crumble when attitudes of adversity, aggravation, and apathy prevail. Many people fight daily battles with folks who do not realize the impact of their bad attitude on those they love, work with, and come in contact with. The attitude we live by becomes attached to our personal identification. People think of us with the way we act rising up in their minds.

Many times employees with attitudes face frustration and feel targeted by employers who feel the need to remove the rotten apple. Harsh as that sounds, it's true. If you've ever been given the assignment of working with people possessing bad attitudes, you understand the necessity to weed out what can ruin a good thing, a growing company, or a great endeavor. Attitude is extremely contagious and can sweep through a congregation like wildfire. Often, churches suffer when attitude creeps in and rears its ugly head. Confronting those who haven't lived long enough to realize the impact of attitude isn't always easy, but it is necessary. It is important to have the right attitude when reminding someone that he or she really does need an attitude adjustment. Most important is keeping a close check on our own attitude.

Remembering that we have a choice every day in the attitude we will embrace for that day gives ownership to our actions. We only have to think of those who make poor choices—and how we are affected—to give grounds for making good choices.

Think of someone who lives life positively and displays an attitude that is appealing. Many people show this enthusiastic spirit in my community. Patty Cherry is one of them. I can never remember a time when she wasn't smiling and serious about spreading good cheer. I have worked with her on committees during the season when Project Graduation was thriving. She always carried an attitude of commitment and charm to each meeting. Her positive attitude overshadowed any problems or predicaments that could have caused her to become negative. She continues to embrace life with an attitude that shows the sweet spirit that thrives inside. Her contributions to our community have made a difference. Her energy and excitement ignite happiness for those who cross her path. Her attitude is awesome—and so are her hats! Patty loves to wear hats and doesn't let anyone deter that passion. It is powerful when we live boldly and bravely with passion—unafraid to get out of the box that binds.

Think of someone who lives life with pessimism and portrays an attitude that is repellent and repulsive. Surely, each of us is thinking of someone who has made a negative difference in our lives, someone we don't enjoy being around, someone we wish would change their attitude.

While reflecting on the importance of attitude in others, we should look at ourselves first. Are we making the choice daily that shows our Lord and loved ones that we take seriously the impact and importance of attitude? While seeking the greatest role model of all times who portrayed the attitude that makes life worthy and wonderful, we only need to look in our Bibles and read story after story of His mercy and His love. His name is Jesus. Look to His teachings and how He lived to see the effects of a right attitude. Listen closely to His calling. Could He be telling us we need to get an attitude adjustment? Don't delay—you're in charge of your attitude. Make it right today!

Loving Through Loneliness

HAVE YOU EVER SUFFERED FROM loneliness? Loneliness is as real as hunger or fatigue. We can get a good night's sleep or enjoy a good meal to satisfy a tired body or growling stomach, but how do we handle loneliness, feeling unwanted, having forgotten what human joy is, even feelings of being unloved? The One who created us knows the best way to fill us with hope and chase away loneliness.

Mother Teresa witnessed and worked all her life to ease the pains of poverty throughout our world. She spoke openly of the great disease of loneliness that is affecting people in places close to home—even in our homes. Feeling unloved or unwanted is real. Being lonely, left out, or looked over is a tremendous poverty in our world today.

Reading of Biblical people who faced loneliness gives insight into dealing with it. Mary, during her pregnancy, showed such strength even when family and friends failed to believe her or stand by her. She pondered things in her heart and stayed true to what God told her.

Ruth surely saw times of loneliness, but persevered from bereavement in Moab. Hannah spent years feeling lonely while yearning for a child. Noah hammered and sawed through season after season with no help from the people who contributed to his loneliness. Yet, in all the stories we read in His Word, God brought revelation, revival, and rejoicing in His time to those who endured lonely times. In story after story, we read of people who suffered from loneliness while living out the plans God had for their lives. Staying close to the One who created us really is the answer to a cure for loneliness.

Jesus even faced trials and tough times when loneliness loomed. Luke 5:16 tells us how Jesus went to withdrawn places and prayed.

Jesus felt the sting of loneliness from his own family and his disciples. Many times, He had to go it alone, when they just didn't understand or stand by Him. You would think His hometown folks and family would have been His most ardent admirers and biggest believers. Yet, we read His own words that declared that a prophet wasn't welcome in His hometown. Jesus could have performed mighty works from His Father, yet the miracles were less because those in his hometown didn't believe and embrace the power of the Messiah.

Jesus sought quiet times to commune with His Father. Getting up early in the morning provided time for uninterrupted prayer. We would be wise to put this into practice in our own lives. Early morning may seem lonely when the world is quiet and interruptions are few, but it's a time when you feel so close to God as you read and pray. Jesus understood the importance of such sacred times with God. His example shows the power of a private, lonely, lovely time of prayer and praise with the One who gave us life. "Very early in the morning—Jesus got up, left the house, and went off to a solitary place, where He prayed" (Mark 1:35).

Do you spend such precious time praying and talking to Jesus? It's a choice we make. We can spend time with Him in places packed with people. While pedaling the bike or walking on the treadmill at the Center for Health and Wellness, I often tune out the crowds and dwell in solitude with my Savior. My favorite place is the treadmill that faces the windows, looking out into the world while walking and running. I watch people come and go, cars whiz by, busses loaded with children on their way to school, the sun rising, bringing warmth and light and showing off colors in the sky that only God can create. I wonder what stories the people out there have in their hearts. How many are headed to work or other destinations with worries and loneliness that keeps them from being close to the Lord and loved ones? Who needs help but knows not where to seek it? How many people have everything this world can offer but are lonely and lost? Who is sharing with them the promise and peace of walking with God?

On that treadmill, I watch my time and wonder what we can do to help those who are lost in loneliness. Balancing time alone and time with family and friends is so important. Jesus loved the crowds, but He sought time to get away and didn't feel guilty about it either. He made use of His time alone to be available so that He might nourish his soul in communion with his Father. Jesus experienced both isolation and alienation. He often asked his disciples if they were going to go away and leave Him too. In Gethsemane, He asked his closest friends to watch with Him! Jesus knew the joy of close friends and family too. Peter, James, John, Mary, Martha, and Lazarus gave comfort and companionship to their greatest friend of all time.

So how do we handle loneliness? St. Augustine taught that we can only be at rest when we are close to our Creator. That is still true. God created us as unique individuals—and He knows the best way to fill our empty places. God is the answer to loneliness or anything else that keeps us from loved ones and our Lord. He fills our deepest longings, never walks out or replaces us with someone He likes better, and promises never to leave us alone.

God is the only one who wants to be—and always can be—the unfailing companion on our journey. Who walks with you daily on your journey? If you don't know Jesus personally, please don't let the sun go down before you find Him. Get reacquainted with Him—and enjoy living life crazy in love with the One who will chase away loneliness and protect your peace, prosperity, and promise of everlasting life in heaven!

We Can Pray

*A*RE YOU PASSIONATE ABOUT THE promises you make to loved ones and to the Lord? Are you one who promises to do this or that with little intention of following through—or are you held in high esteem for being a real promise-keeper? If you've ever been a victim of broken promises, you understand the importance of keeping them. We may break our promises, but God never does. We can count on Him every time? Can He count on us?

Relaxing in the hot tub at the Center for Health and Wellness recently, I closed my eyes and had a little talk with Jesus. The next morning, I could hardly wait to finish my workout and head to the warm water haven. Peeling off my sweaty clothes, I pulled on my bathing suit and walked quickly past the pool to the hot tub. Stepping into the churning waters brought tranquility. Relaxing in the bubbling waters, my body and mind were treated to a short time of freedom from demands of the day—phone calls, beeping messages, packed schedules, dozens of duties waiting to be done, and other stuff that shoos away serenity.

My hot tub visits quickly became treasured times. I felt free to pray, even sing softly in the stirring waters. I pray every time I am blessed to be there—it envelops me with peace and a promise to God. The promise I made was easy to keep when it was just me and God, but the first morning I shared the tub with a young woman I had never met, I considered a silent prayer and a quick departure. My heart stirred as did the waters that brought comfort to my tired body. Knowing what I must do, I broke the silence and we talked until the timer stopped. Then, I extended my hand and a warm handshake led to a short prayer together. Weeks passed with more opportunities in the place where I promised to pray. What an awesome feeling when we share prayer—no matter where we are.

Being bold in our witness is important, but equally important is not chasing people away when we choose to share Christ in places other than church. It may sound silly, but it's true. We expect to pray in church, at the dinner table, or before bedtime, but what about times throughout our days when people need prayer in places where we feel prayer wouldn't be acceptable. Do we shy away, fearful of what someone might think? Does being politically correct take precedence even when the spirit of our Lord speaks softly and tenderly? I can hear the Dove Brothers singing that sweet song as I write. The lyrics tell of times when people feel all is lost and hope is gone, lives are in ruin with no sunshine for their days, but no matter how bad things are—we can always pray.

We must remember how Jesus taught us to pray, especially when we feel led to pray with others. He frowned on those who prayed publically as the Pharisees did. He taught us to pray to our Father, asking His will to be done on earth as it is in heaven, to forgive us and our sins as we forgive others and what they have done that's not pleasing to God, and for what they've done to hurt us. It is tough when the hurt is so deep and time has built walls of isolation. We must pray for strength to say no to temptations and for deliverance from evil; His Kingdom is ours forever and ever. Jesus hears and honors our prayers when spoken from hearts that are in tune with Him. We don't impress people or our Lord with prayers that seek any outcome other than pleasing God and giving glory and honor to Him. It's not how long, how loud, even how beautiful and dignified our prayers are that matters. It is our willingness to open our hearts and pray real prayers that He hears and honors. They may be short—even silent in some situations—but they get the job done when they are spoken in the right spirit.

Do you stop during the day to pray—not just pause while waiting in line or at a stoplight? During a recent Bible Study at Tim's Gift, Elanor Bradshaw shared how her trip to Turkey enlightened her views on praying. She told how five times a day Muslims were called to pray, of seeing prayer rugs wherever they went, of thinking what would happen in our country if all Christians consciously stopped five times each day to pray. Instead, it seems that those against prayer or any Christian witness will not give up. Decisions by people in power demand taking down nativity scenes on town square lawns, Ten

Commandments on the walls of our government buildings, anyplace where someone complains, corporate businesses embracing Happy Holidays instead of Merry Christmas, companies compromising in order to please those who don't believe, our children being denied the freedom to pray in school, and the list is growing as the enemy smiles for a while, but he won't win. God will have victory in the end.

How will our end unfold in our land? Will we flash back in sorrow or smile through the storm knowing God is our personal Savior? Reckoning day is coming. Many will understand the power of prayer and the joy of stopping and communing with our Father. The words to "We Can Pray" will finally be heard in our hearts.

I pray that this story brings you closer to Christ. May you accept this challenge to stop and pray, to keep your promises, and to be passionate about your love for the Lord and your loved ones.

Giving is Great

*D*O YOU PUT YOUR VALUE in the wrong things? Tough times teach lessons that things really are not what matters most in life. The truth is that you get satisfaction from offering others what you have to give—your time, concern, even storytelling. You get respect by offering something that you have. There are lonely people who long to know that someone cares and will come to where they are—hospitals, nursing homes, jails, even the workplace. Devote yourself to loving others. Show people that you truly care about them and their situations. Take a look at where you are placing your values. Is there time in busy schedules for giving to God and to others? God gives gifts graciously. Joy comes when we share what we are given in a spirit of love.

While typing this story, several young faces of students at the Learning Station popped into my mind. Every Tuesday afternoon, I took my older students to Mary Gran to share our time and talents. Isaac Cortez and Spencer Tart loved playing chess and begged to share their gift—instead of singing and dancing. We should encourage people to share their gifts and not force what we think they should do. Visions of them hurrying down the nursing home halls with chessboard in hand still dance in my head. The excited faces of those little boys and old men sharing games of chess, laughing together, challenging one another, and respecting who they were and where they were in life helped me see the beauty of loving and learning. This is how Jesus taught—sharing lessons that touched lives then and now.

Today, those boys are grown and gone, but not far from my heart and the hearts of those they touched . . . here or in heaven. I cherish tender times more with each passing year. This past Christmas, our students brought packages of socks and placed them under our tree. We prayed over the socks, asking God to bless those who would receive them. Each week, we took students to local nursing homes for prayer walks. They gave the residents socks to keep their feet warm and prayers to lift their spirits. Students prayed that God would direct them to those in need of a blessing. We always came back with bigger blessings than we had given. Taking time to share our time is more important that we realize. Finding excuses to dismiss ourselves from offering others what we have to give is easy. But we miss so much! Why have we become so success-driven and selfish in our attempts to find happiness? Without warning, we can become burdened with getting to the next level, passing the test, climbing higher to the top. When we get there, we've often overlooked life's greatest lessons and treasures in our quest for success. When we do things from the heart, happiness follows!

Happiness comes when we care and connect with our Father, family, and friends, and go beyond our comfort to forgive our enemies and befriend strangers, for we could be entertaining strangers unaware. Our community is founded and firm in the fabric of faith and family that keeps us connected. If you're feeling down and depressed, wondering how you will cope with the season of life where you are, there is help and hope when you look to Jesus. Then, get up and get out, become a doer of His Word.

The perfect place to boost your faith and build relationships with people is attending Relay for Life events. Become involved; walk in faith. Meet and mingle. See how awesome God is and the good things He is doing among us. Watch as neighbors and friends pull together and see the fruit of their labor. Watch flames burn in memory and in honor of those loved and looked after by those walking the track and working the event. See bags filled with sand and put in place by people who care. Listen to songs and testimonies from those whose lives have been touched by cancer. Enjoy the food and fellowship of a community of believers. Come close to the Lord as the night sky is lit up with hope. There is joy in our hearts when we commune with our Father, family, and friends in the Spirit He sends. Let sunshine keep you smiling through all seasons.

Do you wonder what family and friends will remember about you when you die or what will happen with your things when you leave this world? Are you afraid to die? Are you ready to die? The theme of this story is one we tend to avoid while life is sunny. When storms send rain and death knocks, we wonder why we didn't spend more time sharing love, laughter, and longing to be close to God and those He gave us to share our lives with. Sadly, many people learn lessons of loving, living for Jesus, and that the most important things in life aren't things . . . when it's too late. Think on these things; make changes that will enrich your life here and reserve your place in heaven.

Share a Tuesday with Someone You Love

*H*AVE YOU EVER HAD A teacher, grandparent, or colleague teach you lessons about life that changed you forever? Teaching is my passion; my students are treasures I cherish more with age—remembering them but not their names. Teaching lessons about valuing life-cherishing love-building character is as important to me as mastering curriculum. I hope that at least one student will remember me as Mitch Albom does his college professor, Morrie Schwartz.

Morrie understood his students; they loved his witty personality and fun attitude. He expected excellence, taking time to teach much more than his subject matter. Mitch adored his teacher who took time from his busy schedule every Tuesday to mentor his student, give him advice about life, and be his friend. Twenty years after college, Mitch rediscovered Morrie in the last months of the older man's life. Morrie knew something was wrong with him long before his doctor ask him and his wife to sit down for the news. I believe we all know when something isn't right with our bodies, especially with our souls. We are given signs that often we ignore. Two weeks before Tim and I sat to hear heartbreaking words from his doctor, I watched Tim sleeping on the couch and felt a sweeping sensation weaken my body. A feeling I can't explain, almost like a warning, a rush of emotions that told me Tim wasn't okay. The same thing happened to me when cancer invaded my body. I believe God sends angels to make us aware—yet, we are so unaware.

Morrie's deadly disease was ALS. It melts your nerves and turns your body into a pile of wax. The doctor's life sentence was five years; Morrie knew it was less. Determined to die with dignity, he decided he wouldn't just wither up and disappear, but he would make the best of the time he had left. Many of you reading this understand that we shouldn't wait to make a bucket list. Enjoy every day . . . prioritize, prepare, play. Knowing he was dying, Morrie spent time with Mitch in his home study on Tuesdays, just as they had during college. Their rekindled relationship turned into one final class: lessons on how to live. Morrie knew his disease would slowly eat him alive, but he wouldn't be ashamed to die. He made death his final project; the world could watch what happened and learn with him. His gift to Mitch was thirteen Tuesdays with Morrie. The last class of Morrie's life took place in his house; the subject was the meaning of life—it was taught from experience.

The lessons in this book taught me things I have taken for granted, things that make life meaningful, things Tim and I learned together. For months, this book seemed to stare at me from my bookshelf while I pecked away at my computer. The same sensation, stirring in my heart, prompted me to write a story about *Tuesdays with Morrie*. Finally, I listened and struggled to share what God would have me write. I pray that the parts I pull from this awesome book will bless you, teach you something that will make a difference in your life, or bring you closer to those you love—and those you don't know. I've read this book twice. The first time it was just another book—but our lives were sunny side up then. The last time it was a masterpiece—hitting home and helping heal my broken heart. My pastor used this book in preaching Tim's funeral. He shared Wednesdays with Tim: prayer, laughter, and lessons of love and longsuffering—another story for another Friday.

Morrie lessons can benefit all of us, especially when we wonder what in the world is going on—and what is important in the great scheme of things. Morrie had much to teach in those thirteen weeks. Morrie talked of how his suffering caused him to feel closer to people throughout the world who were suffering. He said the disease was teaching him that the most important thing in life is to learn to give out love and let it come in. Jesus taught the importance of love when He told us to love neighbors as yourself and do all things in love. If you have the whole world and do great and glorious things but do not do them in love—they mean nothing to the Father. God is love.

The second Tuesday, Morrie talked about being pitiful and feeling sorry for yourself in the midst of your sufferings. He encouraged dealing openly with angry, hostile feelings, but never stewing in self-pity. How easy it is to be pitiful and think the world should stop when we're suffering, dying, and dealing with dreaded things. It's our choice to go on with life or wither away miserably, refusing to accept, adjust, and allow God to help us get through our storms.

The third Tuesday, Morrie reflected on the sadness of putting our emphasis on getting things instead of preserving relationships. He told how people get wrapped up in egotistical things—new cars, money, career, family—trillions of little acts that keep us so busy. He encouraged standing back and asking if something is missing in our lives.

A popular country song made us all stop and think about skydiving, dancing, and doing things before we die. What I learned from this is an appreciation for teachers who care and make us think about what's important in life. We need teachers in our lives. Henry Adams said, "A teacher affects eternity; he can never tell where his influence stops." We should live closely connected to God and those we love—Jesus is our way to happiness forever and ever in heaven.

Mitch asked Morrie if he worried about being forgotten after he died. He told him that many people had been involved with his life in close, intimate ways. Love is how you stay alive—even after you are gone. "You will not forget me after I'm gone, think of my voice and I'll be there." When we live our lives in love—cherishing those who share life with us, networking, never leaving out the One who loves us most, who gave us life—we should have no fear of being forgotten. Love will keep us together—even when we're apart.

Morrie had good and bad days during his sickness. Understanding the beauty of a good day when one you love endures mostly bad days takes going through the process instead of viewing it from the outside. When we experience storms of sickness, sadness, and other situations that drain life from us, having family and friends near us, with us, beside us means the most.

Why not have your own session with someone you love? Everyone has a loved one you can't imagine losing, someone who may appear healthy and happy but is dying on the inside, someone who would love to spend a Tuesday with you!

Living to Die

*D*O YOU TAKE TIME TO talk with people you love or think about what is important in their life? Sharing lessons about life from *Tuesdays with Morrie* is most humbling. Morrie loved life, dancing, and doing daring projects with his students, cherished family and friends. He made sure that they were the focus when together, exercised his body and mind regularly, and honored His Father—even before Lou Gehrig's disease took control. When he became sick, the disease made him a prisoner inside his body, forcing him to give up daily functions and activities we often grumble and gripe about. Morrie's daily declaration of what meant the most to him, before and during his sickness, was having family and friends to share the journey with. Being close to those you love is something we must work at and never take for granted. Cherish each day you are given when your body works, your mind is intact, your heart believes and beats, and you have something to contribute. You can get up and get out; your family and friends are your biggest cheerleaders. Many people dream of having these simple, yet sensational gifts to enjoy every single day. Let us never be guilty of overlooking their importance. Be thankful. Enjoy the journey!

Death was the topic Mitch dreaded discussing, but Morrie handled it with dignity. "Everyone knows they're going to die, but nobody believes it. If we did, we would do things differently. So, we kid ourselves about death. A better approach: to know you're going to die, and to be prepared for it at any time. That way you can actually be more involved in your life while you're living—once you learn how to die, you learn how to live."

He encouraged Mitch to be more spiritual and less ambitious. "I know we are spiritually deficient. We are too involved in materialistic things, and they don't satisfy us. The loving relationships we have, the universe around us, we take these things for granted."

Morrie said he didn't think much about dying before he got sick. We know we are going to die one day but do not spend time thinking about it really happening. Mitch asked why it's so hard to think about dying.

Morrie talked about people going through life as if they are sleepwalking. Tim and I enjoyed every season of our lives together—even those terrible two years when the kids drove us bananas. Only weeks before he died, Tim talked of memories when our sons would wear footed pajamas and run around the house like superheroes. Those are the things you remember and hold dear to your heart. I wiped many tears from Tim's eyes as he talked about the fun times we shared with our sons. He wanted to live but was preparing to die. Living to die is what Morrie taught his student about. All of us should learn that lesson well.

Most of us realize too late that we take precious blessings for granted. The simple things are among our greatest treasures, like a walk on the beach or a day at the park. Enjoying a rainy day cuddled up on the couch with the one you love is priceless. Those are the things we think about when our time together grows short.

On their fifth Tuesday together, the topic was family. "There is no foundation, no secure ground, upon which people may stand today if it isn't the family. It's become quite clear to me as I've been sick. If you don't have the love and support and caring and concern that you get from a family, you don't have much at all.

Morrie realized the value of a family to share the good and bad times with. He told how hard it would be dealing with his sickness if he had no one to go through the daily journey with him. It's wonderful having friends and acquaintances, but having family by your side is a gift that should be cherished.

My husband and I shared a journey that brought us closer together but separated us in the end. We battled cancer for nineteen months. He bravely fought brain cancer. I stuck by him like glue to paper; nothing could take me away from my guy. Yet, the deadly disease that strikes every home at one time or another took Tim away from us in April 2007. As we talked one spring morning, weeks before he lost his voice, Tim shared words about our life similar to what Morrie told

Mitch. Tim talked about the times when we had so little but were so rich. We had fun together, sharing time and making memories. He remembered the little things, the small acts of love that meant the world to him, like rubbing his feet and waiting for him to get home to eat dinner. We recalled the romantic weekends he would surprise me with. We kept faith, fun, and family, romance and real life adventures roaring all our years together.

Morrie's words took me to the afternoon I sat in my doctor's office only two months after Tim died. There was no one to hold my hand when he gave me bad news. My mind fast forwarded to what might be in store for me and my family, with flashbacks of where we'd been! After a long, numb walk to my car, beating on my steering wheel with tears flowing and prayers pleading, I knew I must get myself together, go tell my family, and pull out of the pit where the enemy longed to imprison and destroy me. God blessed me with family and friends to help, but it was God who kept me company when the nights were long and my days uncertain.

Many of you are battling tough times, but they won't last forever. In His time, He works out all things for those who love the Lord. Praise God for your family, your friends, and your Father. You are not alone. Joy comes in the morning for those who wait on the Lord and stand firm. It may feel like waves of despair will crash your happiness and destroy your life. James 4 reminds us to submit to our Father, resist the devil, and to come near to God. He will come near to you. Nothing in the world can compare to being closely connected to Christ.

The sixth Tuesday, Morrie taught a lesson about emotions. This chapter so intrigued me that I read it over and over again. Morrie told how you must detach yourself from the experience. This is important—not just for someone dying, but for someone who is perfectly healthy. When we can detach ourselves, it is much easier when we must leave. We should not hold back our emotions; experience them so that we have no regrets. By throwing yourself into these emotions all the way, you experience them fully and completely. You know what pain is. You know what love is. You know what grief is. When we fully experience these emotions, it helps us move forward to new seasons. This helps us learn to live and to die.

That is a lesson we would all be wise to learn. We let others tell us what is right to do in given situations. Men aren't supposed to cry or we shouldn't share the surge of love we feel for one we love for fear of what our words might do to our relationship. Fear can keep us locked up and left out. When we let it inside us and realize it is just fear, we can conquer that fear. We can truly experience love—and death.

Morrie began coughing uncontrollably, but his friend helped him through the frightening time. Morrie told Mitch he wanted to die—peacefully, not to leave the world in a state of fright. He wanted to know what was happening, accept it, get to a peaceful place, and let go. What a gift when those we love leave this world peacefully—no matter how much it hurts to see them go. Knowing their eternity is secure in heaven gives us peace.

Do you have peace today? If not, heed words from the Good Book and don't let the sun set on any anger—on anything that keeps you from the Father and the ones He gave you to love on this earth. Ask Him to help you, to come into your heart, to cleanse and cure what keeps you in bondage. Be all you can be for Christ, remembering the most important things in life aren't things.

Are you aging with grace or grumbling? I remember when the age I am now seemed so old! Not anymore. I'm thankful to have over half a century under my belt, believing the best is yet to come. It's the spirit in which we age that makes us beautiful in His sight.

Morrie's seventh Tuesday was centered on aging. How do we live? Being over the hill has overlooked benefits and blessings. Age shouldn't consume us; I'm actually proud to order my senior citizen cup of coffee. Morrie's endearing words teach truth to young and old. He talked of caring, sharing, and allowing ourselves to go through experiences—not just endure them. He reminded us that aging is not decay but growth. Enjoying every season of our lives is wise.

Do we long to be someone we're not, live in the past, or propel our lives into the future? Let these words from a wise old man settle in your heart and help you see the beauty of life at any age.

Some people age angrily, becoming bitter and grumpy. We miss many blessings when this happens. It is much better when we accept each season as we age and remember with joy what we used to do—not resent it. Every age is special and gives joy as we grow old.

Do we truly understand the contentment and creativity we possess when we enjoy each season of our lives? Age doesn't matter; how we live at any age makes people recognize our happiness.

Think of someone who may need words of encouragement, someone unhappy with their life—or their age. Share a little love with them. Think of yourself. Are you happy, being all you can be, enjoying life? Do you understand and appreciate God's gifts at each season of your life? Are you living to die?

Love Keeps You Alive

*D*O YOU EVER THINK ABOUT being forgotten after you die? Morrie told Mitch that he didn't worry about being forgotten. His family and many friends kept him loved and lifted. He went on to say that love is how you stay alive—even after you are gone. When we feel we might be forgotten, we can think of the voice of someone you love when you are all alone and they'll be there. And if you want to cry a little, that is okay.

Tears of tender memories can light up dark, lonely nights and bring cheer to cloudy days. Sharing our love is the gift that keeps us in the hearts of those our lives have touched here—when our Father welcomes us home. Don't be stingy; put a lot of love in your heart and pass it on.

Morrie thought being fully present was important. When you are with someone, focus on them. Learning to pay attention was a lesson every student of his mastered by his own example.

"Part of the problem is that everyone is in such a hurry. People haven't found meaning in their lives, so they're running all the time looking for it. They think the next car, house, car—then they find those things are empty, too, and they keep running. Instead of being rushed in all you do, put your energies into people. Really listen to someone without trying to sell them something, pick them up, recruit them, or get some kind of status in return—how often do we get this anymore?"

Morrie's father's sudden death helped prepare him for his own. He wanted lots of holding and kissing and talking and laughter and no good-byes left unsaid—all the things he had missed with his mother and father. Morrie wanted his loved ones around him. Death is something we prefer not to talk about or think about. Yet, it's something that we all must do; how we handle it really will affect our loved ones. This is a very personal issue that should be honored in the way one chooses when their time comes—if given that opportunity. Many leave this world in the twinkle of an eye—with no time to make things right in their hearts or with those they love. What better reason to share love every day and enjoy life to the fullest along the way. Focus on the things in life that are most important. Be ready—and leave the rest up to the Lord. He's got us all in the palm of His hands.

Morrie's last lesson was difficult to deliver. "Forgive yourself. Forgive others. Don't wait. Not everyone gets the time I'm getting. Not everyone is as lucky. I mourn my dwindling time, but I cherish the chance it gives me to make things right. Make peace with living. Death ends a life, not a relationship."

Death comes to each of us. While we wonder how will death come, we should first make sure our hearts are right with our Father, family, and friends. If there is any hatred, resentment, jealousy, or unforgiveness that is stuck inside, we must get it gone in order to enter the promised paradise.

One night, Cameron came upstairs and kneeled beside his father's chair. He talked about unforgiveness and how it keeps us from God's blessings and healing. He read from his Bible and prayed with us. When he went back downstairs to his family, Tim and I were touched that he would talk openly with us about a topic most friends—even family members—avoid. You know someone loves you when they bring such difficult things to your attention. We wrote the names of people we needed to forgive and prayed. We wrote letters and delivered them—hard as it was to do. When we take the first step to forgiving, God takes care of the rest. We take the load off our hearts and do what we know is right and good in His sight. What those we forgive do is between them and God. We must truly forgive and not just go through the motions. If you feel you just can't forgive someone—that what they've done to you or someone you love is beyond forgiveness—go to the Bible and read His words. He tells us to forgive seventy times seven. Please forgive before it's too late.

Mitch asked, "What if you had one perfect day healthy, what would you do?"

Morrie told him he would get up and exercise. Then, he'd eat breakfast, go for a walk, and listen to the sounds of nature all around, take time to talk with friends, spend some time with family at home, and finally go out to a favorite restaurant and enjoy a good meal and dancing with family and friends.

Mitch couldn't believe Morrie's choice for a perfect last day. It was so simple, so average. Then, he realized that was the whole point. We make what God meant to be simple and precious, complicated and perplexing.

Morrie died at home with his immediate family around him. His lessons teach us to embrace what really is most important in life.

Do you value the things in your life? If tomorrow were your last day on earth, what would you do today? Don't keep putting off what matters most—just do it! Live each and every moment crazy in love with the Lord, life, and your loved ones. No matter what season you are in, live out loud in love and give your heart to Him.

Staying in Shape

WHAT IS YOUR PRESCRIPTION FOR health? It's amazing what we'll try in hopes of retaining youth and health. You've heard stories that make your toenails curl of extremes some people encounter in order to keep wrinkles at bay and old age away. Getting old doesn't have to be a horrible thing. Many people don't age well because taking good care of body, mind, and spirit gets out of balance. We must work to stay in shape in all these areas.

Maintaining good habits is the secret to many successes we experience in life. To those who are growing older, there is no better advice than to acquire the habit of daily prayer and daily exercise. Daily is the key my friends. Most of us mean to do these good things daily but get bogged down and good intentions go down the drain. My neighbor is a shining example of doing it daily. She amazes me with her faithful exercise regime. She goes to bed early, rises early, is prayerful, and walks every single day—rain or shine. You'd think she'd miss a day here or there—not Annell. She understands that persistence in making these habits a part of her everyday routine is important.

The prophet Isaiah reminds us to have perfect peace we must stay close to God and trust Him. Trusting in God and worshipping Him in mind and action gives perfect peace. That peace replaces self-centeredness, which is the main cause of personal and social misery in our world today. When we "lift up our eyes unto the hills," we rise above such self-centeredness. When we keep ourselves grounded in prayer and spiritually strong, we benefit in many ways. This balance brings healing to the body as well as to the mind. With a well-disciplined body, we have freedom to develop our mind. A strong body gives us courage and self-confidence. It helps us and inspires others to regard us with respect. When we feel down and out and troubles seem to settle in our minds, we should get out our exercise mat or take a walk. When we really put prayer and daily exercise in place in our daily routines, we can shed tension that troubles us in today's tough times.

When we are closely connected to God, He sends His Holy Spirit to help us keep balance and brings blessings to our lives. The gentle stirring in one's heart, the tugging on your heartstrings, the idea popping in your mind, waking up with a thought or revelation that won't go away, warnings or bits of wisdom grounded in your gut, and unexplainable sensations that guide you are ways the Holy Spirit comes to those who believe. It is awesome how God guides when He lives in our hearts. He speaks, but do we listen? I remember when a sensation came over me driving down the road to call and schedule a doctor's appointment. There was such an urgency I couldn't explain, but I felt something wasn't right with my body. Weeks later, cancer was the news my doctor delivered, saying the outcome could have been deadly had I waited. Some things aren't meant to be explained, but the glory should be given to God.

While growing old is something we all face, we are wise to live out loud and enjoy our journey. Getting old can be weary or wonderful. I chose wonderful; what about you?

When we learn to live with ourselves—being friends with God and people—we find peace in the balance that brings blessings. Work and love can make life easy in old age as in youth. If we learn it when we are young, we will surely know it as we age. Daily exercise can help keep our bodies fit. Daily prayer and staying closely connected to God gives us peace and ease as we face each day of our journey. Devotion to those we love makes us feel loved and wanted. A little sailor sits on a wicker chair in my sunroom. A meaningful message has been sewn into her skirt. Each time I pass by, I am encouraged to grow old gracefully and triumphantly. *Someone will grow old with you and me—and it's true that the best is yet to be.*

God's Word gives reason to believe and be all we can be in any season of our lives. By living a balanced life with God in first place, we rise up above self-centeredness, develop a stronger, sweeter spirit, and live a richer, fuller life. When our time here is done, we will know where we are going and that we have been a faithful servant. What a glorious day it will be when He takes our hand and welcomes us home.

Lessons of the Heart

*D*ID YOU KNOW THERE ARE three great lessons of the heart that can help us prevail in this lifetime and head for eternity in heaven? James 4:14 says, "We are not promised tomorrow. We are but a mist that appears for a little while and then disappears." When I disappear, I'm counting on heading to heaven; how about you?

Lessons of the heart center on head knowledge. This involves things we've known a long time, but they didn't matter so much. One lesson we learned at an early age: sin is ugly. Sin doesn't just affect the sinner. Oh, the heartache families and friends have endured when those they love sizzle in sin. Those little sins seem so helpless until they root inside and rule our lives. Sin sickens and sucks the life from anyone and everyone with no remorse or regard for the damage it does to its victims.

Sin slips in so innocently and slaps defeat in the faces of those who take the bait from the enemy. Temptation works! We hear a little voice inside our heads saying, "It's okay to do this or that," or "Ignore doing this or that." We must realize that little voice says exactly what we want to hear.

The devil is a master of deception. He seeks to steal, kill, and destroy—and will do anything to make us captive to sin. We have to hear another voice that says, "The wages of sin is death." Would we ever knowingly get involved in little sinful acts that would eventually steal our health, loved ones, our sweet relationship with God, our jobs, or our peace of mind? Can we fathom anyone in his or her right mind getting hooked on sin that would kill, destroy, and rob one of eternity in heaven? Sinning is serious business that ends up ugly every time we dabble in it. Dip down a little deeper, dive in head first, and eventually you will drown in it.

If the devil tramped around tempting us in the little red suit with pitchfork in hand, we could easily recognize and resist the rascal. I think of movies where the devil is portrayed in many forms—from a beautiful woman to someone in our past we know and trust. But as the movie ends, the devil rears his ugly head and we see the monster he really is.

Learning to discern and stay away from sin will keep us lifted from the pit and protected from the enemy. James 4 says, "Resist the devil and he will flee from you." We see how sin is suffocating our world. Don't be deceived by the devil. He has no power over us when we don't allow him inside our hearts and heads. Stand strong and resist temptation. The victory will be sweet and everlasting.

Another lesson of the heart is human choice. Our choices can bring good or evil into the world. Choices we make determine if we have joy or pain, life or death; it's up to us. Tough times shove this lesson into our hearts. Many people reject God. In Philippians 3:19, we are told how their end is destruction. We make the choices in life, and every choice has consequences. Heaven is the homeland that awaits those who believe and live life connected to the vine. These words give all the comfort needed to carry us through the tough times we face today. We can't count on tomorrow, but we can count on Him and heaven!

Jesus gave good advice about making choices. In Matthew 7:13-14, we are told of the narrow road that leads to heaven and the wide road of sin that takes one to hell. We wander life's road leisurely as if we have all the time in the world to get our lives in order and make things right with our Maker. What is difficult to understand is that we must be pure in heart to enter that narrow gate. When we stand before God, if there is any unforgiveness or sin in our hearts, we will not enter heaven! Strive to keep tender hearts that beat in tune to our Father and His will for our lives. It's so easy to make bad choices. Sometimes we are thinking only of ourselves when we make choices. Our choice matters as we choose life or death, giving or taking, joy or pain, being together or alone. When we recognize the ugliness of sin and choose the road to *life*, it will be marked with sturdy signs of our Christian *hope*. Pray about the choices you make. Keep God first and let Him guide you in all things. When we walk with Him and talk with Him, He will tell us we are His own and will give us grit and guts to make the right choices.

Finally, the lesson of the heart that we all cling to is *hope*. Romans 6:23 says, "The gift of God is eternal life through Jesus Christ our Lord."

John 14:2-4 shares this hope. "Let not your heart be troubled. You are trusting God, now trust in me. There are many homes up there where my Father lives, and I am going to prepare them for your coming. When everything is ready, then I will come and get you, so that you can always be with me where I am. If this weren't so, I would tell you. And you know where I am going and how to get there."

Thomas told Jesus he had no idea where he was going or how he could know the way. Jesus told him He was the way, the truth, and the life. He shared that the only way to God was through His Son.

Jesus tells his disciples to be happy for Him for He is going away to the Father who is greater than He is. The last verses of John 14 give the greatest lessons of the heart. "I don't have much more time to talk to you, for the evil prince of this world approaches. He has no power over me, but I will freely do what the Father requires of me so that the world will know that I love the Father."

Our head knowledge greatly affects our hearts. Let us stay away from sin, make good choices, and hold tightly to hope. May we triumph over evil, freely choose to trust and obey, and let our lights shine for Jesus!

Holding to Your Faith

*H*OW MANY TIMES HAVE YOU read the story of Job and wondered how he held onto his faith when he lost everything and everyone that he loved. It looked as if he had nothing to live for, but he persevered, embracing patience and purpose while creeping forward in faith. His friends questioned what he had done to make God angry, thinking Job had done something bad to deserve what God was doing to him.

How quickly we condemn his friends, but are we guilty of doing the same to people in our lives? I'm sure by the time the stories about poor Job circulated around town, most folks had condemned him much quicker than they prayed for or comforted him. In fact, they smeared his losses in his face with questions that suggested his faith in God was weak and his woes were his own fault.

You never know how your friends will react when you are treading troubled waters. Interestingly enough, the friends we didn't figure on being there usually surface first and foremost keeping us afloat. Often, our trusted and true mates don't stay the course and leave us treading water on our own. I will never forget the precious people who stayed by Tim's bed day and night. Neither will I forget the friends who followed God's lead by doing things for our family that carried us through the dark valley of sickness and death. Friends who stand by us through sunshine or rain are treasures. Galatians 6:2 says, "Bear one another's burdens and fulfill the law of Christ."

With the difficult days many of our friends are facing, we should remember these words and remain supportive and strong when troubles torment. Every day we hear of more plant closings, job losses, company collapses, and economic woes. When it comes close to home, we sit up and take notice. Many people who felt safe and secure are now jobless and jittery. Family and friends talk about the tough times and wonder what is happening. Everyone has an opinion, many offer solutions, others cringe in fear, but most people press forward praying that they can hold on and take care of their families and fortunes. We may not be rich and famous, but most of us are blessed beyond measure and have filled our barns through the years. How helpless we feel as we watch savings slip away and wonder what happened to that motto we lived and worked by all our lives: save for a rainy day! The rainy days are turning into monsoons for many people.

This determined spirit of Job presents popular theological views that God hands out blessings or curses in proportion to obedience to the law. How many good folks do you know who are having hard times now? Do you believe people are losing jobs, homes, health, and happiness because they did something bad and God is zapping them one by one? God created the world and the people. We are responsible for our decisions. God created us in His own image and one aspect of that is free choice. God created us with freedom and responsibility.

Romans 8:28 says, "God causes all things to work for the good to those who love God." Some people suggest that God is behind everything—planning it all. God is with us through the good and the bad. His amazing grace and unending love can bring goodness from the worst of things.

While we don't fully understand all that happens in life, we can rest assured that God is in charge. We will come out on top when we trust in Him and hold strong to our faith. The storms that are sweeping through our nation and world appear deadly and destructive. Evil is everywhere. God watches and waits for His people to stand and speak to these storms. One person might not make a difference, but one person standing strong and allowing their little light to shine just might ignite a spirit of power and passion that can stop the storms of destruction.

One strong spark here, one spark there, and soon we get a fire going. One Christian stands true to God's Word, another joins, and another, and soon the mighty people who love and serve the Lord will be a force to be reckoned with. My daughter-in-law, Angel, had a vision that all Christians on the East Coast stood together, bearing arms against the enemy. She said the East Coast tilted the United States and the West Coast swayed our way. We scratch our heads and wonder how these special interest groups got such power. They bond together and embrace persistence. Their voice is heard; they don't stop until they get what they want. Who says Christians can't do the same? The good Lord knows our fear of getting involved. *Let someone else do it. People will think I'm a fanatic. What about my safety if I stand up and speak out for my faith in God?* Well, what about our eternity when we stand before God and He asks why we backed down and didn't give our best?

Things may look hopeless for many, but giving up and losing hope and trust in God is not what our nation—and our people—need to do. Job felt hopeless, but he wrestled and worked through his trials and tribulations. God never left Job and spoke words of comfort and guidance to strengthen him.

Job's story ended with him living happily ever after. In fact, the Lord blessed Job at the end of his life more than at the beginning. Job's friends went back to see him and he prayed with them. When Job prayed for his friends, the Lord restored his wealth and happiness. God gave him twice as much as he had before! Then, all his brothers, sisters, and former friends feasted with him in his home, consoling him for all his sorrow, and comforting him because of all the trials he had been through. Job lived 140 more years. He died an old, old man—after living a good, long life.

Job's words give reason for us to hold on in our own storms. We may not understand and talk about things we know little about, but God does. He is ready and waiting to enter our hearts and bless us bigger than we can even imagine. One day we will rejoice and relish the things God has planned that are far too wonderful and are waiting for all who believe!

Great Gifts

*H*AVE YOU EVER THOUGHT ABOUT all the gifts you have given and received in your lifetime? Which gifts are most cherished? Giving gifts and receiving them brings joy when they are given and received in the spirit of love.

At an early age, my mother taught me the importance of giving gifts. She gave with such love and joy, teaching that giving gifts should never be a burden. Mother made it memorable—a happy time when giving others a bit of sunshine. Her lessons about shopping wisely and generosity taught me the thrill of a bargain, the joy of getting, and the rewards of giving.

Gifts received from my parents always came with a personal love note: *To our darling little girl, we love you, Mama and Daddy.* Daddy left the buying to mama. Ironically, the gift I cherish most was from my dad. He traveled to Betty Tew's Department Store in nearby Salemburg to buy his little girl a gift on her thirteenth birthday. I still remember the smile and proud look he wore as I tore into that package and found a pair of brown shoes. I do not know how I covered up my disappointment; they were the ugliest shoes I had ever seen. Yet, they were the first gift my daddy bought by himself to give his daughter. I was proud as a peacock when I hugged him and vowed I would always be his little girl. He taught me the value of gifts often overlooked, humility and perseverance, kindness and compassion, and bravery in the midst of life's battles. He lost both of his legs to diabetes but never complained and walked on prosthesis until the day he died. He is my hero. The price tag—$2.80—still dangles from the stiff shoes he gave me in 1965; those shoes still shine with beauty, reminding me of the great gifts often overlooked in life.

My husband and I loved giving gifts. Christmas was our favorite time of the year. Our second Christmas together brought a sweet memory when we traveled down a dirt path in search of Mr. Dub's little cabin. Our shiny red 280-Z was covered with dust as we drove through the fields headed for a dim light so far away from our world. I talked all the way, telling Tim memories of Mr. Dub. This man would walk two miles to our country store, drink a little Coca-Cola, have my daddy slice him a sliver of hoop cheese, talk with the farmers, and share stories with me about everything under the sun. I remember him being so different; his rough and rugged appearance and lifestyle disguised the beauty and blessings inside—which many missed. We overlook our greatest gifts when they are not wrapped in pretty packages.

Mr. Dub was startled to find friends bearing gifts to his house on Christmas Eve. He invited us into his humble home with only a fire in the small wood stove to provide warmth. He had no electricity, no Christmas tree, and no gifts. He was dressed in coveralls with tobacco juice clinging to the corners of his mouth. His one-room home was filled with heavenly hosts, reminding us of the love within the stable where the shepherds and Wise Men found baby Jesus. We shared our gifts with thankful hearts. I remember his happy grin and big hug; his attempts to postpone our leaving confirmed we had listened to our hearts. As we drove out of sight, Tim and I agreed that we had received more than we gave that Christmas Eve.

Our thirty-first Christmas together brought blessings as Tim battled cancer. His doctor confirmed that his cancer was in remission the first week of December. Our gift came early that year. Still, Tim was weak. We spent more time together at home—another gift that keeps on giving even though Tim is gone.

That Christmas, I was surrounded by piles of gifts ready to be wrapped. Tim was watching television—or so I thought. I talked to myself while placing gifts in stacks for family and friends, and put several things back inside my gift box to wait to be given at another time. Tim was watching me and listening. I looked up to see his smile that told how much he appreciated me taking care of gifts throughout our lifetime. His soft words touched my heart with a powerful message. He said, "I love to see you playing in your gifts and deciding who gets what, but don't put back things and wait to give them another time. Give them now because we don't know if they will be here next year."

Tim watched me do what I had done for a lifetime. I often had wondered if he ever really noticed or understood what a tremendous task it was. Every day is a gift God desires for us to enjoy and cherish. Life on earth does not last forever. Life is delicate and unpredictable, but two things are for sure—the fear of God and faith in God will stand. Whatever you are facing, we must continue to honor and trust God.

Solomon shares valuable lessons on living in Ecclesiastes. He tells us that when we have an opportunity to give and act in faith, we should do it. We should be generous and invest in acts of charity. He reminds us to be a blessing to others. He ends his warning in Ecclesiastes 11:1-2 with a reminder that this could be your last night.

Tim's words are reminders of joyful living and giving any season of the year. Remember to live each day to the fullest. Give those gifts you have stored up for another day, for that day may never come for you—or for those whom you plan to give gifts to. Cherish each day of every season—no matter how hectic or hurried they seem. Prioritize, plan less, and reduce stress that can steal the joy of the season. Relish each gift you receive; one day, you will truly treasure the things your loved ones have given. Remember that Jesus is the reason for the season. He is the greatest gift ever given or received.

The Power of Hope

*A*RE YOU FILLED WITH HOPE? When life looks bleak, leaving us to wonder what fate awaits us, our nation, and our world, we always have the anchor of hope to keep us grounded. Psalm 146 is a powerful reminder to put our hope in God.

Hope produces endurance and perseverance. How else can we explain what happens when our world is turned upside down due to sickness, sorrow, or separation? We have to hold to hope to withstand the storms.

My first mission trip was to Belize the year after my husband died. Ten days of working and witnessing in the small village brought blessings I never expected. My church family bonded as we blessed others. Then, we headed to Caye Caulker to spend a few days resting and enjoying this paradise before returning home.

I strolled the sandy beaches where vendors begged people to buy their wares. A bright blue shirt with hope in white letters fluttered in the wind above a man's table where he was busy bargaining. I introduced myself; we quickly bonded. We both shared a love for Relay for Life. He told how a group of young people from Canada had come to the island a few years earlier, introducing him to the concept and the power of hope. They gave Alberto one of their Relay for Life shirts. He was so touched and wondered how he could join the cause and help spread hope to others. He was confined to this tiny island where he had spent his lifetime watching beautiful sunsets while mastering his trade. Realizing that we can all make a difference, he faithfully hangs the shirt above his stand every day. He shares hope through talking with others. We talked about our lives, blessings, God's goodness, and how building relationships and helping others is more important than having and hoarding things of this world.

I carefully selected some of his original creations to take home to my loved ones. The opal necklace I chose for my mother-in-law looked wonderful but was weighty, like a burden around my neck. This necklace reminded me of how Satan works in our lives. He intrigues, lures, and leaves us without hope when we stumble into his sand traps of sin. The devil dresses up sin, making it look so inviting and lovely while deceiving and weighing us down with a heavy load that steals our joy and destroys our lives.

Sin becomes a burden that refuses to leave until we repent and rid our hearts of the heavy load. Alberto could not understand my choice of a simple necklace with tiny pearls and one simple, green gem centered near my heart. I knew this was the right one for my mother-in-law and no Belizean persuasion could change my mind.

That is the way it is with God's love—once we have experienced it. It is simple and satisfying. We are not heavily burdened or walking around with the weight of the world around our necks. He carries the load; He never leaves and loves us through it all.

Alberto bagged my jewelry and shook my hand. We felt the force of faith and hope swept our souls. The hot sun shimmered on the colorful, blue waters of the Caribbean. A cool breeze swayed the branches of the palms as we joined hands and prayed together in the sand. Spirit was in that beautiful place—and I knew it was the Spirit of the Lord.

I walked away with a good feeling inside. I felt like dancing in the sandy street like penguins do in *Happy Feet*. Then, the enemy tried to steal my joy by reminding me I was walking those foreign streets all alone. I was only one person whose voice would never be heard. I was foolish and feeble to believe I could share love and hope and encourage people to believe. The pit of pity opened wide, waiting for me to take the devil's bait. Every thought he planted made sense in the flesh, but I stomped my sandals in the sand and said, "Get behind me and leave me alone—flee from me for I belong to God."

I looked at the bracelet clinging to my wrist with the word hope glistening in the sun and thanked God for healing and hope. I softly sang a little song the schoolchildren had taught me earlier that week when I was their substitute teacher for the day. "Jesus on the telephone, tell me what you want, tell me what you want right now. Some want silver, some want gold, I want Jesus in my soul."

With sand in my shoes and a song in my heart, I asked God to keep His hand on me, to protect, bless, and enlarge my territory. While some may think that's a selfish prayer, old Jabez prayed it and received exactly what he asked for. When we do not ask, we do not receive.

Sharing God's love and encouraging people to cherish loved ones is what I want to do the rest of my life. God's peace pounded in my heart, my faith soared higher than the seagulls, hope anchored securely in my mind, and love flooded my soul. His Holy Spirit comforted and reminded me that we really can do all things through Christ. He knows the plans He has for us long before we see them unfolding miraculously before our eyes. Our hope is in Jesus Christ.

Someone called my name. I turned to see my church friends waving for me to come join them at the outside café where they had saved a spot for me. My friend, Sandra, brought an extra sweater to comfort me from the chill of the Caribbean night. Someone does care about me, I thought. The devil is a liar and looks for ways to discourage, downgrade, and depress anyone who falls into his trap of torment.

My friends and I feasted on red snapper and yellow fish, the catch of the day reeled in by the men in our mission group. It did not matter that others watched our celebration, our prayers before a delicious meal, or our sweet fellowship. We were closely connected to the Lord and those we love.

The enemy had been defeated; his lies did not weigh me down. People care. I am not alone. I will share His love and teach His Word wherever He leads. Whatever we face in this life, we always have hope when we trust in Jesus.

Who Do You Most Admire?

*C*HOOSING THE PERSON YOU MOST admire is a tough task. We think of family members, friends, and special folks who have made a difference in our lives. Many of us are admired by people and do not even know it. Why not take time to write to a person you admire and share why? What a wonderful gift to bestow on a special person who would remember your uplifting words forever.

In Belize, a school near our camp asked if I would teach for a day while the teacher was out of the village. My passion for teaching must have shown when I visited his classroom earlier that day. I told how I retired years ago, but still loved to teach and reach children. I heartily agreed to care for his class and met with the teacher after school. What a challenge awaited me!

The rectangular room had no air conditioning, two windows that opened with no screens, and forty students from age twelve to sixteen in the class. The teacher told me if I had not been able to come, the students would have been alone in the class because no teacher could be hired. I thought of American schools with no substitute teacher for a day. I had been devoted to my calling and profession for more than thirty years. I was amazed and wondered what awaited me. I walked the dirt path back to camp loaded down with textbooks and a desire to make a difference in those children's lives—even if we would share just one day.

The breakfast bell rang early. My mission friends met to eat and go our separate ways, helping people in this beautiful country. I walked to school with little children who tagged along and asked lots of questions. I carried a large bag of potato pancakes left over from our morning feast, remembering many children who had no food the day before. At mid-morning break, I opened the bag and offered them

Becky Spell

to my students. They ate every morsel and begged for more. I was reminded of the blessings we take for granted in my home country.

I learned more than I bargained for that day. I was amazed at their respect and reverence for doing a good job. They wrote essays about the person they most admired. My writing lesson encouraged them to share from their hearts as I had from mine. I told about my daddy, my hero, who I admired more than any person. I told how he would strap on his artificial legs and work in the garden and operate our store without a complaint—only a slight limp told others he walked in pain most of the time.

While they wrote, I walked and wondered what their papers would reveal. I stopped at each desk to meet each child and give them a message of love.

I walked back to camp with their essays safely tucked inside my bag. I promised to come back the next day with graded papers and a prize for the top three essays. The children were as excited as I was. I sat on our open porch and read papers until my eyes begged for a break. That night, I shared the writing with my friends. We all learned lessons that night about children and their families we were there to bless. We received greater blessings than expected as we read about people they admire.

A small, shy boy wrote about Bob Marley:

> I have met many people I respect, many of which I admire. I also admire many I haven't met. My admiration is equal for most of these people, but Bob Marley takes the cake.
>
> By my standards, Bob Marley was a very skilled artist. Many people immensely enjoy his music. It's a mix between reggae and jazz and appeals to lovers of both styles. His music is played and loved in many parts of the world. He has helped to lessen racism with many of his songs. I'm sure most people who have heard his music would agree with me. If there was a chart about people who helped stop racism, Bob Marley would be as high on the chart as Martin Luther King Junior.
>
> The other reason I admire Boy Marley is for his leadership skills. I think it is quite clever that he tells

> people to be peaceful and not discriminate against people of different races or people that have diseases or anyone for that matter. Many people followed his instructions and became peaceful.
>
> Some people say he is a stupid hippie, but that barely compares to the many that admire him. He is my most admired person who stands for equality and sings how we should all live together peacefully.

Max was as proud of his writing as I was of him when I handed him a certificate with my own words of inspiration for him. His writing sends a message for the entire world to hear and heed.

Another student wrote a paper that tugged at my heartstrings. He talked about his grandfather.

> The one I love the most is my grandfather. I admire him and love him. The reason I admire him is because he never gives up because he is always moving from place to place. Although he was blind, he never gave up. He has a stick that he said guides him to go where he wants. He made a wire from his house straight to the toilet. He made a path to the toilet and never gave up.
>
> He was helping out all the time. When he heard I was to wash my clothes, he would come and help me. When I have to cut firewood, he would always help me. He would always go with me outside at night to the toilet. When we would return, I always told him thanks. That's the reason he is always helping.
>
> He goes with me when I want to go in the bushes to get firewood. That's why he is so loving to me and my family. He passed away lately, but he is still full of love for and me for him. My grandfather is now an admired angel in heaven.

Another student, who took third place, touched my heart also.

> My dad is the one I admire. The reasons of admiring my dad are because he stopped drinking. The days before he stopped drinking were terrible. When we would ask for a dollar, he would not give it to us but would give it to his friends to buy rum. We could not eat while he was drinking because there was no money to buy food. Now that he changed his life, he doesn't do the same again. He does the opposite of the bad things that he was doing before. Now that he is with God, he promised that he will never leave the almighty One. My dad is still living and his gift is to carve slates and carve on wood. I admire my father for all the love he has for my family. I will admire him forever.

I asked my students if I could keep a copy of their writing and share when I went home. They were thrilled to think that their work was worthy of that. I thought of how their writing would be scored by those trained to score student writing back at home. These children wrote wonderfully and did not have to imagine or make up a prompt with make believe elaboration. They lived what they wrote. Their writing was real. I admired them and promised to share my admiration with people in America who would hear their words and be blessed too.

Many people wear crowns for being most admired in our lives. Why not write down a few reasons and send your sentiments to them today. Receiving an e-mail, a letter, a phone call, or even a short note could be the gift that makes someone feel like queen or king for the day. If you put it off, you may not get around to it until it is too late. Being admired by others gives plenty of reasons to be proud and pleased with the life you are living.

Things You Just Can't Do

*H*AVE YOU EVER THOUGHT ABOUT things you can't do? This message unfolded in my kitchen while preparing for Thanksgiving. Memories made in kitchens can sweeten spirits, strengthen family ties, and feed faith to keep us believing and being all we can be.

Memories keep us in touch with the past and link us to the future. Recalling precious memories made with love in my kitchen colors my world. The kitchen serves as the heartbeat of our homes, where we are nurtured and fed, where memories are made with love and happily shared.

I watch the changing of seasons from my kitchen window. My wilted begonias met their fate when an early frost came; brilliant mums take center stage as this is their season to flaunt. My pansies promise to stand me throughout the cold, dark days of winter. When winter gives way to springtime, new life will spring forth from my garden. Preparing for future seasons requires work and wisdom. Yet, every minute of toil brings triumph when the fruit of the harvest is at hand.

Often, I go to my garden alone to have a talk with Jesus and pull weeds from my flowers. There are times when I just kneel to pray and ponder. Listening to the wind chimes makes me smile. Tim gave them to me in a season when our health was good and our happiness was abundant. Sometimes, I declare they sing the sweetest songs when there is no wind stirring. They send a message of love and promise in tones and tunes unknown to our own ears. That's how it is with God's love. We don't understand things, can't figure out the grandeur and guidelines of the changing seasons, or are baffled by our own seasons of change and the promise of tomorrow. How awesome is the sacrificial love of a God who would allow His Son to die so that we might be saved? We live short lives here, worrying about things that will fade away, spending too little time planting and sowing seeds that will bring fruit of the spirit. We should strive to bring beauty and blessings to people's lives as my daffodils and tulips promise to do. We must plant love, joy, and hope that will survive the dark, cold winters of our lives.

One thing we just can't do is to neglect our Lord, failing to sow seeds of Christian love and expecting to reap a harvest and enjoy life everlasting with God. Serving Jesus through all our seasons gives memories of the past to treasure, the present to embrace with gratitude, and the future to face with faith.

This message of things you can't do became real as I searched old cookbooks for holiday recipes. I thumbed through a cookbook given to us as a wedding present in 1975. Smudges and dog-eared pages reminded me that no matter how old and outdated it appeared, this book was filled with recipes that stood the test of time. I thought of how God's Book never changes. The message is the same—past, present, and future.

Man often changes God's Word, but it always fails when we stray from His directions, just as my baking and cooking is a flop when I do not follow the recipe or try substituting what I think will work. We make a mess when we try to do it our way—and not God's way. The recipe for a happy home and peaceful life never fails when we follow instructions from the Good Book and prepare ourselves as directed by God.

One of my favorite cookbooks waited near the bottom of the stack. Opening it brought back memories of our wedding. This book was a gift from good friends who had hoped to help me become a better cook. I ran across the banana pudding recipe and thought of the time I had made it for a family reunion and forgot the bananas. Another page was covered with chocolate fingerprints and memories of Clint's thirteenth birthday. His choice of cooked fudge icing would be a piece of cake—or so I thought. Fifteen layers of cake covered my counters, waiting to be stacked and sealed with fudge icing. I stood over the stove, stirring and stirring and stirring my brew much longer than the recipe called for. Spreading the icing was nearly impossible, a prerequisite of troubles ahead. After a rousing "Happy Birthday to You," Clint tried to cut the first piece of cake for his dad. The knife could not break through the chocolate covering. Clint created a comical scene as he sawed and pounded and finally broke the chocolate force field that held the cake captive.

I wanted to cry but chose to laugh at my mess and enjoy making a memory that would be shared over and over through the years. When we make a mess of things, it's much better for us and everyone else when we face it with faith and forgiveness and move forward.

Turning the page, more chocolate smudges reminded me of the snow day in 1987 when the boys and I made a chocolate cake together while Daddy was at work. Perched on top of our butcher block counter, they took turns adding ingredients. Cameron stirred as Clint adjusted the speed of the mixer. Without warning, one of them raised the head of the mixer and chocolate icing covered my kitchen like snow on the ground.

My chocolate-covered sons wiped the dark frosting from their faces and waited to see what their mother would do. I giggled and grabbed my camera to preserve the memory that would keep us laughing for years to come. Things you just can't do include going back in time to make precious memories with your family. How we handle our journey's jolts makes memories happy or horrible. What types of memories are tucked in the scrapbooks of our hearts? Will you look back to find happy or heartbreaking pictures of time shared with those you love when they are grown and gone? Enjoy your time together; let your children be children. Love and listen to them. Lift them in love and laughter and your memories will bring sunshine in your golden years. There is no substitution for your time and love to saturate their lives. Give graciously and generously to the Lord and your loved ones.

My favorite cookbook shares more than great recipes. On page nine, I found a message that begs to be shared with you about things you just can't do:

Sow bad seeds and reap good character.
Sow jealousy and hatred and reap love and friendship.
Sow deception and reap confidence.
Sow cowardice and reap courage.
Sow neglect of the Bible and reap a well-guided life.

Those words inspire sowing good things in order to reap a harvest pleasing to our Father. We just can't live in sin and expect to reap everlasting life. Between sausage balls and fried onion rings, I found another lesson on feasting and fasting that I had never taken the time to read. These words made me think deeply about my own life, as I hope you reflect on yours:

> Fast from criticism and feast on praise.
> Fast from self-pity and feast on praise.
> Fast from ill temper and feast on peace.
> Fast from jealousy and feast on humility.
> Fast from selfishness and feast on service.
> Fast from fear and feast on faith.

Take the challenge to fast from the things that distance us from the Father and feast on the fruit of the spirit. Taking time to read these bits of wisdom from an anonymous writer can change our views and remind us of the things we just can't do.

As I closed my cookbook and cleared my kitchen table, I thanked God for sending special days when we cooked up good things to eat and gathered together to ask His blessings and make memories with those we love. Searching through those cookbooks brought lessons that will linger much longer than the good food we enjoyed at Thanksgiving. Big helpings of living the good life filled my soul.

Let us sow seeds that will reap a harvest pleasing to our Father, cherish memories of the past, live each day in faith, look to the future with hope, and remember that there are some things we just can't do.

Traveling in the Right Direction

*D*O YOU BELIEVE YOU ARE traveling in the right direction in life? Most of us believe we are, but many are headed the wrong way. A recent road trip brought reality to this message. Often, God gives powerful signs, turns us around, and gets us back on the right track when we are headed in the wrong direction.

Leaving home with plenty of time before my noon appointment, I traveled the familiar highway, taking time to recall fond memories of people and places as I passed their homes and work sites. My happy heart was filled with hope and joy; Christmas was coming and my thoughts were happy.

Satisfaction filled my soul. My heart leaped with joy as I sang along with the Christmas CD for our church cantata. I turned on the road that would take me to my destination with nothing on my mind but that sweet Baby Jesus checking into the barn, into the world, into the lives of boys and girls, never been a baby quite like him, look who just checked in. I sang louder and played the drums on my steering wheel. The music filled my heart as I drove happily down the highway. The songs shared love and compassion, faith and fellowship, honor and glory for the One who came to set us free. I was having the time of my life when I noticed several large signs ahead. Slowing down, I read each of them with wonder. The first sign asked, "Do You Know Jesus?" Several yards on down the road a huge sign said, "Repent of Your Sins." The third sign proclaimed, "Jesus Christ Is Lord of All—Accept Jesus Today and Be Saved." The last sign read, "Are You Going to Heaven or Hell?"

I slowed down and was quiet, thinking how awesome it was that someone would take such a dynamic stand for Jesus. Surely, this bold testimony of God's love and lessons of salvation and eternity encouraged other people to slow down—and to think about their relationship with the Lord and where they were headed.

I talked softly to Jesus about heaven, praying the prayer that frequents my heart, *Lord I ask for your will in my life. I have so much I want to do here, write the newspaper column you birthed, write a book, write and teach Bible Studies, praise and worship, teach about the power of your love and healing power, and enjoy life as you intended. But Lord, when You are ready to take me home—I am sitting on Go.*

A sign that said Grantham was five miles away spelled trouble. *Lord, I'm on the wrong road, heading in the wrong direction, and running out of time for my appointment. I'll be late.*

I whirled my car around, trying to figure out exactly what happened. Not paying attention to where I was headed almost caused me to miss my destination. I changed directions and read the same signs again going the other direction. I pondered why this had happened. Humility hit hard as I promised the Lord to share the message He pointed out on my journey. I made it to my appointment in a nick of time.

Driving home, I did not sing at all. The signs kept popping up in my mind. God was speaking to my heart. The impressions wouldn't stop—even when I helped our kids complete homework and hurried home to Harley and a home filled with plenty of Christmas chores. I spent the evening searching for scriptures about direction.

Proverbs 4:10-14 tells us we have been taught the ways of wisdom and led in the right paths. Our steps will not be hindered and we will not stumble when we run.

Hebrews 12:12-13 says we should mark a straight, smooth path for our feet to follow.

My adventurous day left me exhausted. At three o'clock, I was awakened with the stirring to write. Pretending He wasn't nudging didn't work. The message was for me, but I believe many people might be bitten and blessed as I have been. Bitten with the realization that even believers are too busy doing things we think are right and good in the wrong spirit. We get caught up in our righteousness just as the Pharisees did. We think we are doing right, but we're off the straight and narrow, headed in the wrong direction without realizing it.

We should be bold in our witness like the person who made and displayed those signs, planting them by the roadside for all to see. We become busily burdened with duties and obligations, losing sight of the Spirit in which God expects us to operate. Pride puffs us up and steers us astray. God is pleased when we practice humility, enjoy our relationship with Him, and pay attention to where we are going. When we lose focus, it is easy to be distracted by things we believe are important and distance ourselves from the Lord and loved ones.

Finally, I faced the final sign again. Often, we get caught up in our goodness, working and doing and just believing we are on the right road. God says the road to heaven is straight and narrow. A camel can pass through the eye of a needle easier than a rich man can go to heaven. Surely, many people are headed in the wrong direction. God's grace is our assurance of acceptance.

While seeking the right ending for this story, I stumbled on writings Tim stored in a special folder. Reading his words added meaning to this message. Seeing my husband's handwriting stirred my heart. I thought of his love notes and cards that continue to bless and lift me on lonely days. Writing words of love to someone you care about will never grow cold—as long as you travel the right direction together. Tim's words kept us close in spirit—to one another and to the Lord. "If we could not be saved until we love God, we would never be saved. Realization of God's love for you first is important. Loving God comes naturally when we realize His love for us. Becoming a Christian is so easy that some people stumble over it and cannot realize the way."

Finding the way when facing storms or situations that threaten to steal our joy can be difficult. When one you love and shared your life with is no longer by your side, it is hard to find the way. God promises to stick by our side and show us the way. We must keep moving and remembering that God is a promise keeper. He lights the way and longs for us to follow Him.

If we would work and witness for the Lord as diligently as we work and worry about things of this world, the road to heaven would be heavily traveled. Do you know which direction you are headed?

Stop in the middle of the road you are on; make sure you are headed the right way. Accept Jesus, ask for forgiveness, repent of your sins, and rededicate your life to loving and serving Him in the right spirit. Turn around before it is too late and you arrive at the wrong place. I pray this message touches hearts as powerfully as it did mine. Are we gonna go to heaven? Maybe not today, but the day could come sooner than we might think.

Are You Listening?

*A*RE YOU LISTENING? ARE YOU sure you're listening? Anyone who attended First Baptist Church during the days when Bill Jones was pastor heard those words often. Pastor Jones would regularly insert this in the middle of a sermon. He needed assurance that we really were listening. I can see his sheepish smile and hear earnest pleas to make sure we were listening. He preached the Word with power and shared stories that showed the relevance of listening and looking to God in all things. Mr. Jones was ready to tell the Good News anywhere he went and pray with anyone in his path. He preached the gospel with gusto and yearned for people to listen and learn what matters most in this lifetime—having a personal relationship with Jesus.

Pastor Jones would look you in the eye and say, "Now, Spell, think about what Jesus would do. Don't worry about what they say. It's what Jesus thinks that counts. Just please Jesus." His messages are rooted in my heart.

Seasons of raising our sons in church are precious. Sunday mornings were special; Tim and I would perch on our special pew with our young sons seated between us. Most people have certain places where they regularly sit for worship. Heaven forbid if anyone takes those seats. Our spot was on the second row in the middle section. We heard powerful sermons and spent good times with our church family there.

Tim, Cameron, Clint, and I grew closer to one another and to the Lord in those seasons. We enjoyed seeing our sons draw pictures on the back of bulletins, beg for chewing gum from little old ladies, crawl under benches, wiggle and worry about when worship would be over, fall asleep in Daddy's lap, cuddle up to Mommy, and plunder through family pictures in my Bible, giggle and get in trouble for not listening, play pressing finger games during the prayer, and stand tall on the pew between two people crazy in love with the Lord, one another, and the two little boys He gave us, to sing the benediction. Those Sundays stand out in my mind vividly. Our sons walked the aisle, accepted Jesus, and were baptized as we watched with joy in our hearts. We knew they had been listening.

I treasure those times more than I did when they were happening. Isn't that the way it is? We fail to cherish moments that make the most profound memories. Looking back, it seemed that our lives would always be safe and secure from all alarm—as the words to the hymn we often sang promised. We are safe and secure when we keep our eyes on Jesus and make Him Lord of our lives, but things never stay the same as we grow and go through life.

Now I sit on that pew without my husband or my sons. We are still closely connected to the vine and to one another, but those days when we were so young and in love with two little boys depending on us for everything are gone. I still feel Tim's presence each Sunday and, on special occasions, my sons come home and sit with me during worship. I love those Sundays. Remembering a sermon Mr. Jones shared has helped me move into new seasons without clinging selfishly to the past. He told how someone needed to be rescued from a flood. God sent a boat, a helicopter, and something else (I must not have been listening) to help save the poor man. He refused help from any of them, saying he was waiting for God to rescue him. The man died in the flood and went to heaven. The first thing he did was inquire why God didn't save him. The good Lord told how He had tried three times—but the man refused help from people He had sent. How many times have we been this foolish? It may not have been a flood, but in seasons when storms hit hard, one thing after another seems to leave us wondering if we can survive. Our lives can change forever. The loss of a loved one, a home, or a job can kill our desire to live and look to the future. Listening to Jesus and trusting Him to send help is the way we work through these tough times. He can't do it all. We must listen and obey His voice within. And if we're not securely, sweetly connected to the vine, we cannot hear His voice. Surely, God looks on the rampant sin that has swept through our world and wonders if we are listening. When we listen, He speaks to our hearts and helps us see clearly through the clouds that bring rain and dampen our spirits. He is our sunshine!

God keeps us safe and secure when we put our trust in Him and use good common sense in living our lives. We make choices that pepper our lives with sweet, sensational seasons, trusting the Lord and enjoying our days, or sour, stale seasons when we refuse to budge from our set ways, stubborn mindsets, past mistakes, and heartaches. Abraham made many choices to move ahead and not linger in the past. He didn't know exactly where he was going or what he was doing, but He knew God did and would guide him. What faith! God is pleased when we listen and look ahead instead of overlooking the past and spoiling the present.

Romans 12 gives greater light on the power of listening—and being attentive to what God is revealing in our lives. We are told to be who God made us to be. He warns against allowing things of this world to take over and rule your life. While this sounds easy, most of us fall prey to worrying about what other people think and say. The ways of the world can lead to destruction. Romans 12 shows how we can quickly become victims of doing things the way the world thinks is right. A perfect example is praying in public places. One lady changed the way the world thinks about praying in schools. She stood up and won a fight that never should have gone her way. Hindsight slaps our hand and says you should have been paying attention when that law slipped through the courts.

We should all be paying close attention to what is happening in our world, our nation, and our hometowns. The enemy is running rampant and ruining hearts and homes throughout the land. We can make a difference one voice, one vote, and one victory at a time. Standing up and speaking out in love is vital. Listening and responding in wisdom is necessary. Loving the Lord and rising up to meet challenges with Christian character is important. If we don't do these things, one day we will wonder if anyone was listening.

The Devil Will Get Caught

HAVE YOU EVER FELT THE devil closing in on you? Driving home from Topsail Beach early one morning, I had an encounter with a black vehicle. This experience strengthened my faith while speeding down the interstate and listening to God nudge my heart. I use the term speeding loosely, but most of us do just that nearly every time we get behind the wheel. We go a little faster than the signs say and hope we don't get caught. One thing's for sure: if we keep speeding, there will come a reckoning day.

What joy knowing that the devil will get caught. He slyly sneaks around and tries to lure us into sin and shame. The devil wins many battles—evil lurks at every turn—but the Good Book promises his day is coming to be defeated, and Jesus will win!

I pulled onto Interstate 40 after a leisurely drive down Highway 210. With plenty of time to spare, I cruised at seventy miles per hour, singing along with my favorite tunes. Looking in my rearview mirror, I noticed a black vehicle clinging close to my bumper. The car pulled into the lane beside me, sticking by my side like glue to paper. I sped up, but so did he. I slowed down, but he did too. Then, the car pulled back into my lane and stayed on my bumper. Several miles down the interstate, he pulled in the right lane again and drove beside me. I glanced at his vehicle, but tinted windows hid the driver. I felt as if I was being teased or tempted to go a little faster to outrun him. The uncomfortable feeling didn't go away. I took the bait and pressed the accelerator closer to the floor. Speeding ahead of him was not the answer. He only went faster, passing me with a vengeance I felt in my spirit. Why was this happening to me? My favorite scripture, Psalm 46:10, teaches us to be still and know that He is God and He can take care of anything and everything that comes against us. Today,

I needed to slow down and let this black vehicle move on down the road.

Slowing down was wise. It gave me time to think of things that are lovely, not this black car that wouldn't slow down or stop tailing me. I just wanted him to go away. That's the way it is with the enemy. He just won't leave us alone, sticking right beside us, staying close on our bumper, tempting us to race through life, to bail out on Jesus and miss our blessings. He does not care about our well-being. He loves it when we fall into his trap of sin and ruin our lives. Stealing, killing, and destroying are his trademarks. The enemy pretends to be a friend but will destroy each and everyone who follows him in the end. Slow down and let him pass on by. Don't get caught dealing with the devil.

God spoke to my heart as I drove much slower, actually the speed limit, and slipped in a CD that sent me straight to praise mode. I drove and sang, talked to myself about all the good things going on, and I was enjoying my drive. Then, the message was downloaded. His voice said, "Don't play with the enemy or you will get caught. He may pass you by and tempt you, but he will get the ticket. He will be stopped. Don't try to keep up with him. You will be okay. You will pass him by and know that I am God."

I laughed at the thoughts in my heart, but my head heard the message too. God was speaking to me. The idea of writing a story about my encounter kept stirring in me, but soon I was engaged in singing as one of our favorite songs filled the air. Clint made his dad and me a special CD when he moved to Colorado for a season. The songs playing brought back memories of a time I couldn't call back. Clint's words introduced the song I sang to Tim at his fiftieth birthday. Clint told me he loved me on the CD and the song began. *Love don't come no stronger than yours and mine, I believe in you; you believe in me, that makes us one of a kind.* I kept time to the music on my steering wheel with my little Kia rocking in the wind. Speeding down the highway happened again before I realized how fast I was going.

I spotted the black car farther down the interstate with two vehicles between us. We were approaching the mile marker that told me the exit where I would turn wasn't far away. I was almost home. My heart skipped a beat when I passed a patrolman under the bridge. Looking at my speedometer, I knew I had been caught. I was traveling down the road going seventy-five instead of seventy. When my foot came off the accelerator, my heart pleaded, "Please don't stop me. Please don't give me a ticket!"

The patrolman sat there for the longest time. I watched in my rearview mirror with a sick feeling in the pit of my stomach. Tim always cautioned me about going too fast. He knew the price we paid when the insurance bill came. I didn't slow down too much, not wanting to expose my guiltiness. I thought he would stop me for sure if I slowed to a pace that was slower than it should be on the interstate.

Then, I thought of what God teaches in His Word. We should be in perfect timing in our walk with the Lord, never getting ahead of Him or lagging behind. Today, I was guilty of both while driving the road home. What about the road of life? Do you race ahead of God with little regard to the blessings that pass you by? Do you lag behind what He is calling you to do, waiting and hoping someone else will do it and you can just fade into the background? It is neither wise to get ahead in go-go mode or to wag your tail and lag behind like a slowpoke! God knows the plans He has for us; His timing is perfect, and pleasure comes when we press on with Him leading in love and lighting our paths.

The patrolman's car slowly pulled onto the interstate and the chase began. I prepared myself to pull over and face the consequences, but favor was with me that morning. The patrol car pulled into the left lane and headed for the two vehicles in front of me. They traveled side by side and slowed down for fear they were victims of the flashing blue light. The black vehicle continued to speed ahead of all of us. He was almost out of sight. The patrolman continued trailing behind the two vehicles that blocked the road. I wondered what would happen next. Then, I remembered what God spoke to my heart when the black car teased and tempted me to speed right along with him. I did speed a little, and knew that a little sin is the same in God's eyes. I vowed not to speed again and continued watching the saga that was unfolding. Finally, one of the cars sped up enough to get into another lane—and the chase was on.

The patrolman played no games. The black car had been caught long before he knew it. The patrolman clocked his speed when he passed him by. It took a while to get past obstacles that blocked the way, but the patrolman didn't give up. He pressed on in pursuit of the black car. Finally, the car pulled to the side of the road. The patrolman stood near the car, waiting to proceed with consequences. I passed by with a prayer of thanksgiving that it wasn't me and one for the poor guy who got the ticket.

Exiting the interstate on a road that would take me home was a relief. Driving well under the speed limit on the last stretch to Clinton, I pondered in my heart what God wanted me to see and share.

First, I witnessed that He still speaks to His children. He plainly showed me what was going to happen on that drive home—before it happened. I actually saw myself driving by the black car and saying, "You got caught!"

Being close to Christ has great benefits. When He speaks and we listen, signs and wonders will unfold on our paths. I thanked God for showing me this lesson while driving down the interstate.

He pressed upon my heart that I was guilty too. I had played around with speeding and not wanting the black car to get ahead of me, but I had also backed off. I stopped trying to keep up with what I knew would eventually lead me to a ticket and troubles I didn't want. We are human, sinners by nature. God knows our hearts and motives. He sent His Son so that we can be saved from sin. Yet, He isn't pleased when we play around and dabble in sin. He forgives and wipes our slates clean when we confess and continue to love and serve Him. His message burned brightly in my heart—a little sin is a sin. Don't be like the Pharisees, pointing fingers at others, when there is a telephone pole in your own eye. When we sin—whether it is big or small—we will get caught sooner or later. We must press forward in faith, knowing we will sin. They may be small in our eyes, but our hearts should be cleaned, confessions shared, and lives closely connected to Jesus. He is a loving, forgiving God who keeps His promises.

Finally, we realize that God stands by His Word, keeps His promises, and wins in the end. The enemy may race ahead of us, ride our bumpers—teasing and tormenting—or stick beside us with temptations at every turn, but He cannot make us engage in sin. He has no power over us when we back off and stand on the promises of Christ. When we refuse to play with the devil, we won't be stopped and ticketed. We will rise up; we will win!

The enemy will lose; he will get caught. He will be defeated and God will reign as King of Kings and Lord of Lords forever and ever.

Do You Believe Joy is a Gift

*D*O YOU BELIEVE JOY IS a gift? John 15:11 explains that joy is a gift from God; He gives joy so our joy is complete. Are you joyful or joyless? Is your joy complete? How can we know if we're living and loving with joy? It's in our hearts, heaping helpings that fill our cups to overflowing.

Christmastime's splendor magnifies joy. Each person reading this story sings "Joy to the World" without missing a beat. The songwriter penned the words; God sent the gift. The words convey deep meaning. "Joy to the world, the Lord is come. Let earth receive her King. Let every heart, prepare him room, and heaven and nature sing. He rules the world with truth and grace, and makes the nations prove, the glories of His righteousness, and wonders of His love."

These words remind us that the Lord brought joy that first Christmas. Angels proclaimed joy from the heavens, shepherds from the fields, Wise Men from afar traveled to bring precious gifts and see this bundle of joy. Mary and Joseph's hearts were filled with joy when they welcomed the Christ Child in a lowly stable with smelly animals, itchy hay, and divine connections that would protect and guide them and the Son sent to save the world.

God desires for all His children to be filled with joy, but the choice to be joyful and jolly or pitiful and puny is ours. Mary and Joseph had plenty of reasons to plunge into pity. Being chastised by family and friends ready to stone her instead of standing by them surely stole joy from this couple chosen by God as earthly parents for His Son. Riding a donkey, with child, to a land far away from home was tiring, uncomfortable, and less than joyful. Imagine the pressure on this engaged couple as they faced one trial after another, trying to do what was right and good. Facing the first stages of labor didn't find them in a comfortable room. Instead, they settled down in a smelly stable to share the miraculous birth of Jesus Christ. They made choices that kept them in God's will, being obedient and offering their best even in the worst of times. His gift was the same then as it is today—joy! We face situations when we are forced to make decisions as Mary and Joseph did. It's our choice to follow what God speaks to our hearts—or to ignore and do as we please. Choosing to walk in faith, trusting and obeying, is pleasing to God and gives divine connection to blessings and protection.

John 15:10 explains that Jesus ties joy to obedience. 1 Thessalonians 5:16 says that we should always be joyful. If we don't choose to be joyful, we won't be. Philemon 4:4 reminds us to rejoice in the Lord. Colossians 1:10-12 encourages us to please the Lord in every way, bear fruit in every good work, grow in the knowledge of God, and joyfully give thanks to the Lord.

Decide and determine to be joyful. When we're full of God; we're full of joy.

Let your Christmas be full of joy. Keep God first in all things. Show Him that He is Lord of your life; share His love and joy wherever you go. Sing "Joy to the World" with renewed meaning. Stay closely connected to the Lord and your loved ones—and have yourself a merry little Christmas.

Do Not Wait Expedite

*H*OW DO YOU HANDLE WAITING? Waiting is something we deal with daily at stoplights, grocery stores, traffic delays, doctor appointments, and telephone calls—*hold please, press one for English, listen carefully, our menu has changed.* Waiting is difficult in our fast-paced world.

Watching people wait can be wretched. Some bite their nails, others bang their fists on steering wheels, some sing and talk to themselves, many move from one line to another in grocery stores, often choosing the shortest that takes the longest. Some people get angry and lose their grip, others nervously fidget, some scream and throw phones, others attack receptionists verbally, others grin and bear it, but most just take it in stride and wait their turn.

Synonyms for wait include abide, ambush, anticipate, delay, expect, foresee, hang, linger, rest, remain, stall, stay, tarry, and pray for. Pray for is one we need extra daily doses of in order to handle waiting. I know I did at a recent doctor's appointment.

I understand the significance of waiting in our society. It is understandable that we must wait when one looks at the trends of today's world. I do not mind waiting my turn, but don't you hate it when you feel you have waited long enough and nobody seems to care?

Waiting in a doctor's office can bring out the best and worst of those destined to wait. You enter with all intentions of waiting graciously, but lingering in crowded rooms with a sick loved one is torture. My husband, my son, and I waited at the huge hospital where cancer patients receive excellent care. Tim was not having a good day. Those whose lives have been touched by cancer understand good days and bad days. We settled down in a small room and waited to hear our name. Three hours later, we were still waiting. Tim was weak, I was furious, and Clint was the catalyst that helped us endure the long wait.

The receptionist grew tired of my appearance at her window. I begged and pleaded for them to see my husband. She urged us to get a bite to eat; our wait would be at least forty-five more minutes. Waiting took action on that spring morning; Tim could barely sit and no one seemed to care. He begged me to wait a little longer, but sometimes we must take action for our voice to be heard.

I left my husband and son in the waiting room and headed for the elevators. Of course, I had to wait. Finally, a door opened and I hit the L button. Waiting for the door to close irritated me even more. I felt the power of Rocky Balboa as I punched the button over and over. The door slowly closed; I was headed to find someone who would do something to help.

The large lobby was packed. I felt lost in a world where we hoped to find healing. Facing a little old lady at the admission's desk, I unraveled our miserable morning. She only smiled as my anger mounted. She answered her phone while I waited. I looked to the left of her work station to see a picture of Jesus staring at me. The picture brought peace. His eyes seemed to penetrate my heart. With tears flowing, I looked at that picture and told Jesus how much I loved him. She saw my tears; I felt her hands grip mine with a touch that assured me she knew Jesus too.

A phone call was made; my complaint was heard with a gentle spirit replacing the anger that had brewed inside my heart. The lady assured me that all patients are important and my concerns were appreciated.

Hanging up the phone, I waited to regain my composure before grabbing some food and heading back to the waiting room. Tim and Clint ate and enjoyed their time together. I reflected on my actions and silently prayed that something good would come of my emotional quest.

When Tim's name was called, I noticed a yellow card attached to the top of his folder. "Expedite" had been written in capital letters across the sheet. Instructions were specific: call this number when this patient is seen, document the time.

We waited twenty minutes for the doctor. The visit was a good one, giving Tim encouragement to keep fighting. The nurse apologized for the agonizing day we had experienced.

On our drive home, I replayed the day's events in my mind. Confrontation is not enjoyable, but sometimes it is necessary. It is important to wait, to think, and then speak up for our cause, our situation, and our belief in a manner that brings good change, not regrets.

Expedite popped in my mind like a bright sunshine rising on a new day. The canary colored writing impressed on my heart the necessity to expedite. Waiting is difficult when we want things to move along quickly and promptly in our lives.

Surely, God feels frustration as He waits for us—much longer than three hours! The day's events spoke powerfully to my own heart. Maybe we all need a similar message to remind us to speed up, to perform promptly, to be useful, and to realize that life is short and time waits for no one.

The lyrics to a favorite hymn softly played in my heart. *The Savior is waiting to enter your heart, why don't you let him come in?* I sang while Clint drove through afternoon traffic jams and took us home. I knew God had planted a story in my heart to share with the world. Do not wait—expedite!

Moving Forward

*H*AVE YOU VOWED NOT TO change things in your life? Change is hard. Often, it takes hard lessons to enforce change. God works in all things to teach and touch lives. What have you learned lately that has helped you move forward?

Preparing to leave Topsail Beach, Clint and I followed our routine of making sure everything was secured. I grabbed the key to lock the closet door in our bedroom. Holding the doorknob, I stared into the closet that held things close to my heart. Tim's favorite blue jeans hung on the end of the closet rod where he had placed them two years earlier. I touched his soft jeans and declared that I wouldn't change a thing in my closet. I walked away with a stirring in my spirit that Sunday afternoon.

The following Thursday, our neighbor called Clint with news that water was dripping underneath the house. Clint headed to Topsail. Hours later, he called with ironic news. The hot water heater had burst and water was everywhere. The hot water heater was in the back of my closet. The stirring in my heart brought a message to change my attitude toward holding onto the past; I hope it helps you too.

Watching our house being torn apart inside did the same thing inside my heart. The remodeling process taught me a lesson and took me to a place of brokenness. Early one morning before the workers arrived, I cried out to God with my frustrations, dreams, and desires. He knew it all anyway, but when that closet deep in my heart was unlocked, a cleansing power removed the stains of heartaches, hidden bits of unforgiveness, and uneasiness about moving forward. Stubbornness and sadness seeped out and set me free.

When the plumber arrived, I joined in the restoration by painting our bedroom with Clint. The plumber stopped to show me a new perspective on my painting. I skimped with the amount of paint on my roller. He explained how more paint would make my work easier and the covering more beautiful. We must keep our hearts filled with plenty of love and loyalty, honor and humbleness, happiness and hard work to ensure peace and promise in our relationship with the Lord.

While waiting for the sun to rise and the crew to come finish the last details, I write the ending to this story. I have worked alongside the crew that put my bedroom and closet back together again. I am thankful that God brought good from this bad thing.

My life has changed. I resisted opening my closet and showing how God cleaned up my mess; yet, He tugged and told me there are many people who need this same cleansing experience. Are you holding onto the past so tightly that you can't enjoy today and look forward to tomorrow? God can't bless us when we refuse to embrace change and allow Him to cleanse our hearts and clean up our messes as only He can do.

God has shown me that I never had control of that closet or anything else in my life—neither do you. We must accept change and move forward in faith. Our Heavenly Father is in charge and will keep us safe and secure when we put our trust in Him.

Tim's Gift

*T*IM'S GIFT IS A GIFT that God gave to me after my husband's death. This ministry is a means for us to give help and hope to people in need, a light in our community to draw people to prayer and Bible Study on Tuesdays, a place where children learn about and share the love of Jesus, where widows find comfort, hospice patients and families receive help, and God's love is shared as we grow the ministry and step in faith according to His will and way.

The ministry is about God's gifts—love being the greatest. Tim loved deeply and left a legacy that seeded this ministry of giving and loving in God's name. God gave another gift that helps explain the deep love that grounds this ministry.

One cold, December morning, my feelings were tangled as I plopped on a chair beside my bed. I stared in sadness. I was spending my first Christmas here without my husband; Tim was spending his first one in heaven. Beside my chair, a wooden box with lighthouses held treasures from our lifetime. A strong sensation compelled me to lift it to my lap and look through Tim's things. A red folder caught my attention. Tim's handwriting took me back to 1996 when he was chairman of deacons in our church. Tim had been the bearer of bad news the Sunday morning when our interim pastor passed away. We loved our pastor; this news broke our hearts as we arrived at church for worship. Tim was forced to write quick notes to share with a grieving church family. He loved our interim pastor deeply. Tim's words were from a hurting heart that knew we must hold to hope. I sat on the front pew beside Tim, holding his hand and praying as he stepped slowly to the pulpit. His healing words helped our congregation grasp the reins of hope.

Dr. Hayner's impact—few men in my lifetime had this impact—my dad, Mr. Jones, and Dr. Hayner. He taught us to "Do—Go—Be", that we are not made for mountaintops but for valleys—every day not just Sunday, but Monday through Sunday, going into the real world where people are lost and need to be saved, where people are hurting and need healing, where people weep and need tears dried. My friend, Jerry Hayner, always had the right words for children, elderly, sick ones, for every situation and circumstances. Self was secondary as he continued to work in his own sickness. He even had words for today—in the meantime. His ministry was one of action, teaching us to give and receive blessings. The church is to be in the world, where Jesus would be if He were still with us in the flesh. Our reason for being is to put people in touch with God. The church must seek—not wait. He taught us to have a strong prayer life, to seek God's will. It is hard to understand, but we must remember that God does not make mistakes.

I closed the folder and opened my heart to what God was stirring: a ministry of love. I prayed and praised God for all the gifts He so freely gives. My tears of joy told Jesus how happy I was that He had led me to Tim's gift this Christmas. There was a sweet spirit in my bedroom and in my heart; I knew it was the spirit of the Lord.

God never fails us, for He sent his Son, a gift of sacrificial love for all mankind. He reminds us we aren't made for mountaintops. We are to do, go, and be our best every day, to help those who are lost become saved, those hurting to receive healing, and those weeping to find peace and joy.

Tim's Gift Inc. is a not-for-profit 501C3. It was seeded by friends from The Prayer Connection, and Tim's Hospice nurse, Donna Reedy. They gave love offerings with prophetic words attached. God set the ministry in motion by nudging my heart to step in faith.

Tim's Gift was started in 2008. It is a place where people can come for comforting words of prayer. Our mission is to give help and hope to those in need, to help hospice patients and their families, and to put people in touch with God.

What joy He gives when we make every day a great one and seek mountaintops instead of wandering in the desert. At Tim's Gift, we are doing, going, and being our best every day. We are sharing the Good News and giving help and hope wherever He leads.

Treasuring Time Together

*T*IM'S GIFT IS A FAITH-BASED ministry where sharing the love of the Lord and giving help and hope to those in need is our mission. Every Tuesday, faithful prayer partners come for morning, noon, and evening prayer time.

One cold winter morning while waiting for prayer to begin, my Bible opened to a note scribbled on scratch paper. This note—written by Kurt Borum in memory of my husband, his brother-in-law—has a special spot in my heart and my Bible. This powerful testimony reminds us never to take one another, one single day, or one blessing from God for granted. Stay closely connected to one another and to God. He gives peace and promise. Love Him passionately.

Kurt's handwritten letter stays tucked in Tim's Bible. I am thankful that Kurt shared this special memory with me. I wonder what memories people will share when I am gone to be with Jesus. What memories will loved ones share about you when your work here is done and your time for eternity comes?

Every day we are given the gift of life and free will to make choices that touch tomorrow. Where will we spend eternity? What kind of memories are we making? Those are decisions we make each day. Every decision has consequences. Prayer and time to talk with the Lord keeps us closely connected. The morning I found Kurt's note, I had a little talk with Jesus.

Good morning, God. My family is extremely important to me; I desire for them to be happy and close to one another and to you Lord. I am so in love with you and thankful that you hold my hand as I step in faith for the plans you have for the rest of my days here. I ask forgiveness for anything I have done or said—or not done or said—that has hurt you or others. Thank you for love that binds and brings blessings from you. Help us to give our best to you and make all things right and good in your sight. Let us share your love and enjoy our lives until the whistle blows our name and we head to heaven. I'm ready, Lord, but until you're ready for me, I promise my best and will spend my days praying and pleading for people to love and cherish you and the ones you gave us to love on this earth. Let our memories tell the story of what is most important in life. Kurt's memory of Tim touches my heart every time I read it. I hope it helps others see the power of God's love with those we love. I'm forever yours, Becky.

Kurt's letter teaches a lesson every time I read it. I hope you are blessed by the words of a brother-in-law who loved deeply, yet had difficulty expressing his words orally. His written words are treasures that teach us the value of what we have at home.

> *I remember that Thursday evening when Tim and Becky came to see us after one of Tim's doctor appointments at Chapel Hill. They drove Tim's Corvette. Tim and I took off to the Thursday night car show in High Point. On the way not much was said to each other; we didn't have to. We were entering another world, the world of cars. When we got there, we pulled Tim's Corvette in line with the other Corvettes, proudly as the spectators watched. We got out and started our way down the maze of cars. Personally judging each car in our own way, both of us commenting, "I like that, I want that someday, etc." A young girl walked across the crowd near us, wearing tight short blue jeans. Being the gentlemen we were, we stopped. She passes in front of us. Tim and I looking at each other with a smile but knowing what was waiting at home was much better. We saw some friends of mine. I introduced them to Tim, instantly it was like we had known each other for years. We all came there for one thing, cars. We walked the whole lot of cars in love with our dreams. It was time to go. Leaving with the rev of the engine and squeal of tires, we headed home. We were re-entering the reality world. That night, driving Tim's Corvette, the time we were there . . . cancer or worries did not exist. It was like Tim and I were kids at a toy*

> *store, worry free. That's how I want and will remember my good friend, Tim Spell.*

What is at home is much better! The enemy would have us think happiness is found other places. Home is the core where we come together as a family. What we do in our homes shows our relationship to God and to one another. He works out all things for the good of those who love Him and are obedient to His calling and His Word—and we are part of the happy family of God. When He does call us home, we want to leave precious memories here and be prepared for heaven.

Let us remember our first love, repent of things that have distanced us from our Maker and mate, and repeat the things we did when we first fell in love. He longs for a personal, passionate relationship with us—just as our loved ones crave. He loved us enough to give His Son. I promised God my best one night in May of 2006 when He stirred my heart. He told me He knew I wanted His best—Tim to be healed.

Tim received God's greatest healing when he went to heaven in 2007. Four months later, I received healing from cancer. I have no right to put myself in the place of God and ask why because all the good, the bad, the burdens, and the blessings are part of His plan for my life. I will not forget my promise—or take it lightly. I promised Him my best and I will give it until He calls me home.

God has plans for all of us; His plans are right and good for those who trust and obey. I have never been happier or more excited to get up, to share his love, to serve him, and to look forward to going home.

The End is the Beginning

How do I begin the ending, the final chapters, and the last love stories that will color the sunset years of my life? There is joy in my writing as I recount where I have been and rise up to where I am going. Refusing to move forward selfishly blocks the blessings God still has in store for those who believe and are all they can be—for Him.

I remember the past with a happy heart, enjoy and treasure today, and look forward to my tomorrows with a childlike faith. God guides and gives grace and mercy to light our paths. Rising up and recounting love keeps us grounded and going strong until the last day is done and the victory is won. How exciting to choose living and loving out loud wherever we are in life. The season, the setting, the characters may change, but when you keep love alive and the Lord first, everything else will fall into place.

Timothy Cameron Spell will always be my first, true love. We honored our covenant of marriage and cherished each day together until death parted us. We loved boldly, lived bravely, and believed wholeheartedly that God would bless us with his best forever and ever. He did and the blessings continue in this new season of my life. Our sons continue the legacy that began when we said "I do." I am still saying "I do" to my Lord who has opened the eyes of my heart to love again. He lights my way as new chapters are waiting to be written.

God has tendered my heart to rise up and share stories that recount God's amazing love and grace. I pray that you will cherish love and stay closely connected to the Lord and your loved ones through all seasons and situations.

May you embrace the truth of these last words as you enjoy life and write your own love story. Believe and be all that God created you to be. Love deeply and devotedly. Rise up and recount love!

CPSIA information can be obtained at www.ICGtesting.com
Printed in the USA
BVOW012117220112

280980BV00001B/4/P